Commodify Your Dissent

Commodify Your Dissent

Salvos from

The BAFFLER

Edited by

Thomas Frank and Matt Weiland

W. W. Norton & Company

New York • London

The text of this book is composed in Fournier with the display set in Bodoni
Compositon by Com Com
Manufacturing by Courier-Westford
Book design by Julia Druskin

Library of Congress Cataloging-in Publication Data

Commodify your dissent : salvos from The Baffler / edited by Thomas Frank
    and Matt Weiland.
        p.   cm.
    Includes index.
    ISBN 0-393-31673-4
    1. United States—Civilization—1970– 2. Consumers—United
States. 3. Corporations—Social aspects—United States. 4. Popular
culture—United States—History—20th century. 5. Wealth—Social
aspects—United States.   I. Frank, Thomas (Thomas C.)
II. Weiland, Matt. III. Baffler.
E169.04C648   1997
973.92—dc21   97–34097
                                                            CIP

W. W. Norton & Company, Inc., 500 Fifth Avenue, New York, N.Y. 10110
http://www.wwnorton.com

W. W. Norton & Company Ltd., 10 Coptic Street, London WC1A 1PU

1 2 3 4 5 6 7 8 9 0

Contents

Contents

H.M.S. *Baffler*

OTHER THAN *The Baffler*, I can think of no American journal of opinion—leftist, new age, Ultra, post-modern, Jacobin, conservative, monarchist, evangelical, legitimist, neo-gothic—that could credibly describe its essays and criticisms as "salvos." The less spirited journals produce muffled squibs and tentative ranging shots, sometimes sinister winks, loud coughs, or violent tremblings of the jowl, but not salvos, and never broadsides meant to sink anything larger than the pretensions of a disagreeable politician or the semiotic theory of a rival paraphrast.

Extend the sea-going metaphor to the armada of print that shows up every month on the newsstands or in the mail, and the different rigs and tonnages can be seen and classified as various kinds of ships. The business journals (*Forbes, Fortune, Business Week,* etc.), like deep-laden oil tankers, heavy with the statistics that sustain the faith in late twentieth-century capitalism and fuel the lamps in the temples of Mammon; *Vanity Fair* and *The New Yorker* as festive as Caribbean cruise ships, glittering with strings of colored lights and loud with the music of trendy calypso bands (sometimes a celebrity falls overboard, which is a cause for great excitement and rejoicing); *National Review* and *The New Republic* towing long lines of barges loaded with intellectual waste products and the rusted hulks of political causes long since sold for scrap; the precious literary journals and reviews, too many of them to name or count, like Sunday yachts pirouetting through nimble turns, making a pretty show of running up and taking down their coded signal flags.

But H.M.S. *Baffler* I choose to imagine as a British frigate of thirty-six guns close-hauled on a port tack, temporarily detached from Vice Admiral Lord Nelson's Mediterranean squadron and operating without fleet orders in the Bay of Cant. Targets of convenience and opportunity present themselves at all points of the compass—fat merchantmen sailing under the broad pennants of Condé Nast and Hearst, double-banked galleys rowed by gangs of captive intellectuals chained to the oars of the Cato Institute and the Chase Manhattan Bank, Chinese junks flying the Nike ensign, gilded barges bearing the magnificences of Martha Stewart and Arianna Huffington, high-speed cigarette boats running around in furious circles under the grinning command of George Gilder and Newt Gingrich.

The gunners aboard H.M.S. *Baffler* never miss, and the accuracy of their observation is a job to behold. The cannonade in the present volume falls most effectively on the flotilla that its several authors variously identify as "The Culture Trust," "The Body Demographic," "The Age of Corporate Feudalism," "The Mechanical Yammering" of a consumer society "long since departed from the rails of meaning or democracy." In brief and in sum, the advertised life formed in the firmament of Madison Avenue's brand name strategies and then (after first being processed into a very large wheel of very pale cheese) sold to the American public in the different shapes and packagings marketed as movies, nose-rings, shoes, books, t-shirts, automobiles, music videos, after-shave lotions, alternative lifestyle, cyberspace, punk and post-rock, nihilist poets, and menacing hairdos. But it is all the same cheese, and it's what we have here in the great American "market space" instead of art or thought or politics or literature.

The twenty-one essays in the book fire their grape-shot at different product lines—Thomas Frank talking about popular music, "designated dissidents," and the New Age handbooks of corporate self-help, Keith White leafing through the merchandising catalogues disguised as magazines (*Details* and *Wired*); Maura Mahoney on pre-frabricated, beat generation angst (sold, like black cotton, in six yard lengths of "hip-lit" or "la vie intellectuelle"); Gary Groth on Quentin Tarantino's movies ("the embodiment of living junk"); Tom Vanderbilt on Edge Cities and the syntax (sometimes brutish, always cute) of commercial speech.

Seldom have I come across a book that in so short a space says so much about the shambles of what now passes for the American cultural and intellectual enterprise. But because H.M.S. *Baffler*'s gun crew writes with a marvelous energy of thought and phrase (not to mention intelligence and wit and common sense), I cannot help but think that all is not yet lost. Heartened by the gallant sight of the bombardment in the Bay of Cant, I draw the cheerful moral that other journals luffing up into the scented wind on the nation's newsstands might one day open their gunports and direct their fire at something other than their own mastheads.

—*Lewis Lapham*

Introduction

THE BAFFLER sprang into this world back in 1988 from a very simple idea. Thanks to the forces of academic professionalization, cultural criticism had become specialized and intentionally obscure. The authority of high culture may have collapsed, but the high-culture critics had no intention of allowing their authority to collapse with it. Instead they abandoned the mundane project of enlightenment and aimed for bafflement, for a style that made much of its own radicalism but had astonishingly little to say about the conditions of life in late twentieth-century America. We set out to puncture their pretensions and to beat them at their own game.

Our suspicion of the high critical style quickly merged with a broader analysis of the culture business. If there was ever a time not to be baffling, we insisted, this was it. Between the rise of the Culture Trust and its desire to put an ad on every available surface, a demographic on every face, and an A&R man in every avant-garde, these were times that called for explosive analysis and strong, unambiguous statements.

What we got instead were ten years during which the high critics declared that the production of mass culture was not worth talking about at all, since to do so was to make the distasteful assumption that the public stupidly fell for the commercial ephemera that increasingly made up our cultural surroundings. No, when the subject was everyday life only one interpretation held their interest: that the noble consumer used the dross with which he or she was bombarded to fashion little talismans of rebellion and subversion. And with that polite little moué, a hundred-year legacy was abandoned when we needed it most.

What we thought was really eerie, though, was the way mass culture reflected the high critics' priorities. While they spoke proudly of their own subversiveness and turned out account after account of the liberating potential of each act of consuming, the culture industry itself grabbed with both hands at the golden promise of rebellion-through-consumption. The more closely American speech was brought under centralized corporate control, the more strenuously did our advertising, TV sitcoms, and even our management literature insist on the virtue and widespread availability of revolution. In economic terms, the nineties were years of unprecedented consolidation; in terms of official culture, they were years of unprecedented radical-talk. For us they were a great time to be making trouble.

As *The Baffler* grew, our writing began to focus more and more on business culture and the culture business. For all the flash and cosmopolitanism of contemporary American life, we reasoned, never has it been so directly a product of the corporate imagination. As we waded through the unplumbed depths of management literature, our original suspicions were confirmed: When business advice literature warmly embraces chaos, celebrates the collapsing of high and low, and heralds the demolition of intellectual order as a profit-maximizing opportunity, it's time to dust off those much-vilified meta-narratives. And when the partisans of corporate-sponsored transgression responded by labeling us both reactionary elitists *and* a bunch of Reds, we knew we had hit the interpretative jackpot. Yes, postmodernism *is* the cultural logic of late capitalism.

This is the critique that is collected in the present volume. A number of these essays have been revised, updated, and reworked for publication here. Some—particularly "Dark Age" and "The Problem with Music"—were reprinted extensively and enjoyed significant post-*Baffler* careers, and we have included postscripts detailing their adventures.

The Baffler draws on a long American tradition of dissent, especially the critique of business culture that grew up back in the hopeful days of the teens, twenties, and thirties. When starting the magazine we were inspired simultaneously by Randolph Bourne and H. L. Mencken; we were determined somehow to follow in the paths of both *The Masses* and punk rock. We aimed for nothing less than to revive the old generalist project, to speak about our culture without excessive jargon and as though people cared. We would confront the pomposities of power in the most direct manner we knew, we would call it on its lies and burst the bubble of the moment, whether it was "alternative" culture or the liberating promise of the cyber-revolution.

More importantly, *The Baffler* was our attempt to restore a sense of outrage and urgency to the literature of the Left and simultaneously to unmask the pretensions of the lifestyle liberals. The cultural crisis of our time cannot be understood without reference to the fact that certain modes of cultural dissidence that arose in the sixties are today indistinguishable from management theory. The distance between the new species of business thinkers and the rebel stars who populate our national firmament is almost zero. Our society is blessed with a great profusion of self-proclaimed subversives, few of whom have any problem with the terrifying economic-cultural order into which we are blithely stepping on the eve of the millennium.

But to describe *The Baffler* in terms of the books we read or the records we listened to or the writers we admired overlooks what was, until quite recently, the central, unassuagable fact that dictated the way we did things. To put it simply, we believed in small magazines and in self-publishing because we had to. Until a certain species of cynicism became acceptable in the mainstream press a few years ago, almost nobody else would publish us.

It is also important to point out where *The Baffler*'s critique stops. We make no grand claims about what art or culture can do to transform politics. We confess that we admire certain old avant-gardes, that we like the early writing of John Dos Passos and Edmund Wilson, that we are always looking for a cartoonist like Art Young. But we realize that political change is going to require actual politics. What we are absolutely sure about is that contemporary capitalism has marshalled the forces of culture, whatever they are, to ensconce itself in power and to insulate itself from criticism to an almost entirely unprecedented extent.

It would be difficult to overstate the degree to which *The Baffler* has been assisted over the years by the dozens of readers, writers, editors, musicians, radio producers, and independent bookstore owners who have written to us, encouraged us, argued with us, directed our attention to particular events, and expressed faith in our project. To them as much as to the writers that we have published in our pages we are enormously indebted.

People: Emily Vogt, Brook Dooley, Emily Farmer, William B. Mollard, Kirstin Peterson, Dan Peterman, Thom Powers, Andy Beecham, Erik Bennett, Ed Johns, Paula Cerrone, David Berman, Robert Nedelkoff, Eric Iversen, Gaston de Béarn, Wendy Edelberg, Andrea Laiacona, Lloyd H. Frank, the Pats Mulcahey, the Weilands, Helen White, Mark Meachem, Aloyisius Plantageonette,

Matt Roth, Rob Schrader, Matthew Richards, Gedney Market, Owen Hatteras, Steven Ashby, the late Rev. L. DeLahoussaye, Andy Gregg, and Doug Henwood.

Direction: Dante Germino, Austin Quigley, Ron Sakolsky, Damon Krukowski, Studs Terkel, Vernon White, Artie Shaw, André Schiffrin, Earl Shorris, Fred Whitehead, Lewis Lapham, and Gerry Howard.

Bands: Doom, Empty Box, Fernando Jones, John Huss, Buzzmuscle, Sabalon Glitz, the Galaxy of Mailbox Whores, Ashtray Boy, Magic Hour, the Handsome Family, Thomas Jefferson Slave Apartments, the Goblins, Skinner Pilot, Barbara Manning, the Crown Royals, and Toulouse.

Institutions: The University of Virginia *Declaration, Chicago Review,* The *Grey City Journal,* 57th Street Books, St. Mark's Books, City Lights Books, WHPK, WFMU, Salsedo Press, Screwball Press, Fireproof Press, Gill's Cut-Rate Liquors, Jimmy's Woodlawn Tap, the Illinois Arts Council, the Lounge Ax, the Empty Bottle, the Knitting Factory, the Old Town Bar, the Guild Complex, Big Fish Furniture, and the thoughtful people at the Jackson Park Station of the United States Post Office in Chicago, Illinois.

Thomas Frank, Greg Lane, Dave Mulcahey,
Matt Weiland, Keith White

the law stares across the desk out of angry eyes his face reddens in splotches like a gobbler's neck with the strut of the power of submachineguns sawedoffshotguns teargas and vomitinggas the power that can feed you or leave you to starve.

sits easy at his desk his back is covered he feels strong behind him he feels the prosecutingattorney the judge an owner himself the political boss the minesuperintendent the board of directors the president of the utility the manipulator of the holdingcompany

he lifts his hand towards the telephone

the deputies crowd in the door

we have only words against

—John Dos Passos, *The Big Money*

Opening Salvo

THOMAS FRANK

The New Gilded Age

> It was, indeed, the Age of Information, but information was
> not the precursor to knowledge; it was the tool of salesmen.
> —Earl Shorris, *A Nation of Salesmen*

IN THE UNITED States, where political "change" means finding new ways to redirect wealth into the pockets of the already wealthy, and where political "dialogue" is an elaborate charade that excludes dangerous and difficult topics from public consideration, one must look to the literature of business to find serious talk about national affairs. Here, in the *Wall Street Journal, Advertising Age,* and the steady stream of millennial tracts about the latest leadership practices, is where one hears the undisguised voices of the nation's rulers grappling with the weighty affairs of state, raised in anguish over foreign competition, strategizing against its foes, proselytizing passionately for particular management faiths, intoxicated with the golden promise of new marketing techniques. The jowly platitudes about "bipartisanship," "consensus," or "the vital center" that make up political commentary are thankfully absent: here all is philosophical *realpolitik,* the open recognition that the world belongs to the ruthless, the radical, the destroyer of all that has gone before.

The great earth-stopping subject in business literature of the last decade is the fantastic growth of the culture industry. As the nation advances from the clunking tailfin-and-ranch-house consumerism of the past into a golden era where ever-accelerating style and 'tude fuel ever-more rapidly churning cycles of obsolescence, and where buying things is believed to provide the sort of existential satisfaction that, say, going to church once did, the production and distribution of culture has become increasingly central. No longer is the man of commerce a militant philistine; no longer can any serious executive regard TV, movies, magazines, and radio as simple "entertainment," as frivolous leisure-time fun. These are the economic dynamos of the new gilded age, the tools by which the public is informed of the latest offerings, instructed in the arcane pleasures of the new, and brought warmly into the consuming fold. Every leader of business now knows that the nation's health is measured not by production of cars and corn but by the strength of its culture industry. Nightly business programs gravely discuss the latest box-office receipts; France is threatened with trade war over its protectionist cinema policy; the *Wall Street Journal* publishes long special reports on what naively used to be called "the entertainment industry." This is the glorious Age of Information, a second renaissance in which culture is to be the proper province of responsible executives, the minutiae that were once pondered by professors and garret-bound poets having become as closely scrutinized as daily stock prices.

With its usual foresight, the invisible hand has reacted to the new state of affairs by rapidly erecting a Culture Trust of five or six companies whose assorted vice-presidents now supervise a broad swathe of American public expression. Business ideologists speculate wildly about the potential for "synergy" when "content providers" join forces with "delivery systems." Time Warner unites the nation's foremost mass-cultural institutions under one corporate roof; Sony now produces the movies and recordings you need to make your Sony appliances go; a host of conglomerates battle over Paramount, then over CBS; Disney casts about for its own TV network; Rupert Murdoch acquires an international publishing and broadcasting empire, bringing him cultural power undreamed of by bush-leaguers like William Randolph Hearst. Culture can now be delivered cleanly and efficiently from creator to consumer, without the potential for interference posed by such vestiges of antiquity as bolshevik authors, strange-minded artists, or stubborn anomalies like that crotchety old editor in the MCI "Gramercy Press" commercials who doesn't know how to work his voice-mail. The entire process of cultural production is being modernized overnight, brought at long last out of the nineteenth century and placed in the hands of dutiful business interests.

With the consolidation of the Information Age has come a new class of executives who deal in images rather than triplicate forms. Management theorist Peter Drucker calls them "knowledge workers," former Secretary of Labor Robert Reich dubbed them "symbolic analysts," but the term applied to them by the nation's premier ass-kisser, *Vanity Fair,* in its 1994 "Special Report" on the handful of luminous fabulosities who head up the Culture Trust, seems more appropriate: "The New Establishment." Learn to revere them, the magazine wetly counseled its readers, for these are the new captains of industry, the titans of the future, "a buccaneering breed of entrepreneurs and visionaries, men and women from the entertainment, communications, and computer industries, whose ambitions and influence have made America the one true superpower of the Information Age." As Americans were once taught to regard the colossal plunderings of Rockefellers and Carnegies with patriotic pride, now we are told to be thankful for this "New Establishment": it is, after all, due to figures like Murdoch, Geffen, Eisner, and Turner that the nation has been rescued from the dead end of "military-industrial supremacy" and restored to the path of righteousness, "emerging as an information-and-entertainment superpower." These great men have struggled their way to the top, not just to corner the wheat market, buy up all the railroads between here and New York, or bribe the odd state legislature, but to fabricate the materials with which the world thinks.

As its products steadily become the nation's chief export, the Culture Trust further rationalizes its operations through vertical integration, ensuring its access to the eternal new that drives the machine by invading the sanctum of every possible avant-garde. Responsible business newspapers print feature stories on the nation's hippest neighborhoods; sober TV programs air segments on the colorful world of "zines"; ad agencies hire young scenesters to penetrate and report back on the latest "underground" doings. Starry-eyed college students are signed up as unpaid representatives of record conglomerates, eager to push product, make connections, and gain valuable experience on the lower rungs of the corporate ladder; while music talent scouts, rare creatures once, are seen everywhere prospecting for the cultural fuel that only straight-off-the-street 'tude can provide. Believing blithely in the fabled democracy of the marketplace, the objects of this cultural speculation are only too happy to cooperate, never quite realizing that the only reliable path to wealth in the "entertainment" business starts with a Harvard MBA.

And as every aspect of American cultural production is brought safely on board, business texts crow proudly of the new technologies that promise to complete the circle of corporate domination. The delivery of such glories as interactive media and virtual reality, it is hoped, will open vast uncharted regions of private life to business colonization, will reorganize human relations generally around an indispensable corporate intermediary. Business writers understand that the great promise of the Information Age is not that average consumers will soon wake up to the splendor of 100 high-res channels, but that every imaginable type of human relationship can now be reduced to digital and incorporated into the glowing televisual nexus—brought to you by Pepsico, of course. What Earl Shorris has written of the early promise of TV may finally be accomplished in the near future: "Reality did not cease to exist, of course, but much of what people understood as reality, including virtually all of the commercial world, was mediated by television. It was as if a salesman had been placed between Americans and life." TV is no longer merely "entertainment," it is on the verge of becoming the ineluctable center of human consciousness, the site of every sort of exchange. As the Information Revolution proceeds the myths, assumptions, and folklores of business become the common language of humanity; business culture becomes human culture. Working and consuming from our houses, wired happily into what *Harper's* magazine has called the "electronic hive," we will each be corporate subjects—consumers and providers of "content"—as surely as were the hapless industrial proletarians of the last century.

It seems only natural, then, that as the Dow hits 7000 and Bill Gates knocks off his remaining competitors, an almost staggering triumphalism becomes commonplace in the public proclamations of the communications giants: We hear daily about the "World Wide Web" and IBM's "solutions for a small planet." Microsoft takes as its slogan the imperial query, "Where do you want to go today?" while MCI asks us to imagine the world that it is creating as one without place, race, gender, or age: "Is this a great time or what?"

The world-historical arrogance of the monopolists, though, is a familiar phenomenon, it's something we remember from the days of Rockefellers, Vanderbilts, Goulds, and Fisks. What's remarkable about the new dispensation is the absence of the protesting voices that we associate with the original age of monopoly. The rapid concentration of economic power that followed the Civil War was greeted with a chorus of public alarm. Democratic sensibilities were offended by the prospect of an entire region's or class's impoverishment for the benefit of a small ring of companies. The trajectory from corporate arrogance to public outrage and from there to Populism, Progressivism, Anarcho-Syndicalism, and the New Deal seemed a given, an automatic progression, a product of the normal functioning of political economy.

But cultural economy is different somehow. The rise of the Culture Trust may portend massive cultural dislocation, but since it's being orchestrated by responsible business interests, it's an upheaval with which the self-proclaimed guardians of traditional ways have no dispute (one can imagine their outrage were the government to assume comparable powers). From mainstream journals the only view one is likely to hear is an ecstatic affirmation of the MCI vision: Yes, this *is* a great time! It's an electronic renaissance, a golden age of entrepreneurship and human liberty. The consolidation of cultural power heralds nothing less than a newfound cultural democracy. Not only are the guys who are taking charge of the American cultural economy a bunch of existential individualists— what with their jet airplanes, fabulous homes, virtual offices, and muscular celebrity friends—but the system they're setting up will allow each one of us to be exotic, VR game-playing rebels as well. Since letters to the editor can now be electronic, it seems, the obvious and unavoidable dangers that come with rearranging human life around the cultural needs of business are . . . well . . . insignificant. Since democracy means having more consumer choices, and information technology will vastly increase the power of our channel changers, hey, presto! More democracy!

Baffler #6, 1995

PART I

The Rebel Consumer

THOMAS FRANK

Why Johnny Can't Dissent

The public be damned! I work for my stockholders.
—William H. Vanderbilt, 1879

Break the rules. Stand apart. Keep your head. Go with your heart.
—TV commercial for Vanderbilt perfume, 1994

CAPITALISM IS CHANGING, obviously and drastically. From the moneyed pages of the *Wall Street Journal* to TV commercials for airlines and photocopiers we hear every day about the new order's globe-spanning, cyber-accumulating ways. But our notion about what's wrong with American life and how the figures responsible are to be confronted haven't changed much in thirty years. Call it, for convenience, the "countercultural idea." It holds that the paramount ailment of our society is conformity, a malady that has variously been described as over-organization, bureaucracy, homogeneity, hierarchy, logocentrism, technocracy, the Combine, the Apollonian. We all know what it is and what it does. It transforms humanity into "organization man," into "the man in the gray flannel suit." It is "Moloch whose mind is pure machinery," the "incomprehensible prison" that consumes "brains and imagination." It is artifice, starched shirts, tailfins, carefully mowed lawns, and always, always, the consciousness of impending nuclear destruction. It is a stiff, militaristic order that seeks to suppress instinct, to forbid sex and pleasure, to deny basic human impulses and individuality, to enforce through a rigid uniformity a meaningless plastic consumerism.

As this half of the countercultural idea originated during the 1950s, it is appropriate that the evils of conformity are most conveniently summarized with images of 1950s suburban correctness. You know, that land of sedate music, sexual repression, deference to authority, Red Scares, and smiling white people standing politely in line to go to church. Constantly appearing as a symbol of arch-backwardness in advertising and movies, it is an image we find easy to evoke.

The ways in which this system are to be resisted are equally well understood and agreed-upon. The Establishment demands homogeneity; we revolt by embracing diverse, individual lifestyles. It demands self-denial and rigid adherence to convention; we revolt through immediate gratification, instinct uninhibited, and liberation of the libido and the appetites. Few have put it more bluntly than Jerry Rubin did in 1970: "Amerika says: Don't! The yippies say: Do It!" The countercultural idea is hostile to any law and every establishment. "Whenever we see a rule, we must break it," Rubin continued. "Only by breaking rules do we discover who we are." Above all rebellion consists of a sort of Nietzschean antinomianism, an automatic questioning of rules, a rejection of whatever social prescriptions we've happened to inherit. Just Do It is the whole of the law.

The patron saints of the countercultural idea are, of course, the Beats, whose frenzied style and merry alienation still maintain a powerful grip on the American imagination. Even forty years after the publication of *On the Road,* the works of Kerouac, Ginsberg, and Burroughs remain the *sine qua non* of dissidence, the model for aspiring poets, rock stars, or indeed anyone who feels vaguely artistic or alienated. That frenzied sensibility of pure experience, life on the edge, immediate gratification, and total freedom from moral restraint, which the Beats first propounded back in those heady days when suddenly everyone could have their own TV and powerful V-8, has stuck with us through all the intervening years and become something of a permanent American style. Go to any poetry reading and you can see a string of junior Kerouacs go through the routine, upsetting cultural hierarchies by pushing themselves to the limit, straining for that gorgeous moment of original vice when Allen Ginsberg first read "Howl" in 1955 and the patriarchs of our fantasies recoiled in shock. The Gap may have since claimed Ginsberg and *USA Today* may run feature stories about the brilliance of the beloved Kerouac, but the rebel race continues today regardless, with ever-heightening shit-references calculated to scare Jesse Helms, talk about sex and smack that is supposed to bring the electricity of real life, and ever-more determined defiance of the repressive rules and mores of the American 1950s—rules and mores that by now we know only from movies.

But one hardly has to go to a poetry reading to see the countercultural idea acted out. Its frenzied ecstasies have long since become an official aesthetic of consumer society, a monotheme of mass as well as adversarial culture. Turn on the TV and there it is instantly: the unending drama of consumer unbound and in search of an ever-heightened good time, the inescapable rock 'n' roll soundtrack, dreadlocks and ponytails bounding into Taco Bells, a drunken, swinging-camera epiphany of tennis shoes, outlaw soda pops, and mind-bending dandruff shampoo. Corporate America, it turns out, no longer speaks in the voice of oppressive order that it did when Ginsberg moaned in 1956 that *Time* magazine was

always telling me about responsibility. Businessmen are serious. Movie producers are serious.
Everybody's serious but me.

Nobody wants you to think they're serious today, least of all
Time Warner. On the contrary: the Culture Trust is now our leader
in the Ginsbergian search for kicks upon kicks. Corporate America
is not an oppressor but a sponsor of fun, provider of lifestyle accoutrements, facilitator of carnival, our slang-speaking partner in
the quest for that ever-more apocalyptic orgasm. The countercultural idea has become capitalist orthodoxy, its hunger for transgression upon transgression now perfectly suited to an
economic-cultural regime that runs on ever-faster cyclings of the
new; its taste for self-fulfillment and its intolerance for the confines
of tradition now permitting vast latitude in consuming practices
and lifestyle experimentation.

Consumerism is no longer about "conformity" but about "difference." Advertising teaches us not in the ways of puritanical self-
denial (a bizarre notion on the face of it), but in orgiastic,
never-ending self-fulfillment. It counsels not rigid adherence to the
tastes of the herd but vigilant and constantly updated individualism.
We consume not to fit in, but to prove, on the surface at least, that
we are rock 'n' roll rebels, each one of us as rule-breaking and
hierarchy-defying as our heroes of the 60s, who now pitch cars,
shoes, and beer. This imperative of endless difference is today the
genius at the heart of American capitalism, an eternal fleeing from
"sameness" that satiates our thirst for the New with such achievements of civilization as the infinite brands of identical cola, the
myriad colors and irrepressible variety of the cigarette rack at 7-
Eleven.

As existential rebellion has become a more or less official style
of Information Age capitalism, so has the countercultural notion of
a static, repressive Establishment grown hopelessly obsolete. How-

ever the basic impulses of the countercultural idea may have disturbed a nation lost in Cold War darkness, they are today in fundamental agreement with the basic tenets of Information Age business theory. So close are they, in fact, that it has become difficult to understand the countercultural idea as anything more than the self-justifying ideology of the new bourgeoisie that has arisen since the 1960s, the cultural means by which this group has proven itself ever so much better skilled than its slow-moving, security-minded forebears at adapting to the accelerated, always-changing consumerism of today. The anointed cultural opponents of capitalism are now capitalism's ideologues.

The two come together in perfect synchronization in a figure like Camille Paglia, whose ravings are grounded in the absolutely noncontroversial ideas of the golden sixties. According to Paglia, American business is still exactly what it was believed to have been in that beloved decade, that is, "puritanical and desensualized." Its great opponents are, of course, liberated figures like "the beatniks," Bob Dylan, and the Beatles. Culture is, quite simply, a binary battle between the repressive Apollonian order of capitalism and the Dionysian impulses of the counterculture. Rebellion makes no sense without repression; we must remain forever convinced of capitalism's fundamental hostility to pleasure in order to consume capitalism's rebel products as avidly as we do. It comes as little surprise when, after criticizing the "Apollonian capitalist machine" (in her book, *Vamps & Tramps*), Paglia applauds American mass culture (in *Utne Reader*), the preeminent product of that "capitalist machine," as a "third great eruption" of a Dionysian "paganism." For her, as for most other designated dissidents, there is no contradiction between replaying the standard critique of capitalist conformity and repressiveness and then endorsing its rebel products—for Paglia the car culture and Madonna—as the obvious solution: the Culture Trust offers both Establishment and Resistance in one convenient package. The only question that remains is why

Paglia has not yet landed an endorsement contract from a soda pop or automobile manufacturer.

Other legendary exponents of the countercultural idea have been more fortunate—William S. Burroughs, for example, who appears in a television spot for the Nike corporation. But so openly does the commercial flaunt the confluence of capital and counter-culture that it has brought considerable criticism down on the head of the aging beat. Writing in the *Village Voice,* Leslie Savan marvels at the contradiction between Burroughs' writings and the face-less corporate entity for which he is now pushing product. "Now the realization that *nothing* threatens the system has freed advertis-ing to exploit even the most marginal elements of society," Savan observes. "In fact, being hip is no longer quite enough—better the pitchman be 'underground.' " Meanwhile Burroughs' manager in-sists, as all future Cultural Studies treatments of the ad will no doubt also insist, that Burroughs' presence actually makes the com-mercial "deeply subversive"—"I hate to repeat the usual mantra, but you know, homosexual drug addict, manslaughter, accidental homicide." But Savan wonders whether, in fact, it is Burroughs who has been assimilated by corporate America. "The problem comes," she writes, "in how easily any idea, deed, or image can be-come part of the sponsored world."

The most startling revelation to emerge from the Bur-roughs/Nike partnership is not that corporate America has over-whelmed its cultural foes or that Burroughs can somehow remain "subversive" through it all, but the complete lack of dissonance between the two sides. Of course Burroughs is not "subversive," but neither has he "sold out": His ravings are no longer apprecia-bly different from the official folklore of American capitalism. What's changed is not Burroughs, but business itself. As expertly as Burroughs once bayoneted American proprieties, as stridently as he once proclaimed himself beyond the laws of man and God, he is today a respected ideologue of the Information Age, occupying roughly the position in the pantheon of corporate-cultural thought once reserved strictly for Notre Dame football coaches and positive-thinking Methodist ministers. His inspirational writings are boardroom favorites, his dark nihilistic burpings the happy homilies of the new corporate faith.

For with the assumption of power by Drucker's and Reich's new class has come an entirely new ideology of business, a way of justifying and exercising power that has little to do with the "conformity" and the "establishment" so vilified by the countercultural idea. The management theorists and "leadership" charlatans of the Information Age don't waste their time prattling about hierarchy and regulation, but about disorder, chaos, and the meaninglessness of convention. With its reorganization around information, capitalism has developed a new mythology, a sort of corporate antinomianism according to which the breaking of rules and the elimination of rigid corporate structure have become the central article of faith for millions of aspiring executives.

Dropping *Naked Lunch* and picking up *Thriving on Chaos*, the groundbreaking 1987 management text by Tom Peters, the most popular business writer of the past decade, one finds more philosophical similarities than one would expect from two manifestos of, respectively, dissident culture and business culture. If anything, Peters' celebration of disorder is, by virtue of its hard statistics, bleaker and more nightmarish than Burroughs'. For this popular lecturer on such once-blithe topics as competitiveness and pop psychology there is nothing, absolutely nothing, that is certain. His world is one in which the corporate wisdom of the past is meaningless, established customs are ridiculous, and "rules" are some sort of curse, a remnant of the foolish fifties that exist to be defied, not obeyed. We live in what Peters calls "A World Turned Upside Down," in which whirl is king and, in order to survive, businesses must eventually embrace Peters' universal solution: "Revolution!" "To meet the demands of the fast-changing competitive scene," he counsels, "we must simply learn to love change as much as we have hated it in the past." He advises businessmen to become Robespierres of routine, to demand of their underlings, " 'What have you changed lately?' 'How fast are you changing?' and 'Are you pursuing bold enough change goals?' " "Revolution," of course, means for Peters the same thing it did to Burroughs and Ginsberg, Presley and the Stones in their heyday: breaking rules, pissing off the suits, shocking the bean-counters: "Actively and publicly hail defiance of the rules, many of which you doubtless labored mightily to construct in the first place." Peters even suggests that his readers implement this hostility to logocentrism in a carnivalesque celebration, drinking beer out in "the woods" and destroying "all the forms and rules and discontinued reports" and, "if you've got real nerve," a photocopier as well.

Today corporate antinomianism is the emphatic message of nearly every new business text, continually escalating the corporate insurrection begun by Peters. Capitalism, at least as it is envisioned by the best-selling management handbooks, is no longer about enforcing Order, but destroying it. "Revolution," once the totemic catchphrase of the counterculture, has become the totemic catchphrase of boomer-as-capitalist. The Information Age businessman holds inherited ideas and traditional practices not in reverence, but in high suspicion. Even reason itself is now found to be an enemy of true competitiveness, an out-of-date faculty to be scrupulously avoided by conscientious managers. A 1990 book by Charles Handy entitled *The Age of Unreason* agrees with Peters that we inhabit a time in which "there can be no certainty" and suggests that readers engage in full-fledged epistemological revolution: "Thinking Upside Down," using new ways of "learning which can . . . be seen as disrespectful if not downright rebellious," methods of approaching problems that have "never been popular with the upholders of continuity and of the status quo." Three years later the authors of *Reengineering the Corporation* ("A Manifesto for Business Revolution," as its subtitle declares) are ready to push this doctrine even farther. Not only should we be suspicious of traditional practices, but we should cast out virtually everything learned over the past two centuries!

> Business reengineering means putting aside much of the received wisdom of two hundred years of industrial management. It means forgetting how work was done in the age of the mass market and deciding how it can best be done now. In business reengineering, old job titles and old organizational arrangements—departments, divisions, groups, and so on—cease to matter. They are artifacts of another age.

As countercultural rebellion becomes corporate ideology, even the beloved Buddhism of the Beats wins a place on the executive bookshelf. In *The Leader as Martial Artist* (1993), Arnold Mindell advises men of commerce in the ways of the Tao, mastery of which he likens, of course, to surfing. For Mindell's Zen businessman, as for the followers of Tom Peters, the world is a wildly chaotic place of opportunity, navigable only to an enlightened "leader" who can discern the "timespirits" at work behind the scenes. In terms Peters himself might use were he a more more meditative sort of inspiration professional, Mindell explains that "the wise facilitator" doesn't seek to prevent the inevitable and random clashes between "conflicting field spirits," but to anticipate such bouts of disorder and profit thereby.

Contemporary corporate fantasy imagines a world of ceaseless, turbulent change, of centers that ecstatically fail to hold, of joyous extinction for the craven gray-flannel creature of the past. Businessmen today decorate the walls of their offices not with portraits of President Eisenhower and emblems of suburban order, but with images of extreme athletic daring, with sayings about "diversity" and "empowerment" and "thinking outside the box." They theorize their world not in the bar car of the commuter train, but in weepy corporate retreats at which they beat their tom-toms and envision themselves as part of the great avant-garde tradition of edge-livers, risk-takers, and ass-kickers. Their world is a place not of sublimation and conformity, but of "leadership" and bold talk about defying the herd. And there is nothing this new enlightened species of businessman despises more than "rules" and "reason." The prominent culture-warriors of the right may believe that the counterculture was capitalism's undoing, but the antinomian businessmen know better. "One of the t-shirt slogans of the sixties read, 'Question authority,' " the authors of *Reengineering the Corporation* write. "Process owners might buy their reengineering team members the nineties version: 'Question assumptions.' "

The new businessman quite naturally gravitates to the slogans and sensibility of the rebel sixties to express his understanding of the new Information World. He is led in what one magazine calls "the business revolution" by the office-park subversives it hails as "business activists," "change agents," and "corporate radicals." He speaks to his comrades through commercials like the one for "Warp," a type of IBM computer operating system, in which an electric guitar soundtrack and psychedelic video effects surround hip executives with earrings and hairdos who are visibly stunned by the product's gnarly 'tude (It's a "totally cool way to run your computer," read the product's print ads). He understands the world through *Fast Company,* a successful new magazine whose editors take their inspiration from Hunter S. Thompson and whose stories describe such things as a "dis-organization" that inhabits an "anti-office" where "all vestiges of hierarchy have disappeared" or a computer scientist who is also "a rabble rouser, an agent provocateur, a product of the 1960s who never lost his activist fire or democratic values." He is what sociologists Paul Leinberger and Bruce Tucker have called "The New Individualist," the new and improved manager whose arty worldview and creative hip derive directly from his formative sixties days. The one thing this new executive is definitely *not* is Organization Man, the hyper-rational counter of beans, attender of church, and wearer of stiff hats.

In television commercials, through which the new American

businessman presents his visions and self-understanding to the public, perpetual revolution and the gospel of rule-breaking are the orthodoxy of the day. You only need to watch for a few minutes before you see one of these slogans and understand the grip of antinomianism over the corporate mind:

Sometimes You Gotta Break the Rules	*—Burger King*
If You Don't Like the Rules, Change Them	*—WXRT-FM*
The Rules Have Changed	*—Dodge*
The Art of Changing	*—Swatch*
There's no one way to do it.	*—Levi's*
This is different. Different is good.	*—Arby's*
Just Different From the Rest	*—Special Export beer*
The Line Has Been Crossed: The Revolutionary New Supra	
	—Toyota
Resist the Usual	
—the slogan of both Clash Clear Malt and Young & Rubicam	
Innovate Don't Imitate	*—Hugo Boss*
Chart Your Own Course	*—Navigator Cologne*
It separates you from the crowd	*—Vision Cologne*

In most, the commercial message is driven home with the vanguard iconography of the rebel: screaming guitars, whirling cameras, and startled old timers who, we predict, will become an increasingly indispensable prop as consumers require ever-greater assurances that, Yes! You *are* a rebel! Just look at how offended they are!

Our businessmen imagine themselves rebels, and our rebels sound more and more like ideologists of business. Henry Rollins, for example, the maker of loutish, overbearing music and composer of high-school-grade poetry, straddles both worlds unproblematically. Rollins' writing and lyrics strike all the standard alienated literary poses: He rails against overcivilization and yearns to "disconnect." He veers back and forth between vague threats toward "weak" people who "bring me down" and blustery declarations of his weightlifting ability and physical prowess. As a result he ruled for several years as the preeminent darling of *Details* magazine, a periodical handbook for the young executive on the rise, where rebellion has achieved a perfect synthesis with corporate ideology. In 1992 *Details* named Rollins a "rock 'n' roll samurai," an "emblem . . . of a new masculinity" whose "enlightened honesty" is "a way of being that seems to flesh out many of the ideas expressed in contemporary culture and fashion." In 1994 the magazine consummated its relationship with Rollins by naming him "Man of the Year," printing a fawning story about his muscular worldview and decorating its cover with a photo in which Rollins displays his tattoos and rubs his chin in a thoughtful manner.

Details found Rollins to be such an appropriate role model for the struggling young businessman not only because of his music-product, but because of his excellent "self-styled identity," which the magazine describes in terms normally reserved for the breast-beating and soul-searching variety of motivational seminars. Although he derives it from the quality-maximizing wisdom of the East rather than the unfashionable doctrines of Calvin, Rollins' rebel posture is identical to that fabled ethic of the small capitalist whose regimen of positive thinking and hard work will one day pay off. *Details* describes one of Rollins' songs, quite seriously, as "a self-motivational superforce, an anthem of empowerment," teaching lessons that any aspiring middle-manager must internalize. Elsewher, Iggy Pop, that great chronicler of the ambitionless life, praises Rollins as a "high achiever" who "wants to go somewhere." Rollins himself even seems to invite such an interpretation. His recent spoken-word account of touring with Black Flag, delivered in an unrelenting two-hour drill-instructor staccato, begins with the timeless bourgeois story of opportunity taken, of young Henry leaving the security of a "straight job," enlisting with a group of visionaries who were "the hardest working people I have ever seen," and learning "what hard work is all about." In the liner notes he speaks proudly of his Deming-esque dedication to quality, of how his bandmates "Delivered under pressure at incredible odds." When describing his relationship with his parents for the readers of *Details*, Rollins quickly cuts to the critical matter, the results that such dedication has brought: "Mom, Dad, I outgross both of you put together," a happy observation he repeats in his interview with the *New York Times Magazine*.

Despite the extreme hostility of punk rockers with which Rollins had to contend all through the 1980s, it is he who has been chosen by the commercial media as the godfather of rock 'n' roll revolt. It is not difficult to see why. For Rollins the punk rock decade was but a lengthy seminar on leadership skills, thriving on chaos, and total quality management. Rollins' much-celebrated anger is indistinguishable from the anger of the frustrated junior executive who finds obstacles on the way to the top. His discipline and determination are the automatic catechism of any small entrepreneur who's just finished brainwashing himself with the latest leadership and positive-thinking tracts; his poetry is the inspired verse of *21 Days to Unlimited Power* or *Let's Get Results, Not Excuses*. Henry Rollins is no more a threat to established power in America than was Dale Carnegie. And yet Rollins as king of the rebels—peerless and ultimate—is the message hammered home wherever photos of his growling visage appears. If you're unhappy with your lot, the Culture Trust tells us with each new tale of Rollins, if you feel you must rebel, take your cue from the most disgruntled guy of all: Lift weights! Work hard! Meditate in your back yard! Root out the weaknesses deep down inside yourself! But whatever you do, *don't* think about who controls power or how it is wielded.

The structure and thinking of American business have changed enormously in the years since our popular conceptions of its problems and abuses were formulated. In the meantime the mad frothings and jolly apolitical revolt of Beat, despite their vast popularity and insurgent air, have become powerless against a new regime that, one suspects, few of Beat's present-day admirers and practitioners feel any need to study or understand. Today that beautiful countercultural idea, endorsed now by everyone from the surviving Beats to shampoo manufacturers, is more the official doctrine of corporate America than it is a program of resistance. What we understand as "dissent" does not subvert, does not challenge, does not even question the cultural faiths of Western business. What David Rieff wrote of the revolutionary pretentions of multiculturalism is equally true of the countercultural idea: "The more one reads in academic multiculturalist journals and in business publications, and the more one contrasts the speeches of CEOs and the speeches of noted multiculturalist academics, the more one is struck by the similarities in the way they view the world." What's happened is not co-optation or appropriation, but a simple and direct confluence of interest.

The problem with cultural dissent in America isn't that it's been co-opted, absorbed, or ripped-off. Of course it's been all of these things. But it has proven so hopelessly susceptible to such assaults for the same reason it has become so harmless in the first place, so toothless even before Mr. Geffen's boys discover it angsting away in some bar in Lawrence, Kansas: It is no longer any different from the official culture it's supposed to be subverting. The basic impulses of the countercultural idea, as descended from the holy Beats, are about as threatening to the new breed of antinomian businessmen as Anthony Robbins, selling success & how to achieve it on a late-night infomercial.

The people who staff the Combine aren't like Nurse Ratched. They aren't Frank Burns, they aren't the Church Lady, they aren't Dean Wormer from *Animal House,* they aren't those repressed old folks in the commercials who want to ban Tropicana Fruit Twisters. They're hipper than you can ever hope to be because *hip is their official ideology,* and they're always going to be there at the poetry

44

reading to encourage your "rebellion" with a hearty "right on, man!" before you even know they're in the auditorium. You can't outrun them, or even stay ahead of them for very long: it's their racetrack, and that's them waiting at the finish line to congratulate you on how *outrageous* your new style is, on how you *shocked* those stuffy prudes out in the heartland.

Baffler #6, 1995

KEITH WHITE

The Killer App:
Wired Magazine, Voice of the
Corporate Revolution

The Gateway to the Consumer

IN THE SUMMER of 1994, some sixty slathering publishing would-bes jammed the upstairs of a brew pub in San Francisco's SOMA district to hear the fifth in a series of "soirées" sponsored by the San Francisco writer's guild. The soirée organizers looked warily at their dwindling stack of folding chairs—never before had one of these informal gatherings drawn more than ten or fifteen chronically unemployed writers. Tonight, however, was different; pierced and tattooed writers and artists jockeyed with smartly dressed young execs for a position close to the evening's attraction—a soft spoken man in his forties who was chatting with some lucky, starry-eyed fans. For the focus of this gathering was not just another lecture on such pedestrian aspects of publishing as "copy editing" or "fact checking." This was a chance to meet face to face with the "artistic visionary" behind the nation's hottest lifestyle magazine, a journal that had raced to over 160,000 readers in its first year, pausing only to pick up a National Magazine Award for general excellence and a big injection of cash from Condé Nast's Si Newhouse. This was the magazine that had so successfully captured the zeitgeist that *Newsweek* was breathlessly labeling it the *"Rolling Stone* for the Computer Generation." We were here to listen to John Plunkett of *Wired*.

Plunkett's address, as it turned out, was rather mundane. He divulged such secrets as why the first four pages of each edition are filled by extending a drop quote across computer generated art ("We originally did it to fill up some space."), along with the reason that so many of the magazine's articles are hard to read ("I sometimes have to sacrifice readability when I'm pushing the edge of the envelope on design.").

Wired's distinctive maimed typography and its fluorescent hues may be interesting, but the magazine's truly marvelous feature is its corporate-cultural mission. *Wired* is technology's hip face, an aggressive apologist for the new information capitalism that speaks to the world in the postmodern executive's favored tones of chaotic cool and pseudo-revolution.

Wired's expeditious rise was the payoff of perfect product positioning by its founders and their flawless implementation of an age-old publishing plan. For *Wired* is to the new cyber-samurai of business what *The New Yorker* was to the Organization Man (God rest his soul): at once captious doyenne and encouraging confidante to aspiring members of a new, socially insecure elite. *Wired* works, on the most basic level, by tweaking its readers' anxieties, constantly reminding them that they are hopelessly behind the times on the latest developments in technology and underground hacker culture. It simultaneously offers careful instruction in vocabulary,

47

name-dropping, thinking, and purchasing to allow readers to retrofit their resumes, apartments, and lifestyles in a manner more "on-line" with current techno-opportunities. *Wired* then calms advertisers wary of its "phreakish" posturing by penning gooey appreciations of Silicon Valley CEOs and paeans to the macho individualism of your local cable provider.

Voilà—a magazine with an affluent and impressionable subscriber base, eager to purchase the accoutrements that make up this fascinating new mode of living. *Wired* tells its readers, in great and explicit detail, how to spend their money on consumer luxuries (some expensive, some cheap, all hip). It answers their most pressing info-consuming questions: Which laptop will look the coolest in my meeting? Which on-line service's e-mail address suffix will give me the proper balance between cache and credibility? Whose name should I drop to my boss—Peter Schwartz or Phiber Optik? The magazine's miscellaneous consumption column—"Street Cred"—is full of the types of things that young professionals have the money to buy, month after month. Ordering is as easy as reading, since *Wired* is courteous enough to include phone numbers and e-mail addresses alongside every product they showcase. Big ticket items and limited availability prototypes are covered in a section called Fetish ($10,000 digital Nikons, $49,000 virtual-reality headsets), but if you haven't moved that far up the pay scale yet, there are plenty of ads showplacing what you *can* afford from the likes of Compaq, IBM, Microsoft, Absolut, and Dewar's. This is what's known in the business as "selling up by stepping down"; in others words, I show you the Lexus and you know you'll at least need the Toyota.

But car manufacturers and distilleries are small potatoes in the *Wired* revenue stream. Game manufacturers are where it's at, appearing on the cover more than any other single group. Perhaps that's because *Wired* views these "convergence plays" (where film, games, and merchandising meet)—also known as video games—as the highest form of art, more meaningful than literature, painting, film, or even the internet. The video game, according to *Wired*, is the culmination of civilization, and to play is the ultimate expression of one's self in the Information Society. Or maybe it's just that, as *Wired* often notes, the video-gaming industry takes in over $6 billion in revenues, which makes it the single largest component of the infotainment industry. Either way, each gaming product launch—3DO, Rocket Science, Doom 2, Myst—is welcomed as the future of the art and given generous coverage in *Wired* ("smart money is betting that this audacious upstart might just hold the secret recipe for some of the tastiest thumb candy to come!"), complete with glowing profiles of the game's creators (variously described as "introverted" artists and guitarists who are "gamers, in every sense!") and never leaving out the most important elements ("the per unit margins are huge!"). The favor is generally returned by manufacturers who take out multiple full-page ads over the next few months as they set about hawking their product.

Magazines that cover particular industries are always tempted to let down the wall between advertising and editorial, since the subjects of their articles are also the buyers of their ad pages. Most such publications work hard to at least maintain an appearance of objectivity. But with the chaotically joyous blurring of boundaries accomplished by the Information Revolution, such rules are no longer as binding, a fact that *Wired*, naturally, has been among the first to exploit. The magazine seems to aim, quite simply, to facilitate the moving of product by the technology industry. As such, *Wired* strives to be more than just a magazine; it wants to be a market maker.

The Killer App

Everyone in business now realizes that the changes being brought by information technology are real enough, and plenty of corporate vice-presidential-level effort has been devoted to trying to predict the cyber-future. The big prize for which every Information Age corporate adept is questing is the elusive "Killer App," the computer program that will mesh together all the rapidly converging technologies, will successfully transform life into a jolly interactive game, and will consequently keep consumers happily paying their upgrade and infobahn bills. While the rest of corporate America pursued the grail by debating things like the merits of cable versus fiber optics, the cadre of San Francisco technophiles behind *Wired* were building their own killer app with existing technology. Print, as it turned out, would be sufficient to meet the ideological goals of the great quest, as well as exploit the new affluence of those on the "digital vanguard."

The brilliance of the idea was not readily apparent. What *was* apparent was that the computer industry continued to suffer from a serious public relations problem that had developed during the dark days of the Cold War. In the public mind computers were associated, at worst, with world destruction, the blown tube that caused a nuclear war in *Fail-Safe;* at best with the cold mind of the corporation. After all, that quintessential volume of the 1950s, *The Organization Man,* came wrapped in a dust jacket decorated with IBM cards, emblems of a repressive, number-happy society. As Steven Levy has noted, participants in the counterculture almost universally regarded computers with suspicion: "computers fueled the War Machine, that grinding, wheezing hunk of Kafka that murdered little babies and told us to report to 400 North Broad Street for a physical." But as the ideology of the counterculture became the ideology of corporate America, a major transformation in the image of the computer had to take place. Information technology would have to undergo a gigantic face-lift to achieve proper acceptance in a business world increasingly fascinated with notions of chaos, revolution, and disorder. The famous TV commercial that introduced the Macintosh in 1984 as an implement of order-smashing suggested the course that ideologues of the computer should take; *Wired* simply picked up where the TV advertising left off.

Wired's founders put together an ideological packaging for information technology that screamed nonconformist. The magazine made constant references to an interactive "underground" as a primary means of giving computers the rebellious image they required. Its layout utilizes the now-fashionable fractured, illegible typography that is the calling card of hip publications like *Raygun*. In addition, appearances by leading pop ideologues like Camille Paglia and R. U. Sirius signaled the direction in which the magazine was headed: straight into the hearts of what one Ogilvy & Mather executive giddily describes as the "techno-savvies."

In 1995, *Wired* made public its "HotWired" site on the World Wide Web, and created a media sensation by becoming one of the first web providers to offer advertising. In addition to the plaudits they received from major agencies, the service attracted the advertising of over fourteen big-name clients (including AT&T, MCI, Sprint, and IBM). Ever the rebels, *Wired* restricted the use of its site to those who registered by name and e-mail address, which will no doubt come in handy later for merchandising opportunities. Unfortunately, within two months, HotWired's executive editor had quit. "A glib and probably unfair way to state our differences is that [founder] Louis [Rossetto] wanted to create something cool for the sponsors and I wanted to create something cool for the people on the Web," said the departing executive editor. Needless to say, the advertisers remain.

Wired refers to its readers as "digital revolutionaries," but don't be fooled: the "R" word is being used in the same way it is elsewhere in recent management literature—to signify a particularly unscrupulous type of executive. In fact, according to *Advertising Age*, some 84% of *Wired* readers are made up of managerial professionals with a median household income of well over $80,000. They may be revolutionaries, but they also happen to be the legions of MBAs graduating each year from business schools around the country, where *Wired* is a must read. This group is rooted economically rather than geographically, and must keep up with the latest thinking on the frontiers of Information if they are going to kick ass like their parents did.

Wired has staked out a classic market niche for itself; the kind of ready-made ideological profit-center that only comes along once every ten or twenty years. More than a mere high-end showplace, *Wired* is a full-blown lifestyle guide, like *Vanity Fair* was under Tina Brown, speaking to its status-seeking readers with a familiar but still curious blend of sympathy and exacerbation. It understands what they want, but it is forever scolding them for being slightly behind the curve.

The Rationalizer

Wired's vision of the good life is impressively consistent: money, power, and a Game Boy sewn into the palm of your hand. Equally consistent is the absence of any serious consideration of the problems that come with business control of information technology. In order to reconcile its standard pro-business politics with its rebel image, the magazine makes a great display of embracing a certain strain of extreme information antinomianism.

The perennial favorite issue in this strangely contentless variety of "revolution" is the clipper chip, a device invented by the National Security Agency that would allow them to "listen in" on all on-line conversations. However "radical" *Wired*'s diatribes against the chip may sound, nobody's going out on a limb by supporting this one around the office: business information is as closely guarded as the plots of anarchists once were. Furthermore, the NSA's plan calls for companies to bear a substantial financial burden in installing the chip. By setting itself in opposition to this ludicrous remnant of the Cold War state, *Wired* encourages its readers to imagine themselves revolutionaries when all they are doing is standing up for their First Amendment rights.

Another *Wired* cause célèbre is the outlaw hacker. In almost every issue, it seems, the editors find a new way to stir readers' outrage over the fate of one Phiber Optik, a jailed hacker described as having a "colorful urban style and a near suicidal willingness to demonstrate his prowess at picking the locks on telephone company systems." While *Wired*'s ongoing loyalty to the troubled young man is admirable, its frequent stories do little more than use him to reaffirm the myth of the rebel entrepreneur so celebrated in contemporary management literature. The bottom line, as usual, is that computers are empowering, and that we, too, can best the stodgy Organization Men, à la *War Games*, if we show a little pluck.

For all its radical posturing, *Wired*'s chosen cultural duty (and market niche) is as the Great Rationalizer of the new technology. While *Time* and *Newsweek* might devote special numbers to the internet, every issue of *Wired* blares forth the party line: being wired directly to manufacturers will mean more democracy, increased power for the little guys, greater freedom for consumers who will be able to order goods and talk to their friends (finally!) through an electronic medium. As the magazine maintains, "Life in cyberspace is more egalitarian than elitist, more decentralized than hierarchical. We might think of life in cyberspace shaping up exactly as Thomas Jefferson would have wanted it: founded on the primacy of individual liberty and a commitment to pluralism, diversity and community." Further down the page, the Jeffersonian ideal is said to include "all the dazzling goodies of home shopping, movies on demand, teleconferencing, and cheap, instant databases." And we thought he would have been happy with a mere Northwest passage. But wait—it gets even better. Not only will the new information technology empower each and every one of us beyond our wildest dreams, it will also allow us to implement all those neat Gingrichian platitudes about government that we've been mouthing for so long: "The net is merely a means to an end," *Wired* notes sagely, "the end is to reverse engineer government, to hack it down to its component parts and fix it."

Wired has a simple message from which it never strays very far: computers are not implements of conformity, overorganization, and all those other evils of the 1950s; on the contrary, computers are fun. They are liberating. It will be a good thing—hell, let's go all the way: it will be a bona-fide *utopia* when we are all finally wired electronically together, the big culture conglomerates acting as intermediaries. Rebels with funky hairdos and rockin' attitudes will rule, we'll finally get to tell those stiff gray guys what to do. No, wait, it'll be even better than that, we'll get to choose from *200 channels.* Can you imagine?

Naturally, in *Wired*'s world there is nothing wrong with corporate control of the cyber-future. In fact, *Wired* does its best to present the masters of the "business community" as hip fellow-hackers. A cover story about TCI's John Malone, which featured a photograph of this eminent Captain of Information "raster mastered" (*Wired*-speak for computer imaged) to a picture of Mel Gibson as the Road Warrior, showcases this approach at its wryest. Even though the guy has been screwing consumers with high margins for years (to the point where those meddling Feds had to step in and put an end to his monopolistic plundering), he's still depicted as a self-aware hipster who you can feel comfortable admiring.

The secret of *Wired's* success is rather a simple thing, when you come right down to it.. The magazine's founders identified the direction in which American business was moving, the strange cross between sixties countercultural ideas and the usual exploitative behavior that was coming to dominate the boardroom. And then they put themselves out in front of it. Being a corporation isn't dull and conformist anymore—it rocks! And though it may sound bad to spend all your free time imbibing corporate product, it's really a form of rebellion: just look at those excellent typefaces, the way we've run the lines into one another, stood up to all those guys that insist on readability and other such implements of patriarchy!

Postscript

As it turned out, the Killer App did have one serious glitch. All of that hyper-revolutionary talk made *Wired* extremely vulnerable to cultural outflanking by someone even *more* hyper-revolutionary. As Keith White's essay was reprinted in 'zines and web sites without number, one could feel *Wired*'s smooth, problem-free joining of radicalism and corporate culture beginning to pucker and crack.

We are not unsympathetic to *Wired*'s problems. We understand that it's the nature of the American business class to either ignore people on the Left or to believe them to be extinct (having left behind all these neat words like "subversion" and "revolution"), and that our criticism (and probably our existence) took *Wired* completely by surprise. But their outrage at our pinpricks seemed to make the problem worse. In a discussion of the article that appeared in *Utne Reader* in September–October 1995 one *Wired* editor retorted that "consumerism IS revolutionary" while the journalist who did several of *Wired*'s stories on the information-bosses came after Keith with a barrage of learned disquisitions on the fundamental nature of man and society and then nailed him in the classic trap: In order to agree with our critique, "one must assume that capitalism is . . . inferior to some other approach or economic system." What other "approach or economic system" could he mean? Was a writer for the magazine that equates computing with the millennium calling us bolsheviks?

Our politics aside, *Wired*'s rapid early success built hundreds of reputations and companies. Today from northern Virginia to the San Francisco Bay Area the countryside crawls with a new leisure class made rich on the stock options of internet companies whose reputations derived largely from having been anointed as favorites by none other than *Wired* magazine.

But *Wired* has had trouble turning their kingmaking powers to their own advantage. They branched out into internet and book publishing in 1994–95, but the initial public offering they attempted in early 1996 never got off the ground. The official offering document they filed with the SEC described the company's business as "creating compelling, branded content with attitude" and assured investors that "none of the Company's employees is represented by a labor union." Even if *Wired* does have the bolshevik situation under control, rebel capitalists everywhere were no doubt thinking, how good an idea is it to invest in attitude? *Wired*'s second IPO effort, which also sank, came with a description that bordered on the Baffleresque:

> Site Co-branding. Site co-branding is a format introduced by the Company in 1996 through which the sponsor underwrites and actively co-markets a HotWired Network site in exchange for exclusive long-term sponsorship and deeper integration of brand presence within site content. For example, in September 1996 Levi Strauss & Co. began a 12-month commitment to co-brand the Dream Jobs site with its Dockers® casual-wear brand, and it will co-market the site as part of its planned Dockers® print advertising campaign in Spring 1997.

Let's see: Branded content with attitude, dream jobs, and a union-free work-place. You won't get paid much, and of course your benefits will probably suck, but everyone will respect your (branded) 'tude. Despite such agile zeitgeist mastery, the *Wired* IPO eventually had to be withdrawn altogether, to the hoots of a national media now contemptuous of the hype makers they once cheered.

MAURA MAHONEY

Back in Black:
Here Come the Beatniks!

So you've just completed the inevitable arc from derision to interest to all-out consumer craving over bell-bottoms, and now a
new, or rather, a renewed trend has reared up along the ever-jagged
cutting edge. And worse, this latest expression of the herd—oops,
vanguard—involves more than fond memories of *The Brady Bunch*
recollected in tranquility, or the ability to wear clogs with a straight
face. This is a trend of the hip-lit variety, fashion as totality; in
which the clothes are meant to mirror the artistic soul of the bearer;
sophistication is signaled with the accessory of a dog-eared paper-
back; and *"la vie intellectuelle"* is self-consciously pursued but inevitably condensed to a prefabricated "look."

Well, put away that crocheted cap, turn off the Pearl Jam, forget
you ever heard of Seattle. Your days of automatic street cred sim-

ply for moshing and getting your hair to hang just so over one eye are done. It's time to get serious—break out the black turtleneck, rent French gangster films, and grab your Ginsberg. Beat is back.

But why? And why now? When did the resurgence of this particular brand of ennui and high seriousness first occur? The obvious answer is that beatnicity itself never fully went away, even though the Beatniks themselves ceased to exist as a coherent group about 1960. With the exception of the early Allen Ginsberg, the Beat writers were essentially celebrity-artists, Hemingways minus the extraordinary talent, whose "immortality" was insured not by their work but by their lifestyle. Naturally the Beat image of the rebellious drifter and the antisocial bohemian is a nearly irresistible pose, and it continued to inspire (with mind-bending irony) countless youths to celebrate anarchic individualism by donning a uniform (jeans-and-turtleneck) and gathering (preferably in large groups) in coffeehouses to brood and read bad poetry together— at least until Mom and Dad had paid the last tuition bill. And in the early nineties, this familiar rite of passage blossomed into new-found popularity for urban poetry readings.

The *commercial* rediscovery of the Beats in the 1990s was inevitable, once coffeehouse poetry became one of those "underground" movements that everybody knows about. The culture industry finally recognized in it all the magic ingredients: It's gritty, urban, and edgy; the people's poets can preen (and dress) like rock stars and have even less of a need to carry a tune; it's "deep" enough to seem elitist yet simple enough to be popular; and best of all, the fans can still wear their Doc Martens. Beautiful. Enter Max Blagg.

Blagg is the poet laureate of the ad world, whose verse-spouting Gap commercials in 1992 ("Sky fits heaven, so ride it / Child fits mother, so hold your baby tight," etc.) heralded the commercial dawn of the rebeat era; the commodification of the Rebel Poet had officially begun. Such is the power of advertising and image that Blagg became a bit of a cult-hero himself and people even assumed he was authentic (although perhaps this is not surprising in a society in which Robert Bly's poetry is thought to have merit). At any rate, the message was clear: all it takes to be a poet is the willingness to declaim—and to wear the right clothes.

Since then the Beat-biz just kept gathering steam. *Esquire* announced, "we're deep in the midst of a beat revival," and promoted beat style as "a 90s reaction against 80s self-consciousness . . . Beat has always been a style for people who don't want to be bothered with style." Undoubtedly such antistyle types will be unmoved by the article's accompanying photos of Donna Karan's, Calvin Klein's, and Dries Van Noten's "Beatnik Collections for '93."

Another writer drooled, "the new beat style is cooler than iced café mocha on a warm day . . . . It's affected by Generation Xers and tail-end baby boomers who mix cappuccino with hour-long conversations, poetry readings amid acoustic jazz and blues." (Imagine! An hour-long conversation!) Even Robert Martins, curator of the Costume Institute at the Metropolitan Museum of Art in New York, entered the fray. Noting that the object of the new trend is to look bohemian and intellectual rather than replicate a specific period's dress, he opined that the current look is a blend: "The 50s coming back and the 70s coming back in the 90s, all of which come out of some kind of matrix of existentialism."

Whatever you do, if you're aspiring to Beat-hood, don't leave your matrix at home!

The Gap's 1993 celebrities-who-wore-khakis ad campaign included Jack Kerouac, looking hardened and compelling in pants you too can buy. There's a "Kerouac Jack's Bongo Bar" in Chicago, where upscale bohemians choose from a full array of wines amid enormous murals of Jack himself surrounded by his celebrity friends (whose glorious faces are rendered not in Pollock-style abstraction, but with painstaking clarity so no mistake about Kerouac's cool is possible). Kerouac is clearly the poster boy of Beat nostalgia—perhaps because *On the Road* is such a cherished fantasy ride (and such a quick read) or perhaps because he is conveniently dead and therefore instantly iconic. His aesthetic, the transcendence of sensation and onrushing action, and his pursuit of slick style over substantive content, lend themselves nicely both to advertising and that ineluctable late-twentieth-century "art form"—the video image.

And so, predictably enough, Beatniks on video came to the global coffeehouse when MTV broadcast an all-poetry edition of its "Unplugged" series in 1993. Seven writers, including Maggie Estep (barefoot), Edwin Torres (goatee), and Henry Rollins (tattoo), performed their work in what Caryn James of the *New York Times* described as "a café setting that duplicates the spoken-word clubs that have sprung up in the last few years and pays homage to the days of the Beats (People actually hold cigarettes; definitely retro.)."

In case anyone should fail to recognize that this was very hip stuff, John J. O'Connor, in *another* review of the show for the *Times,* reminded us: "The spirit of Allen Ginsberg and the Beats is palpable." And while most of the reviewers acknowledged that the poetry itself was eminently forgettable, nearly all strained for a solemnity that this display of Beatnik high-mindedness evidently warranted. One critic stated, "You may not admire their wordplay, but you will be impressed with their energy, showmanship, and sheer gall—if anyone can make poetry cool, MTV can." Caryn James even gamely proclaimed that "there's nothing to say an MTV moment can't be poetic, as long as you don't think Matthew Arnold and T. S. Eliot own the poetry franchise" and that "street poetry is a vocal, visceral expression of contemporary life."

Please. While all this interest in and celebration of poetry is laudable, poetry itself is clearly not the point, or surely a little more effort would have been expended on it. Poems do not have to equal Arnold and Eliot to be refreshing, interesting, or insightful; but the producers of the show did not aspire to achieve anything much beyond atmosphere. The "Unplugged" poets offered little more than self-absorbed musings, or pained, soft-headed critiques of the most obvious deficiencies of the modern world. The new Beats proved to be not only derivative, but dull and sanctimonious as well. Their "poems" were merely a gimmick, amounting to nothing but broadsides for correct MTV attitude. New beats "hold" cigarettes because they want to *look* jaded; they borrow cliches from another era because they lack the imagination to dream up anything new.

The fin-de-siècle Beat movement is merely a tired, contrived appropriation of a shallow aesthetic, to be enjoyed on the level of a rejuvenated fashion fad. Kerouac's creed, now devoid even of freshness, is being parboiled to nothing more than performance-art dreck, poetry consumed by commerciality, utter conformity masquerading as rebellion.

It's enough to make anyone want to read Shelley.

Baffler #5, 1993

KEITH WHITE

Burn Down
the House of Commons in
Your Brand New Shoes

I WANTED TO BE a *Details* man. I had recognized my need for bee-stung lips, carefully unkempt hair, a washboard stomach, baggy Versace suits, tattoos—you get the picture. I wanted to pal around with other young sophisticates dressed just as rakishly as I, chatting about the latest trend in alternative music and last week's party with Drew, Ethan, Uma, and Keanu. I couldn't get what I needed from stodgy old *Esquire* or pretty-boy *GQ*. *Spin* might tell me how to dress and behave like Eddie Vedder, but its narrow focus—music—would leave me in the dark about important developments in ice climbing and seventies collectibles. The trio of British men's fashion mags (*The Face*, *Arena*, and *Sky*) were simply too expensive and too derivative for my tastes. *Details*, with its $2 cover price and its relentlessly macho attitude, promised to deliver the new me.

I think of *Details* as the Pearl Jam of the magazine world, the glittery showplace where rebellion, individualism, and nonconformity are conveniently packaged and paired with all of the correct accessories. And like Pearl Jam, *Details* knows how to translate nonconformity into sales. With the combination of Condé Nast's deep pockets, tremendous newsstand clout, and its unifying vision of the rebel as consumer, *Details'* circulation leapt from 150,000 to over 450,000 in less than four years.

The magazine chronicles what I should buy, what I should wear, where I should go, what I should see, and what mass-culture offerings I should choose from. *Details* is a sort of Sears catalog with 'tude, the fabulous intermediary between the latest offering of the nation's clothing and entertainment industries and excitement-starved people like me. And with its utilitarian, punk-inspired type-face and its fractured layout, a reader intent upon learning the secrets of youthful rebellion can be assured *Details* is serious about delivering.

Not that catering to the needs of the status-anxious is anything new. We Americans have long looked to magazines to guide us through the dizzying array of consumer choices. The roots of this tendency, indeed the roots of *Details'* beguiling come-on, are easily traced to the years immediately following World War II. It was then that postwar prosperity and the GI Bill made a college education widely available, thus debasing the undergraduate diploma as the preeminent emblem of achievement and sophistication. When anyone could earn a sheepskin, how were you supposed to prove your refinement? And with so many parvenus blessed with large discretionary incomes, how were you supposed to distinguish yourself from others in the newly monied masses?

A one-word solution was discovered: Taste. As members of the new middle class scrambled to improve their social standing, they were eager to adopt the accoutrements of their social betters. But while spending and acquiring increasingly became sanctioned ends in themselves, questions remained about how to assess individual performance in the new taste wars. Whereas traditionally the rich could rely on the customs of heritage ("Always shop at Brooks Brothers"), the middle class was attempting to camouflage its roots. That's where magazines came in; many publications proved happy to play the role of discriminating doyenne.

For a solid twenty years, beginning in the forties, *The New Yorker* emerged as the dominant voice of taste—a reign remarkable not just for its duration, but for its demographics. *The New Yorker*, after all, catered to the over-30 crowd, not generally the sort insecure enough about themselves to be easy marks. (*Details* wisely targets the more insecure pre- and post-college types.) But the magazine knew its craft. With pronouncements on this book and that art exhibit, ads for the "correct" scotch and "right" clothes, *The New Yorker* functioned as a kind of consumer finishing school. And, helpfully, the products pushed—swanky liqueurs, silk ties—were tantalizingly affordable. Just about anyone could save up and buy a seersucker suit from Brooks Brothers, if only once a year. In effect, *The New Yorker* traded on its literary cachet to play arbiter in the ever-more convoluted status game. As the magazine counseled readers on consumer selections, it grew fat with the ad pages of companies eager to reach this captive and suggestible audience.

Yet as the process of acquiring status became more complicated, readers sought more explicit instruction in the art of the buy. In the late sixties and early seventies, Clay Felker brought to life his vision of the chic, upscale, fantasy magazine for the urban middle class with *New York*, which was designed for a new generation of readers. With king-of-the-mountain bravado, Felker signaled his own magazine's arrival with fillips at the fusty, passé *New Yorker*. What panic and dyspepsia must have set in when hordes of older readers woke to discover that their beacon of chic had been deemed dowdy. Even as it asserted its bona fides, *New York* promised to offer more and clearer signals about how to consume. Recognizing the success of early articles in this genre, *New York* took to offering readers pullout guidebooks on topics that *The New Yorker* would consider too vulgar to mention: where to ski, which summer house to buy, which private schools to send your children to—purchasing decisions new to most readers.

New York provided the goods—the inside dope on how to go about assessing such decisions—but in doing so, it raised the stakes. For implicit in such guidebooks was a new hierarchy. It wasn't enough to know to send your kids to boarding school, it was a matter of which one—and, to be sure, there was always at least one out of the reach of most *New York* readers. Those unattainable schools or apartments or summer homes were there to keep those who might feel they had it sussed just a little off-kilter. That was because *New York* offered a particularly fragile sort of status—the fashionable kind—and it wanted to make sure its reader remained uncomfortable enough to keep coming back for more from those truly in the know—namely, the editors. *New York*'s success was confirmed by a rash of identical glossies that emerged in most American cities.

The eighties saw the advent of *Spy* and *Vanity Fair*, which wove the "how tos" of taste and purchasing into the very text of each article. *Spy*'s innovation was offering helpful consumer hints in the guise of snobbish put-downs. For instance, in a piece about the demise of Times Square, the magazine approvingly sneered that it might "make Florsheim shoes harder to come by." What exactly is wrong with Florsheim shoes—they seem sturdy and stylish enough to the untrained eye—is a question left unanswered, the kind of if-you-have-to-ask omission designed to draw readers in and make them feel happily allied with the magazine's sense of humor as well as its commercial appetites. (The clear implication was that Florsheim shoes were lousy because they were so available, and thus so damn middle class.) Not spelling this out was typical of *Spy*'s approach to what's-hot-and-what's-not journalism. The point was never to argue for the cool; the cool explained itself, or more precisely it was cool because the folks on the masthead had decided it was so.

Vanity Fair writers used the vehicle of celebrity profiles to offer hints to readers about which brands of Italian loafers and mineral water were suitable. Readers are presumably thankful, having been given both valuable information on how to plan their next purchase as well as nifty cocktail-party trivia and handy opinions. As the half-life of fashionable status became ever more compressed, these monthlies strained to stay one step ahead, keeping their readers slightly off-balance and anxious about their own standing on the tote board of hip. *Spy* played this game well, but apparently not well enough. Hemorrhaging talented editors and ad pages for years, the magazine that made its name lampooning the rich of the eighties seemed to wither with the scene that it loved to roil.

Details may also be outpaced by its own definitions of hip, but don't count on that happening any time soon. After all, the magazine had its start as a hip downtown club sheet and chronicler of the Manhattan fashion scene. The magazine added sinew to this potentially effeminate image by adopting the look of the early American punk scene, even recruiting rocker Henry Rollins to become part of the *Details* glitterati. The mannequins on which *Details* hangs its expensive clothes are rebels, with real tattoos to show how close they live to the edge.

Recognizing that *Details* was the real thing, my quest to become a *Details* man was hampered by an unnerving fear. How on earth was I going to reinvent myself month after month with the latest cool identities? How was I going to pass myself off as an aficionado of all these disparate trends when I knew nothing about them? *Details* had the answer. It didn't just fill me in about grunge, it gave me an encapsulated history of the movement, so I could wow my friends with my firm grasp of alternative arcana (Did you know that the Smashing Pumpkins' lead singer had a fling with Courtney Love while Kurt Cobain was sleeping on the Melvins' front porch?). It even had a feature showing me how to alter my clothes so it looks like I've been a punk rocker for years. *Details* never introduces a new youth fashion without painstakingly delineating its rebel credibility.

Despite the whirlwind of trends, *Details* retains a unifying philosophical viewpoint—the archetypal American male is a rebel consumer. A 1994 issue that featured $300 silk Versace shirts also included a revealing apotheosis of Lollapalooza performers Anthony Kiedis and Henry Rollins as the quintessential men of the nineties. "These guys are not only musicians, or even rock stars," the magazine affirmed, "but modern men, emblems of a new masculinity." These "rock and roll samurai live outside the law, but are bound by their own moral codes." The words used to describe this new man were exciting and fresh: explosive, individualist, all for one, self-styled, rebellious, existential, heroic, and—most appealing of all—nonconformist. (These attributes are presented as virtues in themselves. Absent is any sense that the magazine's self-styled, rebellious, existential hero should do or strive for anything beyond consuming.) Furthermore, *Details* was offering to show me how to buy the appropriate gear so I could become just as individualistic.

Other articles further impressed on me the magazine's guiding vision of alternative as a set of consumer choices. When *Details* pushes expensive bathing costumes, it pairs them not with suntanned frat boys, but with skinhead men with tattoos, Doc Marten boots, and leather jackets emblazoned with the names of hard-core bands from the eighties. A $900 silk shirt was photographed with the instructions, "Wear it loose with tight jeans and a rock and roll attitude." Another time it divulged which expensive home video games are preferred by the members of Faith No More. It treated me to a photo spread featuring Perry Farrell, Billy Idol, and a member of the Stone Temple Pilots posing in the latest designer clothes. It showed me that I, too, could show the appropriate level of insouciance by reclining on my office couch while wearing the expensive clothes of designer Calvin Klein.

And *Details* understood my abiding anxiety about falling behind the curve, and failing to purchase and display the appropriate
books and CDs, emblems that would show that I, too, flouted convention. That's a kind of nervousness that is only exacerbated as
one grows older and less daring, feeling further removed from the
latest in youth culture. When Michael Kinsley showed up at a party
for Doug Coupland, anointed voice of "Generation X," Kinsley
told a reporter that he was there because he "wanted to know what
the other generation is thinking." I could just about hear the tension
in his voice as he uttered those words, even as I saw my own future
pass before my eyes.

After drinking in a few issues, I was ready to become a *Details*
man. Setting out right away, I got myself a few baggy suits and
bought a copy of Rollins' poetry to display from my back pocket.
I got a particularly menacing tattoo on my neck, bought the sort of
car Anthony Kiedis drives, purchased some of Iggy Pop's brand of
underwear, and wore one of Michael Stipe's characteristic hats.
While I was spending my money, I thought I'd better pick up a few
packs of Excita condoms, some sex-technique videos, and a few
muscle building machines (all helpfully advertised in the back of
each issue). Unfortunately, all of this paraphernalia cost me
$150,000, and I was still behind the times—the next month's issue
had just hit the newsstand.

But my greatest disappointment came in a more recent issue.
Tucked away in the back pages of the magazine was an elaborate
apologia to all readers who had been led astray by the misfires of
Details' cultural divining rod. "Hypes and Sleepers" was a year-end
scorecard on how the prognosticators had fared over the previous
twelve months. Reading through the list—glam revival, cyberpunk
revolution, girl grunge, Tabitha Soren—brought back painful
memories, like the time I showed up at a party wearing a tight pur-
ple jumpsuit and eyeliner only to find the room full of Beavis and
Butthead manqués. But the people I really felt sorry for were the
folks whose warehouses were full of now-unwanted platform

spaceboots, minidisks, and virtual reality machines—trends that had received countless editorial pages as *Details* valiantly tried to convince its readership of their viability.

Perhaps the real secret to being a *Details* man lies in the magazine's apology: "Mass taste is perverse and unpredictable, [but] that's also why keeping tabs on it is so much fun." This statement of regret seems directed less to readers than to the magazine's true clients, the real *Details* men—the guys who manufacture these trends and make money off them: the editors and the advertisers. Perhaps this shouldn't have been such a shock. After all, it was the dollars of eager advertisers that helped keep magazines like *The New Yorker, New York, Vanity Fair,* and *Spy* afloat despite the development of television and cable. While TV offered the mass marketer the mass consumer, magazines became venues where advertisers could reach a more specific audience, the "top of the pyramid," the segment that would consume their most upscale products. Once advertised in a magazine with trend-setting readers, any product can thus be differentiated and command a premium price from those nervous about their hip credentials. Look what Absolut did for plain old tasteless vodka in the eighties.

The difficulty with this approach in the nineties, of course, has been in developing a new segment, finding a package with the right credentials to slip past the ultrasophisticated media sensors of a younger set of consumers. These are, of course, the fabled "twentysomethings," the monotonous subject of film, news program conjecture, and solemn editorial head-shaking throughout the early nineties. What the media wanted, when it talked about the undefined and mysterious "twentysomethings" in *U.S. News and World Report, Advertising Age,* and *Business Week,* was not cultural expression, but some way of serving us up to the national marketers. The idea was to try to get us to care about and try to quench our own particular status anxiety and, eventually, to part with our money. *Details* saw the opening for a magazine that could accomplish this goal.

If ever thicker copies of the magazine weren't enough to prove its success, the people behind *Details* knew that it had pleased the right audiences when *Advertising Age* named it "Magazine of the Year," citing it for having "established itself as the leading media vehicle to reach Generation X." Indeed, publisher Mitchell Fox boasted of "delivering these twentysomething people to marketers in whatever way we can." Elements of that creativity include a column called "Hardware," devoted to items a would-be urban hipster should own, a monthly travel piece going so far as to give the phone numbers of the *Details*-approved places in which to hang out and spend your money, and an ongoing parade of new looks from the purveyors of too-expensive clothing and attitude.

For all the tattoos, *Details'* message is no different than any other lifestyle magazine: Who you are depends on what you consume, and how hip you are depends on how enthusiastically you keep up with the new. Nonconformity may be the language, but fashion is, as ever, the logic.

Baffler #5, 1993

Postscript

According to an item that appeared in the New York *Observer* for February 17, 1997:

> With *Details* stalled under the 500,000 circulation level and losing millions of dollars, Condé Nast Publications is tossing away its downtown vibe and introducing a heavy dose of work and career into its editorial mix of sex and music . . . .
>
> Apparently, Mr. [James] Truman [former editor of *Details* and current Condé Nast editorial director] experienced a bit of an epiphany when he noticed that the changes of the past few years, particularly in technology, have revolutionized the world of work. "(Young men) can still lead a life of independence and rebellion, but they're doing it through work rather than nose rings and tattoos," he said.

According to an item in the *New York Times* for February 11, 1997, the "epiphany" was that of *Details* editor Joe Dolce:

In June, pop culture addicts are going to see the definition of their favorite subject overturned when *Details* magazine presents work, not leisure, as what defines young men today. "When we started the magazine we thought the young man enacted his rebel pose through rock music," said Joe Dolce, the editor. "I started asking myself a while ago, how is a man rebelling today? Oddly enough, I came up with the idea of work."

THOMAS FRANK AND DAVE MULCAHEY

Consolidated Deviance, Inc.

The Rebel Consumer

INVESTMENT RESEARCH

LeBraff & Lebensart

LeBraff & Lebensart, Incorporated   Investment Bankers   Chicago   Cape Town   London   Tokyo

Buy Recommendation

Robert A. Dobbolina

Sept. 19, 1993
#91993

**CONSOLIDATED DEVIANCE, INC.
(CDEV-OTC)**

Close as of 9/18/93
DJIA: 3630.80
S & P 500:   459.43

Recent Price	$60	
52-Week Range	$61-5/8 -- $33	
Ind. Dividend	$0.28	
Ind. Yield	0.5%	

As of 6/01/93:

Shares outstanding	5.675 million
	(39% is closely held)
Market Value	$340.5 million
Debt/Capitalization	3.7%
Book Value/Share	$6.99

Earnings Per Share:

1994E	$2.98
1993E	$2.40
1992A	$1.90

Price/Earnings Ratio:

1994E	20.0X
1993E	25.2X

Return on Average Equity:

1994E	30.0%
1993E	30.0%
1992A	30.8%
5-Year Avg.	31.2%

Return on Assets: 15.0%

OPINION

Consolidated Deviance, Inc. ("ConDev") is unarguably the nation's leader, if not the sole force, in the fabrication, consultancy, licensing and merchandising of deviant subcultural practice. With its string of highly successful "SubCults™", mass-marketed youth culture campaigns highlighting rapid stylistic turnover and heavy cross-media accessorization, ConDev has brought the allure of the marginalized to the consuming public. Before modern techniques of youth culture fabrication were developed, stylistic subcultures often took years to achieve profitability. Today, by contrast, Consolidated Deviance can devise, package and introduce a profitable SubCult™ into any geographical, class or racial market in a matter of months. ConDev SubCults™ are always designed for full accessorization, ensuring **ample retail profit enhancement**. While the Company's nearly complete domination of contemporary youth culture is garnering widespread media attention as a "one-stop hegemony shop," we do not think ConDev's expansion potential or financial strength has been fully understood by the marketplace. ConDev benefits in unique ways from economic hard times and dismal labor markets. Mounting Inchoate Generational Anomie (IGA), threatening as it may seem to many in corporate America, will **positively impact** the Company's sales. As Company income increases at well-above-industry rates, labor costs continue to fall in real terms. With domestic markets far from saturated and explosive pent-up demand for consumer goods in the newly free East Bloc, we foresee strong earnings growth far into the future. We therefore recommend ConDev as a **strong buy** for accounts seeking aggressive growth.

OVERVIEW OF OPERATIONS

Consolidated Deviance's business, simply stated, consists of translating disparate subcultural signifying practices into easily identifiable and marketable lifestyle consumption configurations, known as the company's trademark SubCults™. The company's staff of lifestyle experts researches, invents, and tests a wide variety of such configurations, concentrating specifically on such market-proven attributes as "attitude," "authenticity," and "street-credibility." And although ConDev intends to positively impact the homogenization and centralization of cultural authority nationwide, the Company has found the greatest measure of success, ironically, in the heavy marketing of the musics, looks and accessories of "local scenes." These geographically particular SubCults™ are presented to the national market as the deeply indigenous and, therefore, 'authentic' expressions of grass-roots alienation.

Merchandise: All ConDev SubCults™ are designed to emphasize distinctive and unusual visual signifiers, which both serve to define in-group status rigidly and to ensure exclusive brand loyalty to company products. Typically the most profitable merchandising spin-offs of any SubCult™ are fashion accessories and musical recordings. Other associated products include hygiene and beauty items; liquor, cigarettes and food; publications; school supplies; and toys.

Intellectual Property: A full complement of signifying practices, including slang, sartorial quirks, physical gestures, and photographic techniques, is the foundation upon which every successful SubCult™ is constructed. While many of these practices remain in the domain of free speech, some are subject to patent.

Rapid Introduction, Rapid Obsolescence: Rapid Introduction, Rapid Obsolescence (RIRO) is the key to ConDev's SubCult™ development strategy. RIRO ensures the profitability of youth culture speculation by allowing a greater number of fully articulated, investment-grade SubCults™ to arise and be liquidated in a given period of time, each one carrying a full payload of accessories and musical products. Accordingly the Company constructs each of its various SubCult™ ventures with a built-in impulse to self-destruction: within two years after their initial deployment, Consolidated Deviance-brand SubCults™ are usually regarded as unfashionable by the very consumers who originally embraced them. High lifestyle turnover velocity (LTV) is achieved by emphasizing the unusual or the awkward in a SubCult's™ visual definition and by emphasizing antinomianism and deviance in its attitudinal definition. Ideally, by the time a SubCult™ has been 'conventionalized', lifestyle consumers have migrated to new SubCults.™

In the past, American youth culture marketers were sometimes able to profit from campaigns with relatively low LTV, such as "Classic Rock" or the "Motown." As consumers in the United States become better accustomed to the rapid turnover of youth movements, ConDev is expected to accelerate its production schedule, aiming through heightened rebelliousness (and with the help of nationwide economic downsizing) to achieve a standard SubCult™ lifespan of less than a year by 1997.

In the aftermath of the marketing success of its highly publicized "Grunge" SubCult™ of 1991-92, *Obsolescence Marketer* dubbed ConDev "the nation's unchallenged leader" in RIRO marketing. The company has succeeded by aggressively rationalizing a process once thought to be the realm of artistic "visionaries." In the past, youth culture fabrication services were performed haphazardly by television producers, admen, clothing designers and music executives working independently and without central direction. ConDev has connected the disparate nodes of cultural manufacturing, and as a result has been able to offer clients a greater number of more coherent potential youth cultures far more rapidly than its competitors.

Marketing Strategy: ConDev launches a new SubCult™ only after exhaustive analysis of key consumer data. Its research department has developed trail-blazing new analytical techniques that focus on the exceptional traits of modern youth. The Company's key consumer indicator, the IGASP ratio, expresses the relationship between *inchoate generational anomie (IGA)* and *spending power (SP)*. The benchmark of the ratio (IGASP=1.00) was set to reflect IGASP levels of August, 1968, when youth rebelliousness and youth spending power were at all-time peaks in real terms.

IGASP curves can be plotted [see figures 1 and 2] to give a picture of the youth culture cooptation possibilities for any market or demographic cohort. Figure 1 shows an IGASP configuration commonly referred to as the "Nike Swoosh," which represents a "bullish" market for SubCult™ positioning. At the low end of the spending-power axis one notes relatively high corresponding IGA values. This condition is typical of the poor and is therefore irrelevant to the marketer. But at the high end of the spending power axis one also sees relatively high IGA values, indicating that the rich are restless and ready for lifestyle experimentation. Under such conditions, ConDev product virtually sells itself.

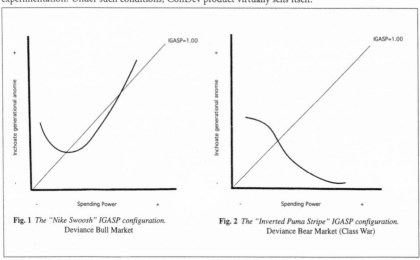

Fig. 1 *The "Nike Swoosh" IGASP configuration.*
Deviance Bull Market

Fig. 2 *The "Inverted Puma Stripe" IGASP configuration.*
Deviance Bear Market (Class War)

Figure 2 shows a more "bearish" market configuration known as the "Inverted Puma Stripe." One notes, as expected, the high corresponding IGA values at the low end of the spending power axis. In contrast to the Nike Swoosh configuration, however, IGA values diminish toward the high end of the spending power axis. This indicates stodgy consumer activity among a relatively complacent middle class. This IGASP configuration, incidentally, also represents social conditions that have historically given rise to class war.

Media Cooptation Strategy: The interest ConDev retains in several large media conglomerates ensures a reasonable amount of large-scale media exposure for any company concept once it has achieved widespread street credibility. But the really important media work comes at a much earlier stage. The launch of each new SubCult™ must be carefully orchestrated to preserve its patina of grass-roots "authenticity." This effect has been facilitated by the company's outright control of a number of smaller publications, DIY-type record labels and thrift store chains.

Academic Cooptation Strategy: ConDev's founder, James Hatt, opened new vistas in the early 1970s when he introduced Poststructuralism™ into several academic markets—working out of his garage! Little did he imagine that this scholarly fashion would spearhead one of the most exciting marketing industries of the '90s. With the 1991 acquisition of the British think tank Lifestyle Partners Ltd., ConDev began a long-anticipated re-entry into this difficult but rewarding market. A new generation of scholars, many of whom have been lifelong customers of the Company's theory products, is quite willing to celebrate, help publicize and lend credibility to certain youth culture ventures *without compensation*. Academics show the most enthusiasm for SubCults™ that accentuate deviance and marginality—the very factors, by happy coincidence, that make the Company's SubCults™ obsolescent and profitable.

While traders and portfolio managers may sometimes find academic prose impenetrable, pedagogical enthusiasm has been found to dramatically increase a culture-product's "credibility" factor significantly in 88 percent of known cases. In addition, it can extend a SubCult's™ shelf life indefinitely by making it attractive to generations of university-aged consumers long after the more discriminating youth cohorts have abandoned it. A popular technique in Britain for decades, academic cooptation helped the beleaguered Madonna Organization maintain market share as its aging customer base entered graduate school.

ConDev has further rationalized the process of academic/SubCult™ synergy by endowing a number of university chairs and departments of "subcultural studies" and acquiring an interest in one of the country's most influential academic presses. The latter effort's first title, a volume of essays seeking to appreciate the "libidinal heteroglossia of Grunge," was perhaps less successful than the Company had hoped. Company managers hope to maximize academic/SubCult™ synergy with PostRock™, a new product planned for launch in the fall of 1995. A *Finnegan's Wake* to the Madonna Organization's *Fanny Hill*, PostRock™ promises an endless feedback loop where incomprehensible music spawns impenetrable exegeses, and vice versa.

"Grunge": In 1992, ConDev proved once and for all the profitability of youth culture speculation with the success of its Grunge SubCult™. In early 1991 the Company was able to unite, name, and accessorize an unruly array of disparate youth culture elements with a single slang, sound and look. Stronger-than-expected American consumption of Grunge™-related product prompted one of the sharpest rallies in the Youth Culture Marketability Index (YCMI) since the "disco sucks" frisson of 1980. In fact, the index reached all-time highs in October, 1992, *less than eighteen months* after the company had introduced the Grunge™ subculture. In early January, 1993, in response to rumors concerning Grunge's™ inauthenticity, heavy selling battered YCMI futures, and Wall Street expected a correction in ConDev shares. Viewing Grunge's™ official obsolescence as irrelevant or even beneficial to overall market penetrability, the Company's risk management department aggressively maintained long positions at the Chicago

Board of Trade and in the end was proved the wiser. The 18 months Grunge™ enjoyed before its demise was in fact quite long-lived by European standards, and allowed ample time for the company to maximize profits and liquidate its Grunge™ inventories. Moreover, the sudden decline of Grunge™ cleared the way for the Company's next SubCult™ introduction, "Baby Fems" and "Riot Grrls." And in the week following the airing of Pepsi's 1993 Super Bowl ads, traders saw three consecutive limit-up trading days in the YCMI pits.

Re-engineering the Culture Industry: Consolidated Deviance has blazed new trails in labor-cost controls. The company's greatest asset is a highly educated and highly motivated work force. The vogue of cultural studies has dovetailed nicely with the conglomeration of the Culture industry and the worldwide assault on the wage, giving rise to a glut of savvy and underemployed pop culture pundits. This work force, though almost exclusively privileged, highly educated and acutely leveraged, is generally willing to work for low wages and few benefits. It is also indifferent, even hostile, to labor organization efforts. And unlike entry-level workers in most industries, the company's fresh post-college recruits are valued for their youth, inexperience and bad attitudes. Nor, in our opinion, is this advantage threatened by a maturing employee base—ConDev benefits from and actively encourages workforce attrition.

Retail Outlook: The most nettlesome issue facing retailers today is how to expand sales as downsizing and stagnant wages are forcing middle-class consumers to tighten their belts. Not only has Consolidated Deviance avoided this problem—it profited richly from the protracted global recession that started in 1990. Of all age cohorts, consumers in the 16-28 year range are the most likely to translate feelings of economic dislocation and personal insufficiency into a frenzied urge to purchase edgy lifestyle accessories. Thus, based on the global economy's dismal prognosis alone, we expect the ConDev product to move briskly well into the future.

True business leaders have always known how to take lemons and make lemonade. Henry Ford knew that the way to stimulate demand for his product was to pay his workers higher wages and make them into reliable consumers. Although critics decried Ford as a heretic, the modern industrial state has prospered ever since under the Fordist paradigm. In a similar fashion, Corporate America is now recognizing the wisdom of ConDev's founder, James Hatt. Jim's unique concept of deviance-driven synergy—the Hattist paradigm, if you will—provides multinational conglomerates the tools to manipulate consumer desire and to shape the articulation of dissent. "Whoever breaks the most rules wins," Jim is fond of saying. We couldn't agree more.

Postscript

Three years after writing about Consolidated Deviance, we received in the mail from one of our subscribers a prospectus for a company called Vans, a California-based shoe manufacture. This company, it turns out, is as adept a lifestyle-and-deviance merchant as anything we could have invented—and as utterly frank about it. Written in a dense and ultra-serious legalistic prose, the document notes that:

> the Company has developed a strong brand image which the Company believes represents the individualistic and outdoor lifestyle of its target customer base. The VANS brand image coincides with what the Company believes is a fundamental shift in the attitudes and lifestyles of young people worldwide, characterized by the rapid growth and acceptance of alternative, outdoor sports and the desire to lead an individualistic, contemporary lifestyle.
>
> The company's success is largely dependent on its ability to anticipate the rapidly changing fashion tastes of its customers and to provide merchandise that appeals to their preferences in a timely manner.

And then, just to make things worse, the prospectus notes nonchalantly how the Company recently "began to source from South Korea" and then determined that a plant closure would be required back in California.

First time as parody, second time as tragedy?

PART II

The Culture of Business

BILL BOISVERT

Apostles of the New Entrepreneur: Business Books and the Management Crisis

JUST BEFORE CHRISTMAS, Wal-Mart workers arrive at their stores to find their boss grinning down at them from a video monitor. Sam Walton, utterly approachable (if only via satellite) in his trademark baseball cap, seems at first to want only to relate a few hunting anecdotes. But then he gets down to business: he's there to launch his crusade for "aggressive hospitality"—a revolution in customer service that will, he promises, catapult Wal-Mart to the pinnacle of discount retail. He gently reassures the faint-of-heart, stressing the *internal* rewards of the new philosophy: "It would, I'm sure, help you become a leader, it would help your personality develop, you would become more outgoing, and in time you might become manager of the store." Finally, he leads his troops in a solemn pledge as, all over America, one hundred thousand Wal-

Mart "associates" raise their right hands: *"From this day forward, I solemnly promise and declare that every customer that comes within ten feet of me, I will smile, look them in the eye, and greet them, so help me Sam."*

The authors of the 1992 management book *Workplace 2000* couldn't resist this vignette, since it enacts virtually every business cliché of the past twenty years. The leader: informal and down-to-earth, insisting that everyone call him "Sam" as they swear their loyalty oaths. The vision: personal growth through abject servility. The program: forget about merchandise—sell them privilege, sell them attention, sell them a coterie of fawning retainers, capering at their every purchase. The workers: they're not employees, they're *associates,* trusted partners in building a fiercely antiunion company.

But damned if it doesn't work. Consider Wal-Mart purchaser John Love, who accidentally ordered five times too many Moon Pies for his Alabama store:

> It was a stupid mistake that could have gotten Love fired if he had worked for any of a number of other companies. Not at Wal-mart. Love's boss just told him: "Use your imagination, be creative and figure out a way to sell it." Love did. He created the first World Championship Moon Pie Eating Contest and held it in the store's parking lot. The contest and the promotion were so successful for the company that it is now held on an annual basis and draws thousands of spectators . . . .

Thus capitalism confronts the specter of postindustrial malaise. As strip-mall revelers fall upon the heaps of faintly toxic snack treats, another tiny crisis of overproduction is transformed into a miracle of overconsumption through the Stakhanovite exertions of a lone-hero salesman. We recognize here a drama of disgrace, forgiveness, and ultimate triumph, revolving around a few primordial themes: trust between supervisor and supervised; the redemptive metamorphosis of clerk into salesman and his centrality in creating a community of consumers; and the community's effort to preserve itself through the yearly reenactment of its foundation epic. And so this spare but exquisite passage from business literature articulates the core motifs of present day corporate ideology, even as it skirts the basic economic issues of efficiency and product quality. It doesn't question the need to manufacture Moon Pies, nor the wisdom of eating a great quantity of them. Instead, with the ancient sonorities of ritual and myth, it infuses sacred meaning into the making and selling of pure junk.

Business literature has always faced two contradictory tasks. It must instruct and prepare its middle-management audience to play a dominant-submissive role in a corporate autocracy; yet it must also inculcate the legend of the entrepreneur who renews the economy by facing, alone and unguided, the inscrutable judgment of the marketplace. Its readers are both fettered within a highly structured business dictatorship, and at the same time devotees of free-market individualism. Business writers massage this tension with elaborate theories of supervision that reassure managers as a class of their indispensability.

Whether they steal fire from the Harvard Business School or find enlightenment through a long pilgrimage in Oriental lands, all popular business books share certain idiosyncrasies. They euphemize their tautologies as "common sense" and their lists of slogans as "practical guides," as if management theories are both self-evidently true *and* arcane enough to require a hands-on primer and costly seminars. Like nursery rhymes, they are fascinated by numerology and alliteration, freeze-drying their "findings" into nuggets of doggerel like "the Three C's: Customers, Competition and Change" or Tom Peters' typically long-winded "Seven S© Framework: Structure, Systems, Style, Staff, Skills, Strategy and Shared Values." And to make reading fun for executives, they eschew logical exposition and an organized search for evidence in favor of brief, happy anecdotes about take-charge department heads, couched always in the cajoling rhetoric of cereal-box propaganda.

Yet these immutable stylistic quirks belie a decades-long up-heaval in the literature, from postwar placidity to post-Communist hysteria. Business books of the 1950s, basking in the noontide of suburban sprawl and Marshall Plan hegemony, offer untroubled systematizations of the role of management that let the organiza-tion man chart his exact position beneath a changeless corporate fir-mament, and fortify himself against tyrant bosses, scheming union reps, sullen line-workers, and other beasts of the field. Best of all, the whole social order rested squarely and eternally on the shoul-ders of management. As Peter Drucker, the Aquinas of manage-ment theory, put it in 1954, "Management . . . is the organ of society specifically charged with making resources productive, that is, with the responsibility for organized economic advance." But in the sev-enties, strange stars appeared in the sky, heralding unforetold plagues—stagflation, trade deficits, and white-collar recession. Sud-denly the management gurus' pious verities of growth and career advancement turned to ashes in their mouths. What if, after all, managers had imbibed the royal jelly of business school training only to preside over economic *decline?*

Little by little, a chiliastic tone crept into business discourse. The book titles changed: Fifties-era sobriety (*The Practice of Man-agement*) gave way in the eighties and nineties to panic-mongering (*Out of the Crisis*) and nihilism (*Thriving on Chaos*). A vast litera-ture on Leadership sprouted up to guide boards of directors seek-ing signs by which they might discern the corporate Messiah. And just when you'd think business writers would be toasting the death of Communism, instead you find them staring into the abyss, vying with each other to evoke images of havoc and doom. In his 1989 book *The Age of Unreason*, business futurist Charles Handy even compared the traditional business world to the Inca empire in that fearful moment when the Conquistadors' sails first appeared on the horizon; he warns hidebound corporate bureaucrats that they too face a juggernaut of unimaginable violence. But to explain all the wailing and gnashing of teeth, you have to look beyond the alarms over "international competitiveness" and the fear of Japan, for these anxieties are dwarfed by one apocalyptic change in the relations of production: *managers are obsolete.*

Rational, All Too Rational

The Vietnam War provided the first great shock to management's *ancien régime,* with the whole world from the Mekong delta to the Mississippi delta seeming to rise up against the corporate imperium. As military defeat segued into economic decline—wage and price controls, inflation, the New Left's challenge to business rule, and the occupation of the United States by Japan in the 1980s—the business community's diagnosis of the Vietnam failure would be repeated almost verbatim in their later critiques of corporate America. Right-wing critics linked the disaster in Indochina to the assembly-line techniques used to fight the war, sneering at the emphasis on "body counts" and "kill ratios." Their complaints about the moral corruption of the army in Vietnam—not the war crimes, of course, but affronts to orderliness like heroin addiction and fragging—prefigured present-day obsessions with random drug testing, disgruntled postal workers, and other symptoms of blue-collar degeneracy. The officer corps was branded a group of careerist hacks who focused on accounting targets and failed to imbue their men with an unshakable will to conquer.

Business critics contrasted the Pentagon's bean-counter mentality with the supposed zealotry of the Vietcong guerilla and his mystical devotion to Ho Chi Minh. They became convinced that the key to an American economic revival lay in worker fanaticism and the cult of heroic leadership, of a sort they believed lay just behind the Iron Curtain. Leadership manuals, whose far-flung quest for potent anecdotes has always bred a certain degree of doctrinal promiscuity, began to feature stirring accounts of Lenin's boyhood alongside the usual profiles of Eleanor Roosevelt and Lee Iacocca. Tom Peters even titled one of his books *Liberation Management,* consciously emulating the rhetoric of left-wing insurgency.

For not even Ho himself could outdo American business writers in their contempt for Robert McNamara, who left the presidency of Ford Motor Company to run the Defense Department and the Vietnam War itself. Granted, McNamara, the epitome of a chief financial officer, was a hard man to warm up to; his favored intellectual pursuit was to spend a quiet evening with his wife and a few friends, taking and retaking the SAT. It took no great leap of the imagination to blame the bloody debacle in Vietnam on the corporate ethos he embodied. So when today's fashionable MBAs pour into the streets waving copies of *Leadership Secrets of Subcommandante Marcos*, they're really locked in a struggle against Fordism itself—the whole complex of assembly lines, mass production, and rationalized bureaucracy that define the American corporation at its apotheosis under McNamara and his ilk. But their insurrection isn't really aimed at the weaknesses of Fordism (or its philosophical generalization, Scientific Management) as a production system, but rather at its implicit assault on managerial privilege.

Frederick Taylor codified the principle of time-motion studies around the turn of the century, and gave his name to the system of Scientific Management that sprouted from it. His ideas were embellished by disciples like Lillian and Frank Gilbreth, who coined the word *therblig* to denote the irreducible physical components of a work routine—simple actions like grasping a tool, releasing a tool, or moving it horizontally. Scientific managers tried to excise unnecessary therbligs from a job and streamline the remaining ones through worker training and rational equipment design. Workers hated the efficiency expert sent out to time their jobs and set the piece rate, who would show up at their coal-shoveling yard with white lab coat and stopwatch, like some satanic avatar of punctiliousness. Taylorism radically de-skilled labor, turning it into a series of robotic motions and suppressing workers' volition and autonomy. Managers loved it, of course—until they realized it was doing the same thing to them.

For supervisors became Taylorized as well, transformed into

narrow specialists with no more inherent *right* to power than the average machinist. The boss's traditional virtues of pluck, fortitude, charisma, and viciousness became entirely irrelevant to the task of organizing production. Any colorless technician with a stopwatch, a movie camera, and a time-and-motion study manual could do the job; boosting profits was a simple matter of speeding up the job and lowering the piece rate. The advent of computers completed the debasement of management, automating the executive suite as thoroughly as the assembly line. As managers found their aura of mystery and prestige dissipating, their psychological dislocation congealed into a sense of political disenfranchisement. Peter Drucker, writing in 1954, compared Scientific Management to bolshevism, observing that "[Taylorism] is usually considered to have been anti-democratic. It was—in intent and direction—fully as much anti-aristocratic," with its soulless enjoinder that "power is grounded in technical competence" rather than the "moral responsibility" that underlies aristocracy. His bitterness at the substitution of "technical competence" for *noblesse oblige* as the legitimating principle behind workplace authority is understandable. It reflects a nervous appreciation that, while powerless workers still have jobs, powerless aristocrats are totally useless and fit only for the guillotine.

Beyond Good and Evil

Taylorism has shattered managers' sense of identity and purpose. Thus, when one surveys contemporary business literature, it's hard to avoid the sensation of being caught up in the aftermath of a nervous breakdown. Psychoanalysis, mysticism, religious tourism—all the traditional enthusiasms of an unhinged mind are represented here.

Some writers have responded to the dissolution of the corporate psyche with an attempt to rebuild a working managerial personality piece by piece. Julius Fast concentrates on the preverbal elements in *Body Language in the Workplace*, which teaches us to project truthfulness or loyalty by obscure physiological clues like handshake pressure and pupil dilation. Much of this work naggingly recaps pointers on corporate hygiene—don't slouch, don't fidget, don't dress like a slut, don't rape your underlings—that apparently need to be learned anew by each generation of MBAs. But Fast also reminds us of just how devalued a skill language acquisition really is in the modern corporation, where so much activity seems to be mediated by pheromone signaling, the reptilian fight-or-flight response, and other hindbrain functions.

Others focus on teaching managers to integrate higher-order cognitive capabilities into a process known as Creativity. You can actually take courses in Creativity at many business schools—Stanford's features exercises in meditation, chanting, dream work, yoga, and tarot-card reading. The acknowledged leader in the field of Creativity is Edward de Bono, whose clients include DuPont and Heineken. De Bono understands that Creativity is both the key to business success and the one faculty in shortest supply among managers. He realizes that managers possess neither the scientist's training nor the worker's long familiarity with production methods; they can draw on little in the way of knowledge or insight to come up with fruitful new ideas. Creativity is thus one area where Scientific Management might still bolster supervisors' status, by letting them intervene in a process for which they have no native aptitude.

In its extreme form, managers' dread of the real world leads them into the embrace of Eastern religions. Zen is the most popular haven for the lost souls of executives; indeed, *Zen in the Art of Archery* is required reading in a University of Chicago course on Management. This classic New Age text narrates the journey of an Englishman from Western Rationalism to the harmony of Buddhism by way of the bow and arrow. Zen archery is elusive and frustrating, the sort of archery where hitting the target is the surest sign of failure. Initiates must give up all thought of the bullseye and attain a state of utter purposelessness; only then can they be one with the universe of arrows-in-flight. The appeal of this philosophy to business writers is obvious. From a Zen perspective, managers' sense of their own purposelessness changes from a burden into a transfiguration. To think of management as a *task* with achievable goals only reveals a certain degree of immaturity and spiritual pollution. Managing is really a *state of being*, a neverending trek inwards toward the purification of the manager's soul; we cannot—*must not*—scrutinize it by rationalist criteria of quality and efficiency.

But many leading management gurus have worked through their denial, bargaining, and rage to *accept* the obsolescence of managers. They acknowledge the crippling inefficiencies of competition, and present a far-reaching critique of the fragmented, hierarchical nature of work in a mass-production economy. According to the authors of the 1993 bestseller *Reengineering the Corporation*, "the old ways of doing business—the division of labor around which companies have been organized since Adam Smith first articulated the principle—simply don't work anymore."

The business-lit consensus wants a new paradigm, one that hearkens back to premodern artisan traditions—with each worker responsible for producing a meaningful artifact or service in a job that fuses labor with planning. Production should be managed by teams of line-workers who organize product design, manufacturing, purchasing, wage levels, and hiring. Specialization must be eradicated—each worker should learn to perform many tasks; the few coordinating positions that remain should rotate among workers. Companies should integrate vertically with their suppliers and customers, sharing information and technology; contracts should be awarded on the basis of a company's willingness to work cooperatively, rather than going to the lowest bidder. W. Edwards Deming, the management *über*-guru who claimed to have invented Japan, even wants companies to team up with their own competitors to jointly develop technology and manufacturing processes. All these writers note impressive gains in productivity and product quality in companies that adopt these principles. Truly rational planning, they say, requires integrated discussion and feedback between everyone from the research scientist to the spot-welder; it can't be done when workers are blinkered and pigeonholed by Scientific Management.

It may seem a strange and hopeful sign when corporate mouthpieces plagiarize Emma Goldman. But despite the iconoclastic tone of their prescriptions, the fundamental impulse motivating business writers is a reactionary one—an attempt by managerial aristocracy to enlist assembly-line democracy in the war against Taylorism. But how can such a bizarre alliance survive its internal contradictions? For in their panic at creeping proletarianization, supervisors seem to have forgotten that in this case, the enemy of their enemy is also their executioner. In the workplace of tomorrow, all the *useful* work—innovation, planning, and production—will proceed in a cooperative and egalitarian way. But then how can capitalism, based as it is on cruel inequalities of wealth and power, survive? How can the business literature rationalize the privileges of a managerial elite while it prophesies the End of Management?

To begin with, where will all the bosses go? To solve this conundrum, management theorists invoke the Law of Conservation of Supervisors: the abolition of middle management will be cancelled out by an equal and opposite reaction—"corporate downsizing." Corporations will shrink—shedding divisions, plants, and employees—while redundant middle managers emerge from their tombs as hard-driving CEOs at a swarm of minuscule spin-off and start-up companies that contract for the services the big companies used to perform under one roof. But while middle managers mutate into a class of small-time entrepreneurs, they still must justify their existence in a world where the CEO is even further removed from useful occupation than the foreman. Even in the Fortune 500, upper management has no *economic* function beyond the traditional boardroom prerogatives of looting the pension fund and relocating to Mexico; in the especially backward, exploitative world of small business, the boss is just the least productive member of the least productive sector in the economy.

The great challenge of business literature is thus to rejuvenate a now superfluous business class by reconstructing the mystique of the entrepreneur. Entrepreneurs must cast off the old husk of managerialism and cultivate their mysterious talents as leaders and visionaries. Part shaman, part huckster, the born-again entrepreneur possesses the gift of oracular communion with the murky forces of market trends, and stands ready to exploit it with the most shameless opportunism. Business missionaries have renounced the old covenant of production quotas and cost-cutting; the central tenets of the entrepreneur's new catechism are "marketing," "sales," "customer service," and "flexible labor markets." But this complex of euphemisms is really just a smokescreen concealing a retreat to capitalism's most antique and corrosive traditions of thought-control and worker oppression. For while business-lit hails progressive reforms in production, it uses the new creed of entrepreneurialism to shackle these reforms in the service of an age-old regime of futile hierarchy and mindless consumption.

Thus Spake Tom Peters

Like all religions, entrepreneurialism requires more than a mere assertion of faith. It carries with it a comprehensive worldview—its own science, its own history, its own art. At its epistemological core it tries to explain managers' sense of disorientation by focusing on the new information technology: The growing flood of knowledge and computing power, far from making things *more* stable and predictable, will make the world profoundly evanescent and unknowable. Around this key non sequitur business writers intone a litany of chance, uncertainty, and upheaval; they decry "planning" as the apostasy of union negotiatiors and government regulators. Only the gods know what the morrow will bring, and only the entrepreneur can divine their intent.

In this vein, Tom Peters draws an analogy between antirational entrepreneurialism's crusade against Taylorism, and the triumph of quantum mechanics, which "has trumped Newtonian physics."

Newton's orderly, calculable landscape of billiard balls and tidily orbiting satellites has given way to the misty, flickering world of wave-particle duality, where companies are both solvent *and* bankrupt until you do an audit. Thus, any attempt to plan and stabilize the corporate world defies the laws of nature *at the subatomic level.* Peters' mind is so hugely blown by Heisenberg's Uncertainty Principle that he recklessly links it with literary post-modernism, demonstrating just how dangerous the uncontrolled spread of critical theory can be:

> To read Max Frisch, Paul Bowles, Gabriel García Marquez, Anton Chekhov, Jane Smiley, Malcolm Lowry, or Norman Mailer is to consume a rich diet of relationships, chance, interconnectedness, muons, songlines, things large within small, small within large, things within things that nonetheless encompass things that are beyond them. Perhaps there are Cartesian novels, hierarchical novels, Newtonian novels. If so, one presumes that they have been quickly—and mercifully—consigned to literature's dustbin.

A bit less hallucinatory, John Naisbitt and Patricia Aburdene argue in *Megatrends 2000* that physics is yesterday's news compared to the even trendier pop-science imagery of "the Age of Biology," where the stale old categories of "gender" and "species" are now up for grabs. Business needs "the models and metaphors of biology to help us understand today's dilemmas and opportunities"—a conceptual shift to buzzwords like "growth," "evolution," "feedback," and "symbiosis" (although they seemed to miss other biometaphors like "parasite" and "lemming"). The real payoff from these new ways of thinking is a psychic openness to novel products and services, from Snow-max, a genetically-engineered protein snow for ski resorts, to a vast unmet demand for ethicists to ponder the morality of harvesting organs from the brain-dead.

Business writers have thoroughly ransacked the literature of pseudo-history in their search for entrepreneurialism's roots. Any historiography maps the preoccupations of the present onto the past; business-lit history does so in a peculiarly charming way, offering guileless anachronisms like "Cortes had a personality that we would describe today as upbeat," and "Louis XI ruled the Dauphiné like an up-and-coming corporate vice president made general manager of a separate division." But disturbingly, the historical role models business writers lionize tend overwhelmingly toward, well, predators—nomadic warriors, to be exact, occasionally sympathetic (as in Emmett Murphy's *The Genius of Sitting Bull*), but usually odious (Wess Roberts' *Leadership Secrets of Attila the Hun*, complete with a cover blurb from H. Ross Perot stating that "the principles are timeless.") Should today's firms emulate civilizations whose history consists of endless cycles of overgrazing, famine, and pillage? Yes (I mean, YES!!!), says Tom Peters, who recommends Genghis Khan's Mongol horde as a corporate model. The Mongols' basic unit of organization, the "group of freelance bandits," admirably adapted itself to conditions of stress and chaos, and fostered a climate of egalitarianism under a heroic leadership. They easily conquered the agrarian civilizations, who foolishly relied on crop-growing to ensure a stable food supply—a mistake that bred timidity, feudalism, and slavery.

Peters uses similar terms to celebrate modern-day entrepreneurs, singing arias to their barbarian manliness and camaraderie as they gallop through burning villages, ponies laden with swag, lords of a "chaotic" economy where bandit companies ride down the dispirited weaklings who crave order and security. From this overarching metaphor, business writers draw an appalling vision of the future. Once, the word "progress" meant a general advance of civilization, a general accretion of wealth, knowledge, leisure, and neighborliness. No more. To the apostles of entrepreneurialism, progress means the constant acceleration of competition as a mystical end in itself, marching towards a zero-sum Valhalla where winners win and losers lose. Humanity's toil has no other end than the carving of new market niches, fetid hatcheries where a cancerous proliferation of product lines germinate and devour one another.

This premise leads business writers to emphasize rapid product introduction as a key to corporate success. According to Peters, healthy corporations are roiling hives of gutsy executives called "product champions," each one enraptured by a delphic vision of superficial novelty—perhaps of a soft drink with an advanced sweetener or unprecedented hue—and willing to go to the wall to bring it to market. But as entrepreneurs offer products increasingly alike and increasingly remote from the satisfaction of human needs, they find it hard to tell if any given product will find a market. Marketing becomes a probabilistic phenomenon, like radioactive decay; all a company can do is accelerate the pace and volume of product introductions and pray that someone, somewhere, will succumb to their advertising and find a use for one of them.

Today's post-modern entrepreneurs thus exhort their minions to a life of unexamined freneticism. "We eat change for breakfast!" sputters one of Tom Peters' favorite executives. "Change something, anything, each day. Just start it, do something!" Peters asks Ted Turner to expound on his business philosophy, and is floored by Turner's guttural response: "Do It!" But doubts sometimes gnaw at executives. Do *what*? they may wonder. And whatever It is, *why* should they Do It in the first place? Peters warns executives never to ask such things, never to let their hands fall idle for an instant lest demoralization and obsolescence creep in. For in the split second it takes merely to pose these questions, their companies have already fallen uncounted generations behind in the cycle of new product development. White-collar employment is driven by the pulsing engine of product differentiation, so executives should be grateful that free markets demand just this sort of anarchic bustle. After all, asks Peters, "What controller would have foreseen the 'need' for 41 varieties of Tylenol?" (with the attendant 41 product champions). We already know the answer: No one with the rational goal of relieving headaches would countenance this "need"— which is why the economy can't be left in the irresponsible hands of "controllers."

Birth of Tragedy

"Half the people, paid double, working twice as hard, with three times the output." According to Charles Handy in his book *The Age of Unreason,* that sums up life for the "high wage, high skill" workers at the small, furiously competitive information-age companies of tomorrow. But what's *really* in it for the workers?

You might be sorry you asked. Business writers warn that only the most fanatical labor discipline can satisfy today's imperious consumers; the entrepreneur's paramount responsibility, indeed his *raison d'être,*, is to enforce that discipline. Boyett and Conn write that "Workers will be expected to do everything absolutely right, the first time and every time . . . . Workplace 2000 will tolerate no mistakes, no errors, no waste, anywhere. Zero. None. Period." Most people will work for small businesses, whose demands for perfection require a complete subordination of the worker's will to the goals of the company. "[T]hese 'work hard, play hard' companies want nothing less than total responsibility and over-the-edge loyalty . . . the line between work and play, the line between public and private becomes fuzzy." Writers return again and again to images of "family" to convey the totalizing character of social indoctrination in the new workplace. But does their mealy-mouthed rhetoric of conciliation, closeness, and self-fulfillment conceal a sinister new totalitarianism? Will the new "quality circles" and "pride teams" really empower workers, or subject them instead to intense exploitation and collective punishment at the hands of a benevolent "leader"?

Tom Peters showcases the new dispensation in a profile of Johnsonville Foods, a sausage company in Wisconsin. If you guessed that this business has something to do with making meat a little easier to swallow, try again. At Johnsonville, self-actualization is Job One. "We're here to give [workers] an opportunity to achieve whatever it is they want to achieve in life," says CEO Ralph Stayer, who adds that "watching people grow is my number one joy." Employees (excuse me, "members") are organized into self-managing work teams that control virtually every aspect of the business; the company even helps pay for continuing education. "Look, anything you learn means you're using your head more," says one line worker. "You're engaged. And if you're more engaged, then the chances are you'll make a better sausage." And make them they do: one worker even cooked up some novel sausages for a new client—in his own basement! Soaring profits, smiling faces, *growing workers*—and yet, is there darkness at noon? Well, Peters admits, "teammates deal harshly with any who choose to opt out of the 'personal growth business' "—those who can't transcend themselves through sausage products. "People who didn't buy into it, given peer pressure, got out," says one executive. "Some needed a little help to make the decision," recalls another. "There were a lot on the fence, there were a lot on the wrong side of the fence. There's a weeding process. Some drop by the wayside." Hmm. "Harsh" peer pressure . . . a big-brotherly CEO . . . that chilling vagueness as to the fate of fence-sitters . . . what exactly is *in* room 101, anyway?

And don't put too much stock in being "paid double." Handy gives us a pointed reminder that blossoming sectors like professional service firms now subcontract their work to the Third World, so that data-entry clerks in London must compete with their Taiwanese counterparts working for a small fraction of the former's wages. High pay is certainly not on their employer's agendas. On the bright side, kids may enjoy a drop in their unemployment rate, say Naisbitt and Aburdene in *Megatrends 2000*, who call for "liberalized" child labor laws. "What's so bad," they ask, "about a 14-year-old working limited hours after school?" Especially given the high-wage, high-skill jobs typically offered to 14-year-olds.

Business writers celebrate the small firms that will overrun the economy as "scrappy" and "innovative"—but "desperate" and "archaic" might be better terms. As liberal economist Bennett Harrison notes in his book *Lean and Mean,* most new small companies fail within a few years, and, unlike the corporate behemoths, few can afford to invest in new technology and research. In the eyes of the business community, their saving grace is labor discipline ("employee commitment"). Small businesses are so precarious that workers put up with low pay and long hours just to stave off bankruptcy. But as corporate downsizing proceeds, job security is a thing of the past. In return for "over-the-edge loyalty," workers can expect a pink slip out of the blue—such is the imperative of "labor-market flexibility." Naisbitt and Aburdene regard the very concept of job security as a perverse joke, snickering that "Loyalty is a quaint memory of the industrial past, a bone in the throat of hundreds of thousands of auto and steelworkers who thought it went both ways." Conn and Boyett explain that employees in Workplace 2000 must prepare for frequent, extended periods of unemployment and expect to "change careers" at least five times before retiring. They suggest that "all Americans will need to keep a close watch on the financial performance of the small company or business unit that employs them," to avoid being caught by surprise when it abruptly folds.

Even in the high-tech sectors, Workplace 2000 looks less like the twenty-first century than the nineteenth. As Harrison points out, the gleaming office parks of Silicon Valley rest on a foundation of Dickensian assembly plants, staffed by poverty-stricken immigrants working under unsafe conditions, for long hours and low pay. And the trendy clothing boutiques that dazzle suburban mall-goers and business writers alike are mainly supplied by Third World sweatshops, where ten-year-olds work sixty-hour weeks so that apparel manufacturers can "make their companies fun again."

But even as business elites hold entire regions of the world hostage under threat of capital strike, their position may be more tenuous than ever before. Most people are inherently conservative, in the best sense of the word. If they're given a chance they may reject the worship of "unreason," "change," and "chaos"; they may refuse to be bits of debris swept along by the latest "megatrend";

they may decide to defend their farms and villages against the Mongol hordes thundering down on them. For as workers take over the shopfloor, what's to stop them from taking over the entire company, or from intervening in the management of the economy as a whole?

If that happens, they may embrace an alternative vision of progress. They may want to channel their surpluses into greater job security and shorter hours; into livable cities instead of shoppable suburbs; into a vibrant natural environment instead of a clear-cut RV park; into a rich, collective public life that all can freely partake of, instead of the pre-processed, rent-by-the-hour lifestyle of the virtual-reality helmet. This is the nightmare that haunts Business: that to the cult of competitiveness, we will oppose the ethic of solidarity; that we will conclude that we can eat *enough* sausage, and drink *enough* beer; that we will gaze at that mountain of Moon Pies and, in the end, just walk away.

Baffler #6, 1995

STEPHEN DUNCOMBE

I've Seen the Future—and It's a Sony!

I FIGURE it's my duty. In earlier times, in other places, I would have consulted the tribal elders, heard the debates at the amphitheater, or gone to the town meeting. But as a good citizen of the overdeveloped world living in the dawn of the age of corporate feudalism, it's my civic responsibility to journey to the centers of ideological propagation and corporate tax abatement and be *edutained*. And so I make my pilgrimage to the "IBM Think" permanent exhibition and the "Sony Wonder" Technology Lab.

These increasingly ubiquitous company exhibits—museums, galleries, learning centers—are where the Gospel According to the Corporate World is set forth. It is here that I can discern the order of the new world, have my questions answered, counsel given, social integration assured. Actually, that's not quite true. I don't want to be integrated into their world. But these are the powers that are running ours, and I want to see the future they have in store for us.

IBM Think is housed in the basement of the granite and glass modernist IBM monolith in midtown New York City. The building is as gray and ordered as the suits once required for all IBM personnel. Everything about it speaks of clean and brutal power: *Fuck with me you'll get a boot up your ass,* except here it will be a wingtip, and it will be done quietly and efficiently.

I walk through the doors, down a flight of stairs, and I am there: subdued lighting, gray industrial carpeting, gray walls, and hushed tones. A temple of reason, a place of contemplation; like a library or perhaps a monastery or, with the ubiquitous presence of hovering guards in neat blazers, a bank. Except for the guards, the place is empty and the only sound I hear is the even cadence and reassuring tones of white male authority that unfold from the rear of a darkened room.

But on my way toward this sacred chamber I'm intercepted. Work stations showing the wondrous ability of computer databases to inform on myriad topics block my path. Sidetracked, I pull up before the "History" monitor. Images of America past scroll across the machine. I put my finger on "Topics," it glows and transports me into another menu. Here I point to "Labor," and again I'm transported. At this menu I can pick labor history topics that range from "Freedom of Contract, 1905," to "Seizure of Steel Mills, 1952."

I press "Freedom of Contract," and over a blur of archival photos meant to bring me back through time, a voice recalls the Supreme Court case of a bakery owner in Buffalo, New York, who won the right to work his employees more than the ten hours a day, sixty hours a week state regulations allowed. Surely a great moment in labor history. "Seizure of Steel Mills," my next choice, recollects President Truman's attempt to nationalize U.S. steel mills during the Korean War. But once again the freedom of business triumphs. Due to the objective and judicious thinking of the

Supreme Court, the President's decision is overruled and, as my electronic tutor informs me, "the mills remained in private hands. A forceful example that the court can limit the expansion of presidential power."

It's a curious sort of labor history that doesn't mention the Ludlow Massacre, the Pullman, Seattle general, GM sit-down, or air traffic controllers' strikes, the Wobblies or the CIO, or anything about labor struggles at all. In fact, IBM's labor history seems solely concerned with the ways that threats to unlimited business expansion were defused. Some of this confusion is cleared up when I back out of "Labor" and light up the "Business" history section. It turns out that four of the five history lessons of labor are also included verbatim in the business division. Synergy, I guess.

But the voice of reason beckons, history calls. So I make my way back through the darkness. Here is the centerpiece of the exhibit, its ideological heart: the IBM Think inspirational/historical video. Like the stained glass windows and tapestries of medieval churches, which once taught illiterate peasants God's word according to whomever was in power, this is where the great order according to IBM is unveiled to the modern masses.

I ready myself. I face a black, slightly concave wall lined with black matte video monitors. A red digital clock on the left wall counts down the seconds 00:03, 00:02, 00:01. The wall lights up and mood music swells. A blur of nature in fast forward, clouds speeding across the sky, the sun rising and setting, nature out of control. An image of Stonehenge. The Voice:

> Imagine standing on that cold plain a thousand years before the pyramids. Alone at that distant dawn. How terrifying the world must have been. And how we responded to the night's dawn, with the dawn of technology. Megaliths carved by hand, shouldered upright, fashioned to create order . . . [dramatic pause] . . . from chaos.

Stonehenge dissolves into an image of a circular shell, which dissolves into a circular staircase. These, in turn, are replaced by a picture of some Conquistadora warship sailing off into space to metamorphose into an Apollo spacecraft. The Voice pontificates some more as pictures of "innovators" appear and fade away; the line ending with IBM scientists.

> .... What is the purpose of this constant need to know? To do? Perhaps it is the discontent of it all. The sense that things can be better . . . more efficient . . . faster . . . more fair. But perhaps it is more . . . .

The video goes on: pictures of deaf children being helped by IBM technology, a woman reading off an IBM screen and smiling contentedly, electromagnetic fields, more kids learning, presumably about order. The Voice reminds us of all the good that the great god bestows upon his children and then issues forth his command:

> And all of this to expand the very power of our minds . . . and our spirits. To define ourselves against . . . the Chaos.

The screen returns us back to nature, which is then superimposed with a fractal geometry grid—bringing proper order to that messy and bothersome thing, nature.

This is the world according to IBM. From apes to IBM scientists—the unfolding spirit of history. There is but one direction and one imperative: all of history, in the words of the accompanying pamphlet, is "a solid record of the human drive to create order."

This fascination with order and the unfolding spirit of IBM continues elsewhere in the building. In the IBM gallery is an exhibit of Sardinian religious art of the fifteenth and sixteenth centuries; art with which the Aragonese colonizers of Sardinia reminded the locals of the great hierarchy of being and the locals' place at the bottom. Upstairs I am treated to 100 Years of Information Technology, with models of computers from the Hollerith Tabulating Machine used for the command and control function of the 1890 U.S. census, to its logical extension, the IBM personal computer, every person a potential order bringer.

And then I'm done. I suppose the Fear of Chaos and the Power of Almighty Order should have me trembling in supplication, but it doesn't. For all its authoritarian bombast, there is something distinctly pathetic—something almost endearingly quaint—about the IBM universe. It's a linear history—one event after the next, all following some internal logic. The end of history is clad in a white scientist's coat; it is a time when IBM has figured out how to control everything. And you're either part of the system or you're chaos. This classic "modernist" notion of history is out of favor nowadays. Too predictable and too square, the po-mo academics cry (while jockeying for place in tenure succession). The exhibit also demonstrates a belief—a creepy instrumental incarnation, perhaps, but nonetheless a real belief—in Reason. It is IBM Think after all, and they (kind of) mean it.

Very square. IBM is out of step. What's missing from their "100 Years" of history is their own eclipse by other computer companies, and their subsequent massive "downsizing": the firing of tens of thousands of employees and plans to close their main suburban New York headquarters. Today's much-touted more-cynical-than-thou audience must find the IBM exhibition woefully naive. In fact, one month after my visit, it closed.

IBM could have learned something from other mega-corps like AT&T, who early in this century had to figure out how to convince the American public that a private monopoly of a public utility would be in the citizenry's best interest. In 1923, William P. Banning, AT&T's assistant publicity manager, put it this way:

> [Our job] is to make the people understand and love the company. Not merely be consciously dependent upon it—not merely regard it as a necessity—not merely take it for granted, but to love it—hold real affection for it—make it an . . . admired intimate member of the family.

To hell with ideas, to hell with Reason. And in a society with feel-good democratic illusions, Machiavelli's old idea about fear being more powerful than love won't wash either. This notion might still do the trick in those parts of the world where the colonels still run things, but what's needed here is affection, understanding, and play-fulness—that just-one-of-the-folks, feel-the-pain, yet ready-to-party spirit. Lights, camera, action. Fun, not fear, is what gets them on their knees today.

IBM scientists in white coats who babble about order over chaos tend to score low on the fun scale. Order is boring, chaos is a blast. The folks at Sony have learned this lesson well. To get to Sony Wonder I leave IBM's solemn modernist Stonehenge, cross the street, and enter Phillip Johnson and John Burgee's pink granite, Chippendale roofed, postmodern playhouse. The building used to be owned by AT&T, and in 1978 they struck an agreement with the city: in exchange for building six more whimsical stories than zoning regulations allow, they would have to provide an educational "public" space, operated by AT&T of course.

So when Sony took over the building in 1991, they also inherited AT&T's public obligation. But whereas AT&T showed no enthusiasm for the task in years past—their "public" plaza was bleak and desolate—Sony has poured money and expertise into the space, in the process interpreting "the public" to mean "their public," a captive audience for fun, excitement, and Sony products.

The heavy weight of IBM's juggernaught History slides away as I enter the Sony Plaza playland. No gray carpets, no somber tones. Here are lights, whistles, products: Sony. Moneylenders would feel at home in this temple. Whereas IBM announced itself softly, their logo on a pamphlet or on a guard's blazer pocket, Sony screams. The name hangs from the ceilings on banners. It's printed everywhere. There's the Sony Signature Store, the Sony Style Store; Sony even gets its name on "Gottfried's Newsstand." (Is "Gottfried" a real person? A fictitious Sony one?) Not really a public space, like the old-fashioned park or square we might have expected, this is a Sonypublic space: the public-private space of the future.

My "adventure" (as the accompanying promo literature puts it) starts at the entry lobby where I extract my Sony Wonder Card—

a simple plastic credit card with a bar code on the back—from a machine that bears an uncanny resemblance to a condom dispenser. A Sony minion then appears and herds me and the other adventurers onto a glass elevator. The doors of the elevator shut and as we begin to glide up, a Voice resonates from the ceiling informing me and my fellows of the wonders that are to befall us on our "Journey of Discovery."

At the top floor the door opens and we enter the Log-in Station of the Sony Wonder Technology Lab. Armatures of steel tubing and wires running from ceiling to floor are scattered throughout a dark room. Each armature is equipped with a keyboard, a small adjustable video screen, and a slot for the card. I walk over to one and enter my plastic. I'm half expecting a terrifying face to appear and bellow "I am Oz," but no, the screen glows and a young white woman, looking vaguely bohemian, appears.

"C'mon, come closer, closer," she beckons. I come closer. She tells me to type in my name, which I do, and then to adjust the screen to my eye level. A brief flash. My picture is taken and my image glows for a few seconds on the screen. Trying to draw me into conversation, she asks me an innocuous question—"What animal makes the best pet?" Trying to share in the warmth and casual good times flowing from my new companion I answer. My response is instantly recorded on the screen as a voiceprint. The woman reappears and says, "Great, you're officially logged in as a media trainee." Media trainee?

I look over my shoulder. A video image of a young black man is cajoling another trainee into logging in her personal information. Throughout the room people are standing in front of the armature apparitions willingly giving away their souls to friendly multi-culti faces. Black, white, red, brown, woman, man, gay, and straight; only the dominant white male, suit and tie, middle class persona of IBM authority is missing (strangely enough, I don't notice any Asian faces either). It's the Rainbow Coalition asking me for my mugshot and voiceprint.

IBM designed the computer pass system that made it impossible for non-whites to travel freely in apartheid South Africa, but that's across the street. This is Sony and this is the new order. Not really an order at all, just friendly folks as diverse as you and me asking for personal information to track you while you're having fun and "training" for Sony.

Leaving the Log-In Stations, I walk across and down the Communication Bridge. It's a funhouse corridor of histotainment, with hundreds of video monitors belching out fragmented bits of history. I pass by a picture of the first telephone, then soon after, Peter Fonda on his hog in a scene from *Easy Rider*. No unfolding-spirit style history here, just a cacophony of simultaneity and banality. And here history isn't distant or remote. No stiff pinkboys telling me about their order; this history is part of me—my favorite TV shows are playing on monitors as I walk by, newspaper headlines from my youth appear, movie stars I had crushes on. To underscore the point that Sonyhistory is our history, they have installed a system whereby the great computer mind that has been tracking your progress inserts your picture into a montage of famous faces on a video monitor as you approach. Who was that jerk who sung about the revolution not being televised? I don't need anybody telling me what history is about, I'm a part of it right now. See, I'm represented, I am somebody. Look, there, next to Marconi, right above Marilyn. Every man a king, Louisiana populist Huey Long once promised; every person an image, this is popular power Sony-style.

Tearing myself away from my place in history I trot down to the "interactive" theater where my media training is to begin. I insert my card at various stations and run through a number of "hands-on" training exercises. The first is a recording studio where I get to "join the team" as a recording engineer and help mix Sonystar Celine Dion's "new hit song," "The Power of Love." Unfortunately, the limits of interactivity prevent me from deleting it from the earth forever.

Next I punch in at the Robotics Engineering Station, where as a trainee I get to operate little metal bugs that wander around in a cage, factory automation that helps get rid of pesky and unnecessary skilled workers, or my favorite, a robotic arm in a nuclear plant. Running the last of these, I get a call on a nearby phone. I pick it up and a voice informs me that there's an energy leak and I get three chances to find it. If I find the leak I get a call offering me a raise and a promotion. If I fail I get a call to evacuate.

Then on to the Environmental Research Station where I get a choice of responding to two environmental crises set in New York: an oil spill and an impending hurricane. I briefly wonder why I don't get a chance to clean up the nuclear melt-down I just created with the Sony robotic arm at the previous exhibit, but I quickly move on to the Sony Wonder Television Studio. Given the option of any number of technical positions, I can help "produce" shows for Sony. Next, in the post-production lab, I can try my skill at re-editing Sonytalent Billy Joel's new video. Again, I'm only sorry that I can't erase it. Maybe I'll bring a powerful magnet next time.

The next room is split in two. On the right is the Medical Imaging Lab, which allows you to experiment with "technological innovation [which] plays a life enhancing role in modern medicine." On the left is the Video Game Production Studio, where you get to work on a Sonygame inspired by the Sonymovie *Dracula*. I weigh my options: life enhancement, vapid entertainment. All value is relative in Sonyworld, right? I head for the video game.

Looking for the exit I cross through the Design Gallery. Here is the closest thing Sony Wonder has to IBM Think's linear sense of history: lining the walls are artifacts chronicling the development, from concept to consumer product, of the Sony Handicam. I marvel at the history of evolution brought down to the level of the development of a video camera.

Finally, exhausted, I make it to the Log-out Station. Here I punch my card into a machine and receive . . . a paycheck? No, a "certificate of achievement" with my picture and skills rating printed on it. I head for the door only to find that after Log-out there is one more skill to be learned: consumption of Sonyproducts. Sony Wonder dumps out into one of the Sony gift shops.

It's not as easy to decipher the philosophy of Sony as it is IBM's. IBM Think comes right out and announces the way it is, Sony Wonder doesn't. At Sony you become part of their vision, participating within it, grooving on it, working for the Man and not even knowing it. You become a Sonycitizen without ever being sure what it is you're a citizen of. My experience with Sony Wonder makes me almost fond of IBM's rigid authoritarianism. At least with IBM you know where you stand: You either wear the gray suit or you're off the bus. It's so ugly, so foreign, so whitebread, so easy to hate . . . so easy to oppose.

Sony Wonder is different. It has no clear and open philosophy, no "bringing order to chaos" mantra; Sony Wonder presents itself as chaos. It's easy to debate a coherent philosophy and to argue against a history lesson—you know what you're up against: something "out there," other and wrong. But it's hard to agree or disagree with something you can't nail down and think about. Sony is amorphous, not caring whether you agree or not (what is there to agree to?). It just is . . . and, by the end of the exhibit, it is *you*.

No abstract ideas, no aloof lab-coated windbags, no distant historical allusions; no polemics that might arouse critical suspicion and disbelief. Sony doesn't lecture, it ingratiates and integrates. Their world starts out as part of mine: the faces at my electronic interrogation look and talk like me and my friends, not Bob Dole; and history on the Communication Bridge is intimate, made up of images I know, including my own. Surrounded by all this familiarity, I begin to cherish Sony and Sonyproducts, like, well, an "intimate member of the family." The message here isn't *Think*, it's *Wonder*. In this era where everybody creates, I get the chance to produce

Sonyproduct and be a part of the Sonyteam. Tapping into popular democratic aspirations, they give me interactive "choice." And then they offer up the ultimate in twentieth-century free-will expression: the opportunity to purchase from the full range of Sonyproduct.

Sony Wonder gets under your skin without you knowing it. The chaos it projects keeps you from seeing any pattern or any political ideology. Instead the Sonyworld envelops you: swirling, dancing, embracing, amusing. As a child of the postmodern world, it's hard not to get off on it at some point. Engaged in Sonyfun, I even find myself forgetting my overarching critical mission and neglecting my birthright cynicism. And meanwhile every action I take and every experience I have brings me closer into the fold. Sony doesn't tell me what to do, I'm already doing it.

The totalizing politics of Sony Wonder are elusive; not because there aren't any, but because they're all too familiar. They are an unarticulated politics we've learned through years of breathing, seeing, feeling, tasting—just living—in an era of unabated hyperconsumerism and corporate rule. And because this experiential catechism is not out in the world presenting itself as a belief system, it tends to go uninterrogated, and to slide by as neutral, or worse, "natural." These ideas are now so naturalized and so much a part of our collective unconscious that Sony didn't even need to employ a Banning or Goebbels to design its Wonderworld, just a prestigious design firm—they "instinctively" knew what to do. And as its message is everyplace, it also seems to be no place. This is the magic of Sonychaos.

Sometimes, when leafing through old magazines, I like to look at the advertisements: brush with Pepsodent or you'll be a spinster. It's hard to believe that these ads ever convinced anybody, their coercive intent and message are so open. IBM Think reads just as plainly. You either buy in or you don't—but you know what it is. It's stern and imposing and gray and paternalistic . . . and boring.

It's also something tangible. It gives you something to reject, to rebel against. Because IBM believes in order so thoroughly they construct one, and in so doing give us an order to tear down.

Their very order also implies that we could build a different one back up. It allows us to imagine that we might replace their vision and their history with something equally coherent and equally grand. In brief: The world according to IBM is utopian. Okay, so we don't like their utopia. It's atrocious, I agree. Good, then let's go out and create our own and try to replace *theirs* with *ours*. It might be difficult, maybe even impossible, but the point is that it's *conceivable*.

It's hard to conceive of how to fight the Sonyworld. There doesn't even appear to be anything there to reject; no coherent order to replace, no grand vision to supplant, no logic of history to rewrite.

Walter Teague's design for the National Association of Manufacturers' exhibit at the 1939 World's Fair might as well have been written for Sony today:

> I do not . . . see it as an historical pageant. I see it as a series of related exhibits which the visitor will review one after another until he arrives at a climax.

In Sonyworld there is no past or future—except relative to the world of media entertainment; no historical progression—except for the Handicam; and, finally, no change—except that moment of "climax" when one becomes a true believer. In other words, for the modern Sonypublic, like for the peasant of years past, the world is fixed, outside of human creation and control. So all that is left for us to do is just sit back and make the best—or worst—of it.

IBM's linear history no longer weighs like a nightmare on the brain of the living. Gone is a historical tradition that excluded whole ranges of people and experiences, ran roughshod over others, and dictated the future from the past. But Sony presents us with something worse: a static world in which humans don't make history and individuals have no place—except as happy diverse worker/consumers integrated within a world already called into being by Sony. For all its sound and fury Sony Wonder is a strangely stagnant universe: everything moves but nothing ventures outside the confines of Sony.

So what do we do? Let's face it, as much as we may need one, we're in no shape to conjure up a utopia nowadays—with or without a solid adversary in mind. In fact, the whole notion of the "we" that's going to do any of this is a bit problematic, as the only universal "we" out there in the open is the public-private corporate one. But the absolute banality and horrible meaninglessness of the World According to Sony is bound to create some heretics, and cracks in the facade can be forced.

It's just too easy (and not much fun) to withdraw into an isolated and self-righteous puritanism. Besides, we can't ignore their world, it's too late for that. Fighting them is important, because hiding beneath the Sonychaos there is an order. It's the social covenant of the coming corporate feudal state. We work for them, they keep track of us, we buy their products, and they entertain us. But at the end of the day, when we turn in our Sonypass, they don't plan on paying us—except with a piece of paper telling us that we're one of them.

Let's make them pay.

Baffler #6, 1995

JENNIFER BROSTROM

The Time-Management
Gospel

IN THE OLD DAYS, we made random lists on sticky notes, forgot
meetings, and preserved our sloth through completely unplanned
time. But there was a brushfire of technological change and team-
based productivity blowing through the land. The officers of our
company were quickly converted by consultants and hucksters who
terrified them with nightmarish tales of "lean, mean companies"
whose ruthless speed-to-market and inhumanly efficient employees
would make short work of our slow-moving operation. We were
warned that the only way to save our jobs was to "reinvent" ourselves and implement a "fast-cycle-time" environment, in which
all activities that "are not directly adding value that a customer will
pay for" are the equivalent of "dead time." Clearly a day planner

would be necessary to organize the demands of this new world, but not just an ordinary day planner. We needed a superior "time-management tool" imbued with a message of hope and outrageous promise to cut through the fearful atmosphere. In short, we needed Franklin Planners.

It was like receiving a Bible after a long and uncomfortable process of confirmation into a church for which we had the utmost skepticism. We had endured the brainstorm sessions, planning meetings, and pep rallies, the rituals that were part of our company's reorganization. At the end of it all, we were each presented with a spanking new Franklin Day Planner to initiate our newly productive, streamlined lives.

At first, we couldn't believe that our penny-pinching company would buy us such an elaborate assemblage. We were given two large binders—one for daily use, and one for "storage"—hundreds of pages with various calendars and graphs, a hardcover book entitled *Time Management*, and an audiotape on "How to Use Your Franklin Planner." My company did not go so far as to send us all to one of the day-long Franklin time-management seminars ($195.00 per person), but we were strongly urged to study the Franklin literature in order to learn the principles and habits of the Franklin system, which promises productivity increases of as much as 29% (although the exact nature of the improvement is not specified).

Time Management, by Franklin Quest cofounder Richard Winwood, lays out the theory behind the revolution, fusing aspects of the self-help, inspirational, and business genres, and declaring time management and self-esteem to be the keys to personal fulfillment and skyrocketing profits—as if the two were somehow interchangeable. The ideal man that emerges from its pages is one of exquisite mediocrity, despite Winwood's claim that the Franklin philosophy is the key to the realization of idealistic dreams. Our hero is lucky to live in such a convenient century in which all sorts of calendars and digital instruments are available for measuring time, because these things help him produce more. But in fact he's not much different from other men who have lived before him, even in ancient times. They, too, being capitalists at heart, simply wanted to produce more, "to get more done," and thus, began to study the heavens and the seasons with an eye toward profit.

But his mind and soul are a grab-bag of vague philosophies and desires. This is his problem. He has no definition, no *control*. He's settling for less, which, for an American, is virtually a sin against nature. Gradually, however, with the help of the Franklin system, he can put his mind in order. First, he can *prioritize* each of his values, and then mold them into affirmations: "I am productive," "I love my family," "I serve others," "I am frugal," "I love God," "I am physically fit," etc. Being of rather dull and conventional character, the Productive Man has no problem selecting the most important values (presumably passed on to him by his parents, school, and church) and writing them in his Franklin Planner, where they will provide the basis for his newly emerging mind. Luckily, none of his values contradict one another.

His new mind—a Franklin mind or "productivity pyramid"—assumes the simple shape of a triangle. It is an aerodynamic mind. Uncluttered by passion or confusion, it is driven like a missile to achieve its goals. The Productive Man documents specific long-term and short-term goals in his Planner, and from these he formulates the pointed tip of his consciousness—his Daily Task List. This will give his existence structure, direction, and meaning.

The goals he has selected for himself are in perfect harmony with his company's goals, although it's unclear what his job actually is from his "Daily Record of Events," which serves as an example in *Time Management*: "New procedure for handling petty cash; B-phase prototype on sched.; Inventory of alum. back plates in question; Mentioned dislike of Paul's attitude at mtg." His "Daily Task Lists" are a combination of business and household chores:

"Reading—20 minutes; Clear in-drawer; Do expense summary; Prod. committee mtg.; Take in dry cleaning; call mom re. dinner; Clean hall closet." From various examples, we gather that he has a wealth of basements and closets to organize, and being the nice, clean sort of person he is, he keeps himself busy with these nagging tasks rather than dallying with the devil's handiwork. Occasionally, he even spends some time with the kids: "Talked with Julie tonite re. basketball et al."

Once in control, our hero is on the lookout for the "dysfunctional interruptions" and "time robbers" that will attempt to lure him away from the achievement of his daily objectives. He skirts ingeniously around "lengthy, unproductive social calls" with a "cheerful, outgoing greeting" calculated to make his coworkers get directly to the point without the unnecessary exchange of language formerly known as conversation. ("Hi Lynn. I'm trying to finish this report for the finance committee. *What can I do for you?*") His thought processes are governed by "return on investment" analysis that determines the priorities that structure his life. In this way, he remains in control, which elevates his self-esteem, which in turn increases his productivity. Higher productivity means he feels even *better* about himself. While his psychological profile increasingly resembles an addict's, he has confined his addiction to the legal drug of time management.

→►◄┼

The tape-recorded voice of Franklin CEO and Chairman Hyrum Smith surges and wanes like a televised sermon throughout his seminar on "How to Use the Franklin Planner." The rhetoric of power and control dominate the seminar: "[With the Franklin method] you'll not only scare yourself, you'll intimidate everyone on your block!" He chides an employee who earns $600,000 with the comment, "Well, if you ever got organized, you'd really be *dangerous.*" While clichéd appeals to aggression flood the business world,

Smith's power rhetoric is remarkable in its pettiness. "[What] gives you power," he drones, is "knowing where the information is [in your Planner]." Forget charisma and daring; the Franklin system extols the robotic—mindless efficiency, synchronization, and precision.

In one example of what he apparently considers to be an impressive managerial show of force, Smith suggests that a supervisor could "stun" an employee by successfully following through on a promise to call him in ten days at exactly 8:43. "Will you be thinking about that call for the next ten days? No way. It'll *resurface* in the Planner," he says. Smith takes a slightly sadistic pleasure in the ability to annoy people with perfection. "Actually, you'll start to drive people crazy," he says cheerfully. "You won't forget *anything.*"

Not one to risk being accused of neurosis or compulsion, Smith reluctantly admits that sometimes "we need to vegetate for an hour or two," although he blithely assumes that "we're constantly fighting the emotion of guilt all the time we're doing it." Fortunately, the Franklin Planner also provides absolution for time-management transgressions. Witness the case of the executive who arrives home after a long day at work only to discover a family crisis that demands his undivided attention. What a dilemma! He had several tasks *already planned* for that evening! What to do? Not to worry, says Smith. "The first thing you do is go to the planner and move the tasks [to another day]. . . . You're still in *control.*" By forwarding tasks to another day in the Planner, he claims, "the guilt goes away."

As I completed *Time Management* and Hyrum Smith's seminar, the feeling of induction into an unconvincing religion became overwhelming. There is something familiar yet bizarre in the combination of capitalism, traditional family values, and idealism that pervades Franklin Quest. Something quintessentially American— simultaneously wholesome and insane. The company's rhetoric evokes a world of maternal secretaries with perfect nails, serenely separating their boss's appointments from those of their children with different colored ink in their pristine Franklin Planners; of men with names like Tom Green and Bob Garf landing great deals on expensive cars and trying to squeeze in a bit more time for "the wife and kids" in their Planners. It depicts a world of church picnics and corporate takeovers; of Donny and Marie and Senator Orrin Hatch. Not surprisingly, the Americana, the "traditional values," and the doctrines of unlimited profit and growth promoted by Franklin Quest bear a distinct resemblance to the culture of America's best-known home-grown religion.

A great-great-grandnephew of Joseph Smith, founder of the Church of Latter-Day Saints, Franklin CEO Hyrum Smith is well-versed in the corporate savvy that plays an essential, even exalted, role in the Mormon Church. In contrast with the cultish and blasphemous image that dogged its tumultuous beginnings, today the Church of Latter-Day Saints enjoys a conventional, nonthreatening, all-American reputation. But beneath its bland surface, many assert, the Church aggressively pursues economic and political power. The theological basis for this materialism is the Church's post-millennial doctrine, which holds that the Second Coming is quickly approaching, but that the Mormon Church must first prepare the world—economically and politically, as well as spiritually—for the arrival of Christ, and the subsequent establishment of a theocracy.

Based in Salt Lake City, Utah, Franklin Quest is one of many multi-million dollar success stories that contribute to the Mormon corporate empire. Although all its donations to the Church are made on a private, individual basis, they are known to be enormous. And as corporate theory became more evangelical in recent years, Hyrum Smith was poised to make millions. Like the frenzied "soul gathering" crusades that used to sweep through the states of the northeast, Franklin Quest spreads the good word about time management, appealing at once to the uncertain identity, greed, and superficial morality of the business community.

+>-<+

As the central role model and marketing image for the Franklin Quest Company, Benjamin Franklin is both an appropriate and ironic choice. The Franklin promotional literature proclaims, "The same powerful principles and techniques that made Franklin one of the most productive and respected men of his time can now help you reach your goals and achieve success and fulfillment in your own life." The supposed principles and techniques in question originate from a brief section of Franklin's *Autobiography* in which he relates a youthful "quest for moral perfection," and describes his plan to keep a "little book" in which he employed an elaborate system to record his daily success or failure to maintain the "virtues" of Temperance, Silence, Order, Resolution, Frugality, Industry, Sincerity, Justice, Moderation, Cleanliness, Tranquility, Chastity, and Humility. Franklin's many subsequent allusions to his various indiscretions, though, give the lie to the Franklin Institute's suggestion that Franklin succeeded to any degree in upholding the virtues he advocated for himself. Franklin was a notorious flirt, for example, especially during the years when he served as emissary to the French court. Furthermore, while it is true that Franklin carried a "little book" in his pocket in which he made appointments, it is unclear whether he in fact arrived at his engagements on time. During his political mission in Paris, he was reputed to be punctual only for dinner invitations. Pierre-Georges Cabanis, a French physician who became a close friend to Franklin, observed: "[Franklin] would eat, sleep, work whenever he saw fit, according to his needs, so that there never was a more leisurely man . . . . [His house] was always open for all visitors, he always had an hour for you."

While Franklin's exhortations to industry and frugality in such publications as *Poor Richard's Almanack* may have had an important influence on American identity, the Franklin Institute's rather priggish Benjamin Franklin bears only a shadowy resemblance to the highly paradoxical man. In addition to historical inaccuracy, the marketing image of Benjamin Franklin promotes a superficial and dehumanized conception of what it means to be a "successful" American. Franklin's respect for productivity is deified, while the philosophical inquiry, experimentation, humanism, inspiration, and lack of regimentation that characterized his life are ignored.

➤➤◄◄

It has become a very different world at my company since our initial baptism into the world of Franklin Planners. As far as I can tell, most people don't spend any time with the sections on values and goals, but their daily task lists are full of notes attempting to structure their ever-increasing work loads. There's less "meaningless" conversation and more stress, but this unites us in rueful sympathy and codependency. A typical exchange in elevators and hallways: "How are you doin'?" "I'm so busy!" "I know, I'm so fried!"

I begin each work day in quiet meditation with my Franklin Planner, the all-important "planning period," during which tasks for the day are listed and prioritized in detail. After establishing the most important work to be done, I typically begin with what I most *feel* like doing—a definite violation of the system, which is designed specifically to encourage the hard logic of business priorities and ambitions to supersede the soft lethargy of human moods. My "Daily Record of Events" is a combination of industrial jargon and inappropriate outbursts, which, along with my non-work-related "values and goals" make it imperative that my Franklin Planner never fall into the hands of a coworker.

In the world of fast-cycle time, the Franklin Planner becomes a savior, or at least a security blanket. Many of my coworkers believe that they would be completely lost without it. One employee, describing her habit of hiding the Planner in her car to protect it from potential kidnappers, commented, a bit too seriously, "I would have to *commit suicide* if I ever lost my Planner!"

When the unthinkable happens, and a Franklin Planner actually does depart from its corporate home, there is much grieving and a generous extension of sympathy. Great emotion is vented, in contrast with the nervous and tentative office apologies that follow the death of grandparents and other relatives: "Oh my *God!* You poor thing! I would be so *lost* without my Franklin!"

Baffler #8, 1996

DAVE MULCAHEY

Leadership and You

SUCCESS AND HOW to achieve it. Try to imagine the vast amount of time and human energy wasted pondering this topic, the money people have spent on books, tapes, and seminars that teach "success" like some sort of 12-step program. To the American middle manager, "success" may be a lifestyle, a matter of correct handshakes, of wearing the right color tie; or it may be a dark mystery, requiring the uttering of the right shibboleths, the ablutions of Positive Mental Attitude, and the study of pseudo-sacred texts like *The Leader as Martial Artist*. It may even be the Rotary Club Nietzscheism elaborated by the author of *21 Days to Unlimited Power*.

The secrets of success, however, are hardly mysterious—we learn them on the school playground: Leadership is usually little more than the systematic exploitation of the weaknesses of others. Hardly a profound insight, but a definition conspicuous for its absence from the ponderous library of business and career advice.

Recently I happened across the psychological profiles of two men competing for a promotion within the management hierarchy of their employer, an international computer marketing company. Both men are currently area sales managers, and each has fixed his eye on the next rung on the ladder to the executive suite—yes, they both want to be *regional* sales manager. The job was not simply there for the taking: Each candidate has survived a months-long process of scrutiny and winnowing, dinner interviews with the wife, and golf games, back-slapping, and thank-you note writing. Now, as one of the final hurdles, the candidates must submit to a psychological evaluation. In an introductory handout given to the candidates (unthreateningly titled "Development and You"), the presiding "professional"—a psychologist who runs his "consulting" business out of his house with the assistance of his wife and a college student intern—explains rather misleadingly that his task is merely to "identify and assist in the development of the potential of the company's people."

The assessment consists of three parts: a personal interview, an intelligence test, and a series of paper-and-pencil exercises. All information gleaned from these examinations, the applicants are assured, will be analyzed "in a careful, professional manner in our efforts to assist you and your company." The applicants are also promised a debriefing at the conclusion of the process, at which time they will have ample opportunity for "communicative interchange." And since at each stage of the evaluation the applicants will be asked to divulge personal—and often highly sensitive—information, they are told that, "All of the information you provide will remain in our offices and only we will have access to it."

Oops, trust betrayed. When will we learn that even the experts lie? But more about that in a moment. Let's meet the contestants.

At first glance, we seem to have come upon a rather fortuitous snapshot of the diversity of the American managerial elite. One of the applicants—we'll call him Chad—comes to the table with all the advantages of a suburban East Coast upbringing. He indicates that his father was a successful lawyer and an avid sailor. Like his siblings, Chad did well in high school and went on to attend an Ivy League college where he studied economics and business administration. The fondest memories of his college days, Chad tells his interviewer, were his athletic exploits and care-free fraternity highjinks. A 6′3″ blond, blue-eyed stud, Chad must have cut *some* figure. But Chad has a sober, responsible side as well: He comes from a strong, stable family background where bedrock values of hard work and play figured prominently. Imbued with a deep affinity for the comforts of a prosperous home, he expresses a desire to reproduce those conditions for the next generation of Chads with his fiancée, a doctor (bonus points!).

Chad's rival presents a more problematic case. This man—let's call him Vern—has struggled to make his way in life. His father was killed in the Korean War when Vern was very young, and his mother later remarried to a rather undependable, emotionally distant man with a drinking problem. In spite of these handicaps, Vern persevered. After an unremarkable high school career, he worked his way through a couple of junior colleges and ended up at an obscure state university, where he picked up a bachelor's degree in business administration for his trouble. Thus endowed, Vern answered the call of salesmanship, hawking swimming pools and copier equipment before settling in the company where he currently works. During his ten years of service, Vern allows with manly confidence, he's built up a track record of "proven sales ability." Vern is an all-American type of success—the backwoods individualist who creates his own opportunities by dint of raw intelligence, hard work, and determination to overcome adversity. But success has not come without a price—Vern expresses regret about the breakup of his first marriage and would like to spend more time with his current family.

While the dossiers fail to record the firmness of Chad's handshake or the shine of Vern's tassel loafers, they do provide the more quantifiable particulars. For example, the Ivy Leaguer boasts an impressive IQ of 126; no mere hick, Vern clocks in at 115. This being America, earning power doesn't necessarily correlate to brain power: Vern's $54,000-a-year salary will take him to Vegas a few more times than Chad's $47,000. Not to worry for Chad, though; his fiancée's $85,000 salary looms on the horizon to help him whittle away the $320,000 mortgage on his suburban Colonial. Vern's mate takes home a modest $25,000, but one gets the feeling that's the way Vern likes it.

These data tell us much, but the psychologist's challenge is to divine those intangible, ineffable traits of personality that make one a leader among men—or in this case, that make a regional sales manager among area sales managers. Subtle tools of discernment are called for. In the case of our psychologist they are: the Thematic Apperception Test, which presents respondents with pictures and requires them to compose explanatory narratives; the Cornell Index, a list of 127 yes-or-no questions querying the respondents about their moods, emotions, and psychosomatic symptoms; and an exercise called "sentence completion," wherein respondents are given a set of opening clauses, from which they are to construct sentences.

Of all the exercises, the latter turns out to be the most important in determining the fate of the two applicants. In fact, the final evaluations submitted to their company—the document that gave the final word on their respective abilities to manage the sale of computer equipment on a regional basis—amounted to little more than a cobbling together of the phrases that each man wrote down in an exercise each probably completed quickly and thoughtlessly. Sentence fragments like, "I get down in the dumps when . . . ," "I lose my temper if . . . ," "She became irritated when they . . . ," and "He suffered most from . . . " are calculated to elicit inevitably negative responses. These are then dutifully transcribed by our "careful, professional" psychologist as potential emotional weaknesses of the candidate.

Other fragments in the exercise trawl for motivational deficiencies ("It's fun to daydream about . . . ," "In spare moments I . . . ," "On weekends I . . . ," "My greatest ambition . . . "); inappropriate social or political attitudes ("Careers for women are . . . ," "A husband should . . . "); and willingness to adopt a bourgeois lifestyle ("Having to care for a house is . . . ," "On vacation I like to . . . "). The most telling fragments are those that directly engage the respondent on power issues in the workplace. "I like the sort of worker who . . . ," "Bosses seem to think . . . ," "Company policy is . . . ," "Taking orders . . . ," "Having to work overtime . . . "— these are nothing other than attempts to see how pliable, how willing to kiss ass, how unwilling to make waves, the candidate is. And then there is this corker—"A leader is . . . "—which gives the candidate a chance to flex his rhetorical muscles.

If at first glance, Chad and Vern seemed to be cast as stock characters in the age-old clash between Old Boy and Can-Do Bastard, the result proved less interesting. In fact, Chad's and Vern's evaluations were remarkably identical—and identically inadequate in revealing anything important about either man. Despite their divergent backgrounds and education, the key information these two contenders related in the crucial sentence-completion exercises was framed in exactly the same jargon. While both are considered to be competent for their current positions, their potential for further advancement is judged to be marginal. They are adequately qualified to remain in their present capacities, reads the final verdict, but every effort should be made to avail them of the proper "managerial firming."

The dark irony of the evaluations is that Chad and Vern were judged not on relevant psychological data—on those innate, definable characteristics that make each of us special in our own way— but on their failure to adequately think about or tailor their responses for the "expert" into whose hands they have foolishly placed their professional fates. Innocently, thoughtlessly, Chad admitted that he sometimes sweats excessively and becomes frustrated in traffic; Vern confessed he sometimes envies others. By answering truthfully, these two men have failed a simple test of common sense. They didn't recognize the examination for what it was: an opportunity to parrot the platitudes of corporate correctness. When dealing with the gatekeepers of power, honesty is *never* the best policy. It's best to tell them what they want to hear, and make it believable. Vern's father, the dead G.I., probably understood this too well, even without the benefits of managerial firming.

Baffler #6, 1995

TOM VANDERBILT

The Advertised Life

> He would forget his fine disgusts, cease to rage against the
> tyranny of money—cease to be aware of it, even—cease to
> squirm at the ads for Bovex and Breakfast Crisps. He would
> sell his soul so utterly that he would forget it had ever been
> his.   —George Orwell, *Keep the Aspidistra Flying*

Lessons in Life

LAST SPRING, I wandered through "Lessons in Life," a photography exhibit at the Art Institute of Chicago. As I gazed at the photographs, an unstated unifying theme of the show began to emerge: each work was either a comment on consumer culture or looked a part of it. I was not surprised to see shopworn deconstructionist statements by Barbara Krueger and Richard Misrach, nor was I surprised by the "lesson" that accompanied these works: "Beware of the Media." But it rang dated and rather naive—after all, what was the "media," some snarling and brutish dog tucked safely behind a fence? What set me thinking about the intricacies of life in an image-based consumer society far more sharply than did the connect-the-dots symbolism of the postmodernists' belabored collages, were Joel Sternfeld's photographs, rather plainly depicted portraits of what the curator called the "respectable middle class." In one, an attorney reclined in his office; in another, a pink-clad woman clutched shopping bags on a Santa Monica street. Their faces were earnest and full of vigor, and if you looked beneath each portrait's hyper-real veneer you could discern something quirky about each subject: the attorney was barefoot; the pink-clad woman carried a pet rabbit housed in a pink container. Like the man in the Hathaway shirt ads, whose perfectly ordinary visage betrays the startling fact that he is wearing an eye patch, they were strikingly distinct, yet something about them could appeal to everyone.

It occurred to me that these subjects could have been culled from the portfolio of an idealized ad campaign. I wondered how the unique energy that these achievers possessed could be channeled into a suitable product line, and I groped loosely for a tag line, a hook. Had they each "found their own road"? Was it a "Just Do It" spirit that crackled in these characters? As soon as the thought had crossed my mind I shrank back in disgust: Why did I choose those words, that idea? I had, in fact, only hours before, visited Chicago's NikeTown, a giant "sports-retail theater" filled with images of people engaged in Nike's "total body conditioning" lifestyle, a shrine to the possibility of Nike-accessorized athletic greatness and to the poetry of William Blake. It is a palace of emulation. Now I thought maddeningly of the entire Nike pantheon, of Dennis Hopper, and every photo in every magazine and on every bus stop. Faced with Sternfeld's images, I looked in vain for a message, a brand, a campaign. Surely there was a product for sale here. But they were deafening in their commercial silence.

Suddenly the connection between NikeTown and the pictures in the exhibit became clear: They were both aspects of the *advertised life*, an emerging mode of being in which advertising not only occupies every last negotiable public terrain, but in which it penetrates the cognitive process, invading consciousness to such a point that one expects and looks for advertising, learns to lead life as an ad, to think like an advertiser, and even to anticipate and insert oneself in successful strategies of marketing. The advertised life is not merely what you see on television, it is what the television sees. It is now everything that is around you. That beautiful person standing next to you in that upmarket bar who just ordered a Hennesy martini might be a live product spokesmodel, part of that brand's effort to reach elusive style makers. That mildly humorous dog race you read about was an imitation of a beer ad in which two television programs—drag racing and a dog show—are made into one with the help of a can of beer, an event that proves that "the TV mnemonic," as Miller Lite's brand director puts it, "has really permeated the fabric of the culture." One day, you may dial your telephone and hear an ad instead of a ring. Your friends are going on-line to "interact" with the fictional employees of the MCI commercial's "Gramercy Press."

These are just a few signals of a realignment of society in which advertising has become an ingrained function of daily existence, an "Absolut Environment," as the ad says. A visit to another city today is a visit simply to another set of franchises in the stable of a few national corporations. A meal once eaten in a small local diner is now eaten, from New York to Santiago, in what a corporation, in its neatly packaged estimation, considers to be "The French Bakery Cafe"; or, in one of their "multi-themed food and entertainment outlets," whose only link to its environs is to provide paltry service-industry wages. The consumer, feeling that life has become easier in the land of superstores and familiar logos, responds eagerly to the promise that nothing need happen in life that is not the finely contrived end product of an agency meeting.

It is in Madison Avenue's firmament of campaigns and brand awareness strategies, rather than contemporary art, that "lessons in life" are being forged, and they are reinforced at every juncture where consumers are, in the advertiser's delightful euphemism for delivering a message, "hit." The penetration is so complete that a simple trip to a museum becomes a mental battle against the corrosive power of the commercial aesthetic. At the "Lessons in Life" exhibit, even a powerful, decidedly anti-consumerist work like Margaret Bourke-White's "World's Highest Standard of Living" was not immune. It's a famous image, contrasting a breadline against a billboard that portrays a shining, airbrushed family in a new automobile, driving toward the future, emboldened by the words "There's no way like the American Way." Today, however, the work can hold little impact. The clashing of images is but a tool for holding viewers' attention, and Bourke-White's greatest legacy, the Gap now informs us, is that she wore khakis.

And now that the underbrush has been cleared, advertisers, armed with visions of their own future, proclaiming the benefits of "new media," and the "virtual brand," prepare to usher in an interactive future in which every individual—the terminus in the long march of market segmentation—can be personally "hit" with their very own message. "In this hyper-customized world," writes Andrew Susman, an associate at Chapman Direct, in *Advertising Age*, "the inter-relationship of advertising and programming increases because customer tastes and preferences are known in advance. Programming and advertising become interchangeable, as consumers are *living inside a perpetual marketing event*." (italics added)

Through the same media lens that allows us to observe military actions unfold on CNN, we can watch in wonder and dismay as these lessons in life are crafted. The exploits of their creators is the stuff of the daily business pages, where we read panegyrics to the latest doings of the hip, young agencies, whose brash creative directors play frisbee in office hallways and plot wholesale cultural upheaval. This is not business; this is art, and rest assured, the Madison Avenue mandarins of hip—the spotniks—are more interesting than their vulgar Wall Street brethren. Just listen to *The New Yorker* rave about the "young and hip-looking" thirty-four-year-old copywriter who (gasp) sports an earring, who (hold steady now) has an impressive collection of punk rock records, and who (this is getting very counterhegemonic) was able to listen to a Japanese noise band until 3 A.M. and still present five campaigns later that day. Such boardroom bohemianism reveals another shift: the "Madison Avenue boys" once wrote up the Beats because they were both fascinated and miffed by their lifestyle of unscheduled casualness, sloppy clothes, good records, and the fact that they "got away with it," as Paul Goodman writes in *Growing up Absurd;* today, however, Madison Avenue has become the Beats, or whatever the counterculture is, and through their works they establish the limits on how far out the fringe can go.

They may be young, but as the mobilizers and disseminators of lessons in life they have been granted enormous resources. If the latest model of the twenty-to-thirty demographic has moved away from drinking hard liquor, and your annual profits on sales of scotch are down 12%, you do not simply sit on your hands and assume cultural changes in diet and health are taking place. You unveil a $23 million campaign, with ads in magazines and "sampling events" at 1,000 bars and nightclubs on the East Coast. Or, if you're going after a bigger target, you bring in the heavy guns. In China, for example, you need the tools mentioned above but you've also got to worry about not breaching *guo qing,* i.e., respect for the local customs. Luckily, regional specialists can be snatched from academia, as in the case of Kellogg's foray into the republics of the former U.S.S.R., where cultural expertise is duly necessary when you're trying to "teach people a whole new way to eat breakfast." In regions where consumer products are widely available for the first time and consumers are "learning how to buy," as an adman in Mexico put it, advertising must point out the correct paths of consumption. A century ago the same breakfast lessons were applied in the U.S. to get people to switch from their "heavy" traditional breakfasts to the "simple yet satisfying" Quaker Oats.

Nowadays, when presented with these lessons in the advertised life, American consumers react with a fairly instinctual irony. The young especially, we are told, have developed an ability to shrug off advertising, and they are said to stray warily from overly blatant attempts to sell them. And yet they still buy the products. The *New York Times,* discussing MTV's new shopping network, reported that "by using sarcasm and irony to sell products (instead of the saccharine sincerity of QVC or HSN's hard sell and emphasis on bargain prices), MTV is effectively co-opting critics by not taking itself too seriously." Critics held securely at bay, MTV gleaned more than $1 million from a trial-run "Woodstock" promotion. Does anyone still believe that the MTV generation is "suspicious" of advertising? The article assumes, matter-of-factly, that sarcasm and irony are enough to placate critics. What it does not explain is why this is even possible, now that we are all aware that advertisers have seized upon irony as the cultural in-joke of the century. As everyone stands around winking and nudging, why does no one see fit to question irony itself? Of course they are trying to sell me something, the ironic response begins, but *I know that, and isn't it a funny ad?* The use of irony is shrouded in another, more distant, form of irony: since ads are now viewed with sneering, condescension, and the assumption that they are in no way effective, it then comes as little surprise that no one is disturbed or even really notices when advertising begins to appear in new places.

Indeed, the advertised life has settled in around us as though it were just another part of culture, with the myriad voices that once railed against the consumerist onslaught reduced to a nervous whisper on the pages of small magazines. As Mark Crispin Miller has noted, it is now much more difficult to discern this encroachment because the media has become the surroundings. MTV is the bellwether of this change, and it is a perfect model. MTV is what the *Harvard Business Review* calls a "marketspace," a consensual hallucination where "product becomes place becomes promotion." In the "marketspace" the *context* or cultural surroundings—not the *content* of the actual programming—is what attracts advertisers, and once brand loyalty has been formed at the context level the number of promotional opportunities blossoms exponentially. In the MTV marketspace, the network sells its identity with the same tactics it uses to sell products, and, at last, vehicle, style, and the language of the quarterly report have become one. Thus does the network's outlook "for a radically different future" derive directly from the business imperatives of the most conservative past.

Brand Fetishism

In the advertised life, the paradoxical relationship between consumer passivity and active public consumption has been consummated. In terms of how many goods are purchased, today's consumer is more active than ever. But in another sense the consumer has also become more passive than ever, having arrived at the necessary end of a historical process in which people in Western countries have become gradually removed from the goods they purchase. Where buyers and sellers once argued over the price and quality of necessary goods in marketplaces, today's consumers act out a pre-written script, purchasing the most heavily-advertised brands, no longer even needing to leave the house to buy. Marx's famous fetishism of commodities, once considered a radical notion, is now readily accepted on Madison Avenue as the modern way to sell products people do not actually need. When people began to define their inner selves through outward appearance, Richard Sennett has noted, the products they purchased began to acquire great meaning. After 100 years of mass consumer culture, we identify ourselves by our goods more publicly than ever—you can see it represented most neatly in the emergence of see-through shopping bags. But as brand awareness and advertising campaigns become larger than the products themselves, we increasingly identify our place in society through advertising. Not only is it difficult to imagine the labor that goes into products, it is now difficult to see the products aside from the brand or the lifestyle they represent: The "product idea" is more important than the product. Marketers fully realized the brilliant utility of this strategy long ago, recognizing that once they have successfully launched a brand into the daily vernacular, it is no longer necessary to sell "goods."

Brands are also a handy device for papering over nasty ambiguities like how things are made and what product is "right" for a person's socioeconomic standing and lifestyle. This strategy has been taken to ridiculous extremes, as in the case of sunglasses, hiking shoes, water, beer, and countless other cases where the most everyday products are socially totemized according to price and the identity with which the brand has become associated. As Sal Randazzo, senior vice-president and director of DMB&B, put it in his book, *Mythmaking on Madison Avenue: How Advertisers Apply the Power of Myth and Symbolism to Create Leadership Brands,* a brand is "a perceptual entity that exists is a psychological space in the consumer's mind." The advertiser believes the brand fills some sort of primal need and that, with the right orchestration, the brand eventually becomes part of the consumer's "psychic makeup." The old credit card ad began, "You may not know me," but the brand dispels such anonymity: I smoke Merits. I drink Pepsi. I drive a Pontiac. You do know me.

In the advertised life the power of brands allows the traditional formula of companies paying for advertising to reach consumers to be reversed. Consumers will now pay corporate sponsors for the right to display the detritus of corporate marketing on their person. What advertisers call "promotional wearables" is perhaps the most perverse example: people actually turn their own body into a marketing vehicle by wearing a t-shirt emblazoned with "The Gap," or, as was the fashion a year ago, by physically "branding" a corporate logo on their body. Madison Avenue insists there is deep myth and symbolism going on here, or worse yet, it makes ridiculous claims of distinctiveness: Describing their entrance into the premium bottled-water market, a Donna Karan New York executive said that "it just seems so right. Water is international. It's real. It's part of you." Or, as the ad director for another designer-water brand said, "Pure. Refreshing—all those adjectives that go with it describe both us and the water" (one wonders if "shallow" and "transparent" are among those adjectives). And yet, as the *Wall Street Journal* pointed out, DKNY uses the same water as Sierra Gold, which is available in stores for under a dollar a bottle.

For the passive consumer, economic activity is reduced to choosing between the advertised life offered by Brand A or Brand B, proudly trumpeting their individuality in this "consumer democracy" by putting either the Coca-Cola or Pepsi-Cola poster on their wall. The entrepreneurs behind a company called Posters Preferred, which actually sells advertisements to college students, told the *New York Times* that, when asked why they chose to purchase the posters, people usually answered, "To express something about myself."

Alexander Abrams and David Lipsky, authors of "The Boomlet Generation," an editorial that appeared a while back in the *New York Times,* epitomize the ontological squalor of the advertised life. Presenting the article as a "notice to advertisers," they decry the failure of marketers to notice the "irresistible purchasing power" of their generation (aged 24 to 32) amongst the hoopla over their "noisier, younger siblings." No, they plead with advertisers, we are not the grunge kids, those harbingers of "true nihilism." We are the ones with the real jobs, the real apartments, the real girlfriends, and we'll gladly drink your real drink if you would just reciprocate a bit and direct some ads our way. And, please, do not let our passage into adulthood (that is, once Abrams and Lipsky are done "waiting for the economy to give us a chance to become the adults we hoped we could be") proceed without appropriate advertising mirroring and guiding every step we take as we grow up absurd. But they need not worry. The market will see that their needs are met, thanks to the efforts of people like youth marketing director Jane Rinzler, who said in one interview that "Gen-X'ers . . . spent $95 billion in 1992, which is a significant market. It's time they started building brand loyalty."

The Closing of the Frontier

The manifest destiny of American business is not a matter of occupying vast tracts of empty land, but of seeking out new frontier territories of the mental and the built environments in which to plant their brand-label flags. With pioneering fervor they stalk the last few stretches of logo-free America, hoping to get a piece of the rapidly filling market-niche frontier with a new round of "place-based," or "out-of-home" advertising.

"Place-based media is like the Wild West of the American frontier," David Verklin, director of Hal Riney and Partners, San Francisco, said in *Advertising Age*. "It's an exciting freewheeling brawl, and there's a new idea coming to town every week." These ideas are, just to name a few, the "Good Health Channel," a television channel providing health information and advertising to be placed in 1,500 pediatric offices, modeled on Whittle Communications' now-defunct Medical News Network; NBC On-Site, which is "being positioned as an 'out-of-home TV network' to be packaged as another 'daypart' of NBC . . . the goal is to reach a critical mass of supermarkets and other mass retailers nationwide"; and, courtesy of Food Court Entertainment, Cafe USA, a television channel intended for shopping mall food courts, which is boasting a consumer recall for ads "about three times higher" than conventional broadcast media, and is, according to the company's president, "hitting the people when they are relaxed, sitting down to eat with $100 in their pocket."

There are few boundaries to the search for market share. And yet, if anything should challenge the eminent domain of advertising, its makers rush to dispose of the threat with free speech rhetoric and legal intimidation. Efforts to crack the public sphere with anything but advertising are done so at great risk these days. Several years ago, the New York-based artist Michael Lebron attempted to rent space in New York's Penn Station to display his artwork. Fine, Amtrak said, until they learned that the mural was a satire of the

Coors Brewing Company's support of right-wing causes. The mural, which featured a Coors can streaking like a missile toward a village in Nicaragua over a caption that read "Is it the Right's Beer Now?", was now a problem, and Amtrak officials, no doubt lobbied by Coors officials, decided that regulations prohibited displaying politically-based advertising. Lebron challenged Amtrak in the Supreme Court on First Amendment grounds, but he faced an ultimate challenge from Coors: Since the can is trademarked, they argued, it cannot be reproduced without permission.

Lebron, who himself worked in advertising, thus encountered the Golden Rule of the advertised life: You will be exposed to nothing but commercial speech. Coors spokespersons respond haughtily, "It's just unfortunate that some people want to advance their own agenda with unfair swipes at the brewing company." But can one mural overcome the agenda of identity-making that Coors has sculpted through countless hours of commercials, inserts, and promotional giveaways, all celebrating a cult of vibrant youth sipping the purity of the Rocky Mountains? Coors, like any corporation in the advertised life, is able to squash dissent through the sheer bulk and frequency of its message. It is appropriate that the company's recent campaign fantasizes about a mythical "Coors Light Channel," which is "always on"—an effective metaphor, really, for the boundless saturation of the public imagination that corporate consciousness demands. Should this reach be threatened with restrictions on advertising, corporate lobbyists in Washington are ready. Private individuals may cling desperately to the First Amendment, which protects speech in public places, but there are very few "public places" left.

And so, with the rules of the game firmly set, the boundaries of the advertised life expand. Children too can be "in the demo," with the "My First Sony" and "Baby Guess" lines teaching children their first consumerist lessons in life and allowing parents to accessorize infants to their own designs. Place-based advertising is even moving out of the retail arena and into what used to be known as "films." The tie-in (or "integrated marketing") campaign arranged between McDonald's and the *The Flinstones* was about more than just getting a Big Mac into a few frames; as a marketing exec told *Business Week,* the fast-food chain wanted "to be integrated into the property." A seemingly less commercial film such as *Forrest Gump,* which was heralded as a film that spoke to America's "traditional values," was actually, as *Advertising Age* noted approvingly, "providing positive image enhancement for the Nike brand."

With imperial arrogance advertisers feel that if there is space in society that is not currently being used to sell a product, then it is theirs to exploit. You can hear it in the voices of the "place-based pioneers." The president of New Jersey-based Quantum Systems Inc., the company that has taken out a patent to put ads on phone lines, said in one interview, "We're talking about the nooks and crannies of dead space where companies can play advertising and not offend customers." In describing their low-watt radio station that reaches 92,000 people per day stuck in traffic near New York's Lincoln Tunnel, Atlantic Records' vice president of promotion said, "It's a completely unused, radical new form of advertising."

But marketers have only recently discovered the public space with the greatest potential of all: the information superhighway. Once the government has stopped funding it, advertisers realize, commercial interests will be the only ones who can sustain its vast infrastructural and administrative needs. At that point we can justifiably say that the electronic frontier will have been closed. Just as the closing of the geographic frontier in 1890 paved the way for nationally standardized brands, markets, and products, the closing of the electronic frontier means that the decades-old anarchic and weird electronic subculture depicted by Thomas Pynchon and others will be replaced by a smooth, well-heeled cybermall. There will be little room, if any, for experimentation or unscripted events, only products and services for sale in a slick graphic environment that will seek to capture the consuming imagination in the same way mass retailers did a century ago when they unveiled the glass, sound, and lights of their giant commercial palaces. At a recent industry convention a chief executive at Time Warner told the crowd assembled to "Stop thinking about it as the 'information superhighway' and start thinking about it as the 'marketing superhighway.' " While hackers may have temporarily checked the appearance of ads in cyberspace, ad agencies are already meeting with Microsoft and other companies to discuss ways to reduce consumer opposition to "interactive" ads on advertiser-supported data networks. By couching the accumulation of demographic data in the democratic-sounding shibboleth of "interactivity," marketers can foist the burdens of identifying, targeting, and "hitting" the consumer onto the consumer himself. The consumer will now be able (and, no doubt, willing) to internalize the focus-group process and deliver by their mouse-moving hand their very own demographic profile. To reconfigure Mark Crispin Miller's reconfiguration of Orwell, Big Brother will be you, interfacing.

The Body Demographic

If advertising has indeed become more pervasive, the reasons for its expansion have little to do with a logically arranged cabal of agencies and their designs to inflame the desires of the American consumer. The significance of advertising's encroachment is not in the power of Madison Avenue, but in the near-complete inscription of consumerism into the national life. The appearance of these ads and marketing strategies should not simply trigger an angry response against the advertisers, but rather an appraisal of how the American cultural landscape has changed. It is easy to attack people like Chris Whittle who seek to reform society through purely mercantile means, but we should be prepared to answer when he asks: "Should capitalism be in the public sector?"

Actually the question is a bit moot: Capitalism now virtually owns the public sector. Many found a victory for "the past" in the Disney corporation's decision to refrain from building a Civil War theme park in Virginia, but it may have been a pyrrhic one. Why save a vision of the past from corporate redesign when the present and the future face no such salvation? With little of the controversy it drew from its Civil War project, Disney has built a town called "Celebration" in Florida. This is not a mere tourist attraction, but an actual functioning town of 20,000 whose residents live among the pre-World War II architecture of yuppie fantasy. The residents' children attend a model school linked to a Disney-run national teacher training academy, which Disney in turn uses to market educational software and other innovations. Like the Puritans, Disney seeks a City on the Hill where the dystopian public sector problems that impede American progress can be solved by "imagineering," Disney's entertainment-cum-management philosophy.

Should capitalism be in the public sector? If the public believes government to be corrupt and inefficient—and if there has been, as Christopher Lasch has argued, a "revolt of the elites," in which those who traditionally were called upon to fund and build public institutions have revolted against the ideals of public service and community, sending their children to private schools, insuring themselves against medical catastrophe, and locking themselves in high-security private residential retreats—who will support the public institutions that were once considered the cornerstone of liberal democratic achievement? Surely the poor cannot afford such a task, and the middle class has taken refuge in tax revolts and the House of Gingrich. Who then is left? The Cold War consensus has collapsed, the labor movement is a shell of its former self, postmodern fragmentation has reduced ideology and culture to a host of special-interest groups clamoring in the trading-pits of pluralist relativism. Amongst these ruins, only the rapidly consolidating corporations of late consumer society maintain their form and cohesiveness, their vision and drive; and as their brand managers and image consultants and creative directors spin their seamless narratives they gain the trust of a disenchanted public that sees few alternatives to the advertised life. Recently a Colorado school district that was strapped for cash agreed to lease pieces of school property to advertisers. Rather than criticism they received hundreds of inquiries from other schools wondering how they too could add Burger King logos to the sides of school buses.

Almost through default consumerism has become the reigning ideology in American society, and its health is gauged by the way we now understand "freedom of choice." Choice is a catch-all notion in a "consumer democracy": It can mean school choice, where the problems of public schools are somehow solved by allowing the children of the wealthy to opt out; and it can signify personal choice, which, as Lasch noted, has increased in those matters where most people see the need for solid moral guidelines rather than further choices. But above all it refers to an ever-expanding choice of consumer products.

The consumption of goods is now so closely linked to identity that a new form of social analysis has emerged in which classes are defined not by property or profession or even income but by what products they purchase. These new social groupings are part of the elaborate schemata of marketers, where demographics and psychographics are merged to create mythical profiles of who buys what and for what reasons. In SRI International's Values and Lifestyles System, an industry staple, there are eight basic classes into which all Americans fall. There are no rich, no poor, only those with more resources and less resources. From the low-demo "Strugglers," who are "brand loyal" and "read tabloids and women's magazines" to the "Experiencers," who are on top in the "Action Oriented" category and who "buy on impulse" and "listen to rock music," there is a category for everyone. The information gleaned with the "new media" will provide marketers the building blocks of a new Leviathan. The old behemoth of Hobbes gave human form to the "bodies politique," but the new Leviathan is the consumer society's Body Demographic: an individualized mass of consumers, grouped in the humanized portraits of market segmentation, joined by passive observation of a sovereign lifestyle.

The new consumer society will no longer need the general advertisements broadcast from without at the entire populace; it will, rather, speak to consumers directly from within. "Aftermarketing" will attempt to make the purchase the first step in the advertised life, rather than the last, and other novelties, such as "relationship billing," will hit consumers with ads based on the kinds of purchases recorded on their credit card statements. As *American Demographics* put it, new media consumers will "be more tolerant of advertising because it will be more appropriate and customized." In the new media, the goal of the marketing message is not the "purchase," but "further interaction." As life becomes a "perpetual marketing event" we will no longer be able to discern where advertising begins and where it ends. In a realm that could have been designed by Kafka, we shall all awake not as giant insects but as "productive reach" targets of an innovative marketing plan. The next time around it will begin: *Someone must have been telemarketing Joseph K . . .*

Baffler #6, 1995

PART III

The Culturetrust™

Generation

THOMAS FRANK

Alternative to What?

It's Not Your Father's Youth Movement

THERE ARE FEW spectacles corporate America enjoys more than
a good counterculture, complete with hairdos of defiance, dark
complaints about the stifling "mainstream," and expensive accessories of all kinds. So it was only a matter of months after the discovery of "Generation X" that the culture industry sighted an
all-new youth movement, whose new looks, new rock bands, and
menacing new 'tude quickly became commercial shorthand for the
rebel excitement associated with everything from Gen X ads and
TV shows to the information revolution. Consumers have been
treated to what has undoubtedly been the swiftest and most profound shift of imagery to come across their screens since the 1960s.

New soundtracks, new product design, new stars, new ads. "Alternative," they call it. Out with the old, in with the new.

Before this revelation, punk rock and its descendents had long been considered commercially unviable in responsible business circles because of their incorrigible angriness, their implacable hostility to the cultural climate that the major record labels had labored so long to build, as well as because of their difficult sound. Everyone knows pop music is supposed to be simple and mass-producible, an easy matter of conforming to simple genres, of acting out the standard and instantly recognizable cultural tropes of mass society: *I love love, I'm sad sometimes, I like cars, I'm my own person, I'm something of a rebel, I'm a cowboy on a steel horse I ride.* All through the seventies and eighties the culture industry knew instinctively that the music that inhabited the margins couldn't fit, didn't even merit consideration. So back in 1977, at the dawn of punk, the American media, whose primary role has long been the uncritical promotion of whatever it is that Hollywood, the record labels, or the networks are offering at the time, lashed out at this strange, almost unfathomable movement. "Rock Is Sick," announced the cover of *Rolling Stone* in 1977. The national news magazines pronounced the uprising to be degeneracy of the worst variety, then proceeded to ignore it all through the eighties. Its listeners were unmentionable on TV, film, and radio except as quasi-criminals, and in the official channels of music-industry discourse—radio, MTV, music magazines—this music and the tiny independent labels that supported it simply didn't exist.

Of course we all know what happened next. Thanks to the turning of generations and the inexorable logic of the market—and the wild success of Nirvana in 1991—the industry was forced to reconsider, and it descended in a ravenous frenzy on the natural habitats of those it once shunned. Within weeks high-powered executives were offering contracts to bands they had seen only once, college radio playlists became the objects of intense corporate scrutiny, and longstanding independent labels were swallowed whole. *Rolling Stone* magazine began making pious reference to the pioneering influence of defunct bands like Big Black and Mission of Burma, whose records they ignored when new, and MTV hastily abandoned its pop origins to push "alternative" bands round the clock. By 1993, the mass media had risen as one and proclaimed itself in solidarity with the rebels, anxious to don flannel, head out to Lollapalooza on the weekend and "mosh" with the kids. The pinnacle came when *Time* magazine finally smelled green in the music, too. In its issue of October 25, 1993, *Time* sent Christopher John Farley headlong into the kind of reckless celebrationism the magazine usually reserved only for the biggest-budget movies and the most successful TV shows. Salivating over the "anxious rebels" of "a young, vibrant alternative scene," Farley breathlessly detailed every aspect of the youngsters' deliciously ingenuous insurrection: They're "defiant," they're concerned with "purity and anticommercialism," they sing about "homes breaking," and—tastiest of all—they're upset about "being copied or co-opted by the mainstream."

Strangely, though, Farley's *Time* story on "alternative" rock barely mentioned a band that is not a "co-optation," that still produces records on an actual independent label. As per the usual dictates of American culture, only money counts, and indie labels don't advertise in *Time*. So Pearl Jam, the major-label band that has made a career out of imitating the indie sounds of the late eighties, won the magazine's accolades as the "demigod" of the new "underground," leading the struggle for "authenticity" and against "selling out."

Of course this is poor reporting, but journals like *Time* have always been more concerned with industry boosterism and the hard, profitable facts of making credible the latest packaging of youth culture than with a vague undefinable like "news." Thus while we read almost nothing about the still unmentionable world of independent rock, we are bombarded with insistences that Pearl Jam is the real rebel thing, the maximum leaders of America's new youth counterculture—assertions that are driven home by endless descriptions of the band going through all the varieties of insurgent posturing. They have a "keen sense of angst," and singer Eddie Vedder feels bad about the family problems of his youth. He rose to success from nowhere, too: He was a regular guy with a taste for living on the edge (much like the people in ads for sneakers and cars and jeans), a "gas station attendant and high school dropout," who thought up the band's lyrics while surfing. But Eddie's real sensitive also, a true Dionysian like Mick Jagger, with a "mesmerizing stage presence" that "reminded fans of an animal trying to escape from a leash." In fact, he's so sensitive that certain of the band's lyrics aren't included with the others on the album sleeve because "the subject matter is too painful for Vedder to see in print."

The gushing of official voices like *Time* make necessary a clarification that would ordinarily go without saying: Among the indie-rock circles, which they mimic and from which they pretend to draw their credibility, bands like Pearl Jam are almost universally recognized to suck. Almost without exception, the groups and music that are celebrated as "alternative" are watery, derivative, and strictly second-rate; so uniformly bad, in fact, that one begins to believe that shallowness is a precondition of their marketability. Most of them play predigested and predictable versions of formulaic heavy guitar rock, complete with moronic solos and hoarse masculine poutings. There is certainly nothing even remotely "alternative" about this sound, since music like this has long been the favorite of teenage boys everywhere; it's just the usual synthetic product, repackaged in a wardrobe of brand new imagery made up of thousands of fawning articles and videos depicting them as "rebel" this or "twentysomething" that. The sole remarkable feature of these otherwise stunningly mediocre bands is their singers' astonishing ability to warble the shallowest of platitudes with an earnestness that suggests they have actually internalized their maudlin, Hallmark-worthy sentimentality.

As ever, the most interesting aspect of the industry's noisy clamoring and its self-proclaimed naughtiness is not the relative merits of the "alternative" culture products themselves, but the shift of imagery they connote. Forget the music; what we are seeing is just another overhaul of the rebel ideology that has fueled business culture ever since the 1960s, a new entrant in the long parade of "countercultural" entrepreneurship. Look back at the ads and the records and the artists of the pre-Nirvana period: all the same militant protestations of nonconformity are there, just as they are in the ads and records and artists of the seventies and the sixties. Color Me Badd and Wham! once claimed to be as existentially individualist, as persecuted a group of "anxious rebels" as Bush now does. But by the years immediately preceding 1992, these figures' claims to rebel leadership had evaporated, and American business faced a serious imagery crisis. People had at long last tired of such obvious fakery, grown unconvinced and bored. No one except the most guileless teeny-boppers and the most insecure boomers fell for the defiant posturing of Duran Duran or Vanilla Ice or M.C. Hammer or Bon Jovi; especially when the ghettos began to burn, especially when the genuinely disturbing sounds of music that was produced without benefit of corporate auspices were finding wider audiences.

By the beginning of the new decade, the patina of daring had begun to wear thin on the eighties' chosen crop of celebrity-rebels. Entire new lines of insolent shoes would have to be designed and marketed; entire new looks and emblems of protest would have to be found somewhere. Consumerism's traditional claim to be the spokesman for our inchoate disgust with consumerism was hemorrhaging credibility, and independent rock, with its Jacobin "authenticity" obsession, had just the things capital required.

Out went the call for an "alternative" from a thousand executive suites, and overnight everyone even remotely associated with independent rock in Seattle—and Minneapolis, Chapel Hill, Champaign, Lawrence, and finally Chicago—found themselves the recipients of unsolicited corporate attention. Only small adjustments were required to bring the whole universe of corporate-sponsored rebellion up to date, to give us Blind Melon instead of Frankie Goes to Hollywood; 10,000 Maniacs instead of Sigue Sigue Sputnik. And suddenly we were propelled into an entirely new hip paradigm, a new universe of cool, with all new stars and all new relationships between the consumer, his celebrities, and his hair.

And now Pepsi is no longer content to cast itself as the beverage of Michael Jackson or Ray Charles or even Madonna: These figures' hip has been outdated suddenly, convincingly, and irreparably. Instead we watch a new and improved, an even more anti-establishment Pepsi Generation, cavorting about to what sounds like "grunge" rock, engaged in what appears to be a sort of oceanside slam dance. *Vanity Fair*, a magazine devoted strictly to the great American pastime of celebrating celebrity, hires the editors of a noted "alternative" 'zine to overhaul its hipness; *Interview*, the great, stupid voice of art as fashion, runs a lengthy feature on college radio, the site of the juiciest, most ingenuously "alternative" lifestyle innovations in the land. Ad agencies and record labels compete with each other in a frenzied scramble to hire leading specimens of the "alternative" scene they have ignored for fifteen years. Even commercial radio stations have seen the demographic writing on the wall and now every city has one that purports to offer an "alternative" format, featuring musical hymns to the various rebellious poses available to consumers at malls everywhere.

But the most revealing manifestation of the new dispensation is something you aren't supposed to see: an ad for MTV that ran in the business sections of a number of newspapers. "Buy this 24-year-old and get all his friends absolutely free," its headline reads. Just above these words is a picture of the 24-year-old referred to, a quintessential "alternative" boy decked out in the rebel garb that the executives who read this ad will instantly recognize from their market reports to be the costume of the "twentysomethings": beads and bracelets, a vest and t-shirt, torn jeans, Doc Martens, and a sideways haircut like the Jesus and Mary Chain wore in 1985. His pose: insolent, sprawled insouciantly in an armchair, watching TV of course.

His occupation: consumer. "He watches MTV," continues the ad, "which means he knows a lot. More than just what CDs to buy and what movies to see. He knows what car to drive and what credit cards to use. And he's no loner. What he eats, his friends eat. What he wears, they wear. What he likes, they like."

Thus with the "alternative" face-lift, "rebellion" continues to perform its traditional function of justifying the economy's ever-accelerating cycles of obsolescence with admirable efficiency. Since our willingness to load up our closets with purchases depends upon an eternal shifting of the products paraded before us, upon our being endlessly convinced that the new stuff is better than the old, we must be persuaded over and over again that the "alternatives" are more valuable than the existing or the previous. Ever since the 1960s hip has been the native tongue of advertising, "antiestablishment" the vocabulary by which we are taught to cast off our old possessions and buy whatever they have decided to offer this year. And over the years the rebel has naturally become the central image of this culture of consumption, symbolizing endless, directionless change, an eternal restlessness with "the establishment"—or, more correctly, with the stuff "the establishment" convinced him to buy last year.

Not only did the invention of "alternative" provide capital with a new and more convincing generation of rebels, but in one stroke it outdated all the rebellions of the past ten years, rendered our acid-washed jeans, our Nikes, our DKNYs meaningless. Are you vaguely pissed off at the world? Well, now you get to start proving it all over again, with flannel shirts, a different brand of jeans, and big clunky boots. And in a year or two there will be an "alternative" to that as well, and you'll get to do it yet again.

It's not only the lure of another big Nirvana-like lucre-glut that brings label execs out in droves to places like Seattle, or hopes of uncovering the new slang that prompts admen to buy journals like *The Baffler*. The culture industry is drawn to "alternative" by the more general promise of finding the eternal new, of tapping the very source of the fuel that powers the great machine. As *Interview* affirms, "What still makes the genre so cool is not its cash potential or hype factor but the attendant drive and freedom to create and discover fresh, new music." Fresh new music, fresh new cars, fresh new haircuts, fresh new imagery.

Thus do capital's new dancing flunkeys appear not in boater hat and ingratiating smile, but in cartoonish postures of sullen angst or teen frustration: dyed hair, pierced appendages, flannel shirt around the waist. Everyone in advertising remembers how frightening and enigmatic such displays were ten years ago when they encountered them in TV stories about punk rock, and now their time has come to be deployed as the latest signifiers of lifestyle savvy. Now it's executives themselves on their days off, appearing in their weekend roles as kings of the consumer hill, who flaunt such garb, donning motorcycle jackets and lounging around the coffeehouses they imagine to be frequented by the latest generation of angry young men. Of course every other persecuted-looking customer is also an advertising account exec or a junior vice president of something-or-other; of course nobody would ever show up to see a band like, say, the New Bomb Turks or Prisonshake in a costume like this.

So on we plod through the mallways of our lives, lured into an endless progression of shops by an ever-changing chorus of manic shaman-rebels, promising existential freedom—sex! ecstasy! liberation!—from the endless trudge. All we ever get, of course, are some more or less baggy trousers or a hat that we can wear sideways. Nothing works, we are still entwined in vast coils of tawdriness and idiocy, and we resolve not to be tricked again. But lo! Down the way is a new rebel-leader, doing handstands this time, screaming about his untrammelled impertinence in an accent that we know could *never* be co-opted, and beckoning us into a shoe store. Marx's quip that the capitalist will sell the rope with which he is hanged begins to seem ironically incomplete. In fact, with its endless ranks of beautifully coiffed, fist-waving rebel boys to act as barker, business is amassing great sums by charging admission to the ritual simulation of its own lynching.

Come Around to My Way of Thinking

Perhaps the only good thing about the commodification of "alternative" is that it will render obsolete, suddenly, cleanly, and inexorably, that whole flatulent corpus of "cultural studies" that seeks to appreciate Madonna as some sort of political subversive. Even though the first few anthologies of writings on the subject only appeared in 1993, the rise of a far more threatening generation of rock stars has ensured that this singularly annoying pedagogy will never become a full-fledged "discipline," with its own lengthy quarterly issued by some university press, with annual conferences where the "subaltern articulations" of *Truth or Dare* are endlessly dissected and debated.

Looking back from the sudden vantage point that only this kind of image-revolution affords, the scholarship of academia's Madonna fans now appears as predictable in its conclusions as it was entertaining in its theoretical pyrotechnics. After careful study of the singer's lyrics and choreography, the professors breathlessly insisted, they had come upon a crucial discovery: Madonna was a gender-questioning revolutionary of explosive potential, a rule-breaking avatar of female empowerment, a person who disliked racism! One group of gaping academics hailed her "ability to tap into and disturb established hierarchies of gender and sexuality." Another celebrated her video "Vogue" as an "attempt to enlist us in a performance that, in its kinetics, deconstructs gender and race," an amusing interpretation, to be sure, but also one that could easily have been translated into academese directly from a Madonna press kit.

The problem is not that academics have abandoned their sacred high-culture responsibilities for a channel changer and a night at the disco, but that in so doing they have uncritically reaffirmed the mass media's favorite myths about itself. Discovering, after much intellectual twisting and turning, that Madonna is exactly the rebel that she and her handlers imagine her to be, is more an act of blithe intellectual complicity than of the "radicalism" to which the Madonna analysts believe they are contributing. After all, it was Madonna's chosen image as liberator from established mores that made her so valuable to the culture industry in the first place. It doesn't take a genius to realize that singing the glories of pseudo-rebellion remains to this day the monotone anthem of advertising, film, and TV sitcom, or that the pseudo-rebel himself—the defier of repressive tradition, ever overturning established ways to make way for the new; the self-righteous pleasure-monad, changing identity, gender, hair color, costume, and shoes on a whim—is more a symbol of the machine's authority than an agent of resistance. But academics seem to have missed the point. For years the culture industry has held up for our admiration an unending parade of such self-proclaimed subverters of middle-class tastes, and certain scholars have been only too glad to play their part in the strange charade, studying the minutiae of the various artists' rock videos and deciding, after long and careful deliberation, that yes, each one is, in fact, a bona fide subversive. How thoroughly had they come around to the Industry's way of thinking; how desperately did they want to, *want to* get along!

But thanks to the rise of "alternative," with its new and vastly improved street cred, sneers, and menacing hairdos, the various postmodern courses by which each scribbler arrived at his or her conclusion that Madonna is "subverting" from within, and the particular costly academic volume in which they presented their "findings" are now, thankfully, finally, and irresistibly made irrelevant. Just as Madonna's claims to rebel authenticity have been made suddenly laughable by an entirely new package of much more rebellious rebel imagery, so their works are consigned to the same fate. Academia's Madonna fans have built their careers by performing virtually the same task, with a nice intellectual finish, as the toothy hosts of *Entertainment Tonight,* and now they are condemned to the same rubbish bin of instant forgetting. Their embrace of corporate culture has brought them face to face with *its* unarguable conclusions, the steel logic of *its* unprotestable workings: obsolescence.

In at least one sense, then, the triumph of Urge Overkill is a liberation. At least we will never, ever have to hear this favorite Paglian (or, should we say, all-American) platitude chanted for the thousand-and-first time: "I admire Madonna because she's a woman who's totally in control of her career." And since it will take at least three years for the first close readings of the "Sister Havana" video to appear in assigned texts, let us enjoy the respite and ponder the strange twists of history that brought academia so closely into line with the imperatives of mass culture.

In this spirit I offer the following observation.

Perhaps the saddest aspect of all this is not scholars' gullible swallowing of some industry publicist's line, or even their naïve inability to discern Madonna's obvious labor-fakery. The real disappointment lies in their abject inability to recognize "popular culture" anywhere but in the officially-sanctioned showplaces of corporate America; their utter dependence on television to provide them with an imagery of car miracles qua dissidence. Even as they delved deeper and deeper into the esoterica of poststructuralist theory, investing countless hours scrutinizing bad rock videos frame by frame, they remained hopelessly ignorant of the actual insurgent culture that has gone on all around them for fifteen years, for the simple reason that it's never made MTV. And academics, the wide-eyed, well-scrubbed sons and daughters of the suburbs, cannot imagine a "counterculture" that exists outside of their full-color, 36-inch screens. So in TV-land as well as the academy, Madonna was as "radical" as it got. Thus did the role of criticism become identical to that of the glossy puff magazines, with their well-practiced slavering over the latest products of the Culture Industry: to celebrate celebrity, to find an epiphany in shopping, a happy heteroglossia in planned obsolescence. As for their interpretations, the professorial class might just as well have been proclaiming the counter-hegemonic undercurrents of *Match Game* or the patriarchy-resisting profundity of Virginia Slims advertising.

Imagine what they could do if they only knew about Borbetomagus or Merzbow!

Fuck You and Your Underground

At the center of the academics' intricate webs of Madonna-theories lay the rarely articulated but crucial faith that the workings of the culture industry, the stuff that comes over our TV screens and through our stereos, are profoundly *normal*. The culture-products that so unavoidably define our daily lives, it is believed, are a given—a natural expression of the tastes of "the people." This has long been a favorite sophistry of the industry's *paid* publicity flacks as well: mass culture is fundamentally democratic. The workings of the market ensure that the people get what the people want; that sitcoms and Schwarzenegger and each of the various sneering pop stars are the embodiment of the general will. Thus, as the academic celebrators of Madonna were always careful to assert, those who insist on criticizing Madonna are deeply suspicious, affected adherents of an elitist and old-fashioned aesthetic that unfairly dismisses "low" culture in favor of such insufferably stuffy pastimes as ballet and opera.

This anti-elitist theme is, quite naturally, also a favorite in sitcoms and movies, which establish their hegemony over the public mind by routinely bashing various stock snobs and hapless highbrow figures. Advertising repeatedly strikes the same note: a drink called "Somers" is to gin, one ad asserts, as a bright green electric guitar, implement of transgressive cool, is to an old brown violin, squeaky symbol of the slow-moving. A Pizza Hut commercial similarly juxtaposes a moralizing, old-fashioned, stuffed-shirt man who is filmed in black and white, with a full-color, rock 'n' roll rendition of the restaurant of revolt. And when the straw man of "cultural elitism" is conjured up by the academics for its ritual stomping, the feeling is exactly the same. There is only the dry, spare, highbrow of the privileged and the lusty, liberated, lowbrow of the masses, and between these two the choice is clear.

This, then, is the culture of "the people." Never mind all the openly conducted machinations of the culture industry—the mergers and acquisitions, the "synergy," the admen's calculations of "penetration" and "usage pull," the dismantling of venerable publishing operations for reasons of fiscal whimsy. What the corporations have decided we will watch and read and listen to has somehow become the grassroots expressions of the nation. The Cultural Studies verdict is crucial financially as well, since the primary business of business is no longer, say, making things or exploiting labor, but manufacturing culture, finding the means to persuade you of the endless superiority of the new over the old, that the solution to whatever your unhappiness may be lies in a few new purchases. It is a truism of the business world that Coke and Pepsi don't make soda pop, they make advertising. Nike may pay Indonesian laborers absurdly low wages, but their most important concern is convincing us that it is meaningful, daring, and fulfilling to spend over one hundred dollars for a pair of sneakers. If you feel a burning need to understand "culture," get out of the coffeehouse and buy yourself a subscription to *Advertising Age.*

The media-flurry over the definition of the "twentysomethings" provides an interesting example of the ways in which "popular culture" is made, not born. Between the multitude of small presses and independent record labels that were founded, produced, and distributed by young people over the last decade, we have been an unusually voluble group. But this is not what was meant when the various lifestyle journalists and ad agency hacks went looking for "Generation X." The only youth culture that concerned them was the kind that's prefabricated for us in suites on Sunset Strip and Madison Avenue, and the only question that mattered was how to refine this stuff so that the young could be lured into the consumer maelstrom. Take a look at the book *13th Gen* by Neil Howe and Bill Strauss, the most baldfaced attempt to exploit the culture industry's confusion about how to pigeonhole us. What matters and what deserves to be reported are the movies, TV sitcoms, and major-label records that are targeted our way. The book's press kit explicitly cast *13th Gen* as a useful guide for executives in the advertising, public-relations, and election-winning industries. We are to be sold, not heard.

Under no condition is "popular culture" something that we make ourselves, in the garage with electric guitars and second-hand amplifiers, on the office photocopier when nobody's looking. It is, strictly and exclusively, the stuff produced for us in a thousand corporate boardrooms and demographic studies. "Popular culture" sells us stuff, convinces us to buy more soap or a different kind of shirt, assures us of the correctness of business paternalism, offers us a rebel fantasy world in which to drown our never-to-be-realized frustration with lives that have become little more than endless shopping trips, marathon filing sessions.

"Popular culture" is the enemy; rock 'n' roll is the health of the state.

The true culture war has nothing to do with the clever *pas de deux* of affected outrage acted out by sputtering right-wingers and their blustering counterparts in Soho and Hollywood. It is not fought out over issues like "family values" or "cultural elitism," but with a much more basic concern: the power of each person to make his own life without the droning dictation of business interests. If we must have grand, sweeping cultural judgments, only one category seems to matter anymore: the adversarial. The business of business is our minds, and the only great divide that counts anymore is whether or not we comprehend, we resist, we evade the all-invasive embrace.

But between the virtual monopoly of business interests over the stuff you spend all day staring at and the decision of the academics to join the burgeoning and noisy legion of culture industry cheerleaders, very little that is adversarial is allowed to filter through. Our culture has been hijacked without a single cry of outrage. However we may fantasize about Madonna's challenging of "oppressive tonal hierarchies," however we may drool over Pearl Jam's rebel anger, there is, quite simply, almost no dissent from the great cultural project of corporate America, no voice to challenge television's overpowering din. You may get a different variety of shoes this year, but there is no "alternative," ever.

We may never be able to dismantle the culture of consumption nor achieve any sort of political solution to the problems of this botched civilization. The traditional organs of resistance, enfeebled by decades of legislative attack and a cultural onslaught they do not comprehend, have either made their peace with consumerism or cling to outdated political goals.

But through the deafening mechanical yammering of a culture long since departed from the rails of meaning or democracy, through the excited hum of the congregation gathered for celebrity-worship, there is one promising sound. Its scream of torment is this country's only mark of health; the sweet shriek of outrage is the only sign that sanity survives amid the stripmalls and hazy clouds of Hollywood desire. It is proof that just beyond the silence of suburban stupidity, the confusion of the parking lots, the aggression, display, and desperate supplication of the city streets, the possibility of a worthy, well-screamed *no* survives. That just behind the stupefying smokescreens of authorized "popular culture" seethes something *real*, thriving, condemned to happy obscurity both by the marketplace, to whose masters (and consumers) its violent negation will be forever incomprehensible, and by the academic arbiters of "radicalism," by whom the "culture of the people" is strictly understood to be whatever the corporate donors *say* it is. Unauthorized and unauthorizable, it clamors in disgust amid the pseudo-rebel propriety of the cultural avenues of the empire. For official America it's fantasies of the comfortable cul-de-sac with state-of-the-art security equipment, the fine car, the airborne curfew enforcement unit, the Lake Forest estate, the Westchester commute; for us it's the secession, the internal exile, the thrashing release, the glorious never never never.

For this expression of dissent there has been no Armory show, no haughty embrace by aesthetes or editors. The only recognition it has garnered is the siege equipment of the consumer age, a corporate-sponsored shadow movement that seeks to mine it for marketable looks, imitable sounds, menacing poses. A travelling youth circus patterned, of course, after the familiar boomer originals of Woodstock and Dead shows, is invented to showcase the new industry dispensations. With their bottomless appetite for new territory to colonize, the executives have finally come around to us. For years they were too busy to be bothered, but now what we have been building has begun to look marketable.

But we will not be devoured easily. Few among us are foolish enough to believe that "the music industry" is just a bigger version of the next-door indie label, just a collection of simple record companies gifted mysteriously with gargantuan budgets and strange powers to silence criticism. We inhabit an entirely different world, intend entirely different outcomes. They seek fresh cultural fuel so that the machinery of stupidity may run incessantly; we cry out from under that machine's wheels. They manufacture lifestyle; we live lives.

So as they venture into the dark new world of hip, they should beware: The natives in these parts are hostile, and we're armed with flame-throwers. We will refuse to do their market research for them, to provide them amiably with helpful lifestyle hints and insider trend know-how. We are not a convenient resource available for exploitation whenever they require a new transfusion of rebel street cred; a test-market for "acts" they can someday unleash on the general public. And as they canvass the college radio stations for tips on how many earrings and in which nostril, or for the names of the "coolest" up-and-coming acts, they will find themselves being increasingly misled, embarrassed by bogus slang, deceived by phantom blips on the youth-culture futures index, anticipating releases from nonexistent groups. It has taken years to win the tiny degree of autonomy we now enjoy. No matter which way they cut their hair or how weepily Eddie Vedder reminisces about his childhood, we aren't about to throw it open to a process that in just a few years would leave us, too, jaded and spent, discarded for yet a newer breed of rebels, an even more insolent crop of imagery, looks, and ads.

Baffler #5, 1993

What is Alternative?

Business Man: "Here is one of the best employment makers we have. Since its co-optation the alternative lifestyle has created over 20 million jobs, and increased business volume to more than 100 industries nation-wide."

Police Chief: "Alternative lifestyles are on the side of law and order. The culture industry is actively cooperating with law enforcement officials to stamp out conditions not in the public's best interest."

Poet: "Ah, Alternative! The lifestyle of the rebel...endlessly questioning authority. Not accepting of mediocrity, continually striving for something different. Unafraid to weep, blazing new paths to liberation of the soul."

Tax Collector: "The alternative industries are mighty important to the taxpayer. Public revenues from alternative industries exceed four billion dollars a year...more than 10 million dollars every day. And remember what is good for the culture industry is good for America."

Teacher: 'Alternative lifestyles make good sense. By giving children a safe and productive outlet to vent their negative energies, it frees their minds to focus on what really matters... citizenship in our consumer-industrial state."

A+R Rep: 'It took the alternative industries decades to perfect the simulation of deviance. Now we want to keep alternative lifestyle retailing as cutting-edge as the product itself. We have a mighty interesting program and we'd like to tell you all about it. Write us."

Average Citizen: "Say listen, you fellows. You think you know what alternative is. I'll tell you what alternative really is. To me, and millions like me alternative is just one thing...a grand lifestyle".

Alternative...

A LIFESTYLE OF MODERATION FOR THE NATION

The Problem with Music

WHENEVER I TALK to a band who are about to sign with a major label, I always end up thinking of them in a particular context. I imagine a trench, about four feet wide and five feet deep, maybe sixty yards long, filled with runny, decaying shit. I imagine these people, some of them good friends, some of them barely acquaintances, at one end of this trench. I also imagine a faceless industry lackey at the other end, holding a fountain pen and a contract waiting to be signed.

Nobody can see what's printed on the contract. It's too far away, and besides, the shit stench is making everybody's eyes water. The lackey shouts to everybody that the first one to swim the trench gets to sign the contract. Everybody dives in the trench and they struggle furiously to get to the other end. Two people arrive simultaneously and begin wrestling furiously, clawing each other and dunking each other under the shit. Eventually, one of them capitulates, and there's only one contestant left. He reaches for the pen, but the lackey says, "Actually, I think you need a little more development. Swim it again, please. Backstroke."

And he does, of course.

A&R Scouts

Every major label involved in the hunt for new bands now has on staff a high-profile point man, an "A&R" rep who can present a comfortable face to any prospective band. The initials stand for "Artist and Repertoire," because historically, the A&R staff would select artists to record music that they had also selected, out of an available pool of each. This is still the case, though not openly.

These guys are universally young (about the same age as the bands being wooed), and nowadays they always have some obvious underground rock credibility flag they can wave. Lyle Preslar, former guitarist for Minor Threat, is one of them. Terry Tolkin, former New York independent booking agent and assistant manager at Touch and Go is one of them. Al Smith, former soundman at CBGB is one of them. Mike Gitter, former editor of *XXX* fanzine and contributor to *Rip*, *Kerrang*, and other lowbrow rags is one of them. Many of the annoying turds who used to staff college radio stations are in their ranks as well.

There are several reasons A&R scouts are always young. The explanation usually copped-to is that the scout will be "hip" to the current musical "scene." A more important reason is that the bands will intuitively trust someone they think is a peer, and who speaks fondly of the same formative rock-and-roll experiences.

The A&R person is the first person to make contact with the band, and as such is the first person to promise them the moon. Who better to promise them the moon than an idealistic young turk who expects to be calling the shots in a few years, and who has had no previous experience with a big record company. Hell, he's as naïve as the band he's duping. When he tells them no one will interfere in their creative process, he probably even believes it.

When he sits down with the band for the first time, over a plate of angel hair pasta, he can tell them with all sincerity that when they sign with company X, they're really signing with *him,* and he's on their side. Remember that great gig I saw you at in '85? Didn't we have a blast.

By now all rock bands are wise enough to be suspicious of music industry scum. There is a pervasive caricature in popular culture of a portly, middle-aged ex-hipster talking a mile a minute, using outdated jargon, and calling everybody "baby." After meeting "their" A&R guy, the band will say to themselves and everyone else, "He's not like a record company guy at all! He's like one of us." And they will be right. That's one of the reasons he was hired.

These A&R guys are not allowed to write contracts. What they do is present the band with a letter of intent, or "deal memo," which loosely states some terms, and affirms that the band will sign with the label once a contract has been agreed on.

The spookiest thing about this harmless sounding little "memo" is that it is, for all legal purposes, a binding document. That is, once the band sign it, they are under obligation to conclude a deal with the label. If the label presents them with a contract that the band doesn't want to sign, all the label has to do is wait. There are a hundred other bands willing to sign the exact same contract, so the label is in a position of strength.

These letters never have any term of expiry, so the band remain bound by the deal memo until a contract is signed, no matter how long that takes. The band cannot sign to another label or even put out its own material unless they are released from their agreement, which never happens. Make no mistake about it: Once a band has signed a letter of intent, they will either eventually sign a contract that suits the label or they will be destroyed.

One of my favorite bands was held hostage for the better part of two years by a slick young "He's not like a label guy at all" A&R

rep on the basis of such a deal memo. He had failed to come through on any of his promises (something he did with similar effect to another well-known band), and so the band wanted out. Another label expressed interest, but when the A&R man was asked to release the band, he said he would need money or points, or possibly both, before he would consider it.

The new label was afraid the price would be too dear, and they said no thanks. On the cusp of making their signature album, an excellent band, humiliated, broke up from the stress and the many months of inactivity.

What I Hate about Recording

1. Producers and engineers who use meaningless words to make their clients think they know what's going on. Words like "punchy," "warm," "groove," "vibe," "feel." Especially "punchy" and "warm." Every time I hear those words, I want to throttle somebody.

2. Producers who aren't also engineers, and as such, don't have the slightest fucking idea what they're doing in a studio, besides talking all the time. Historically, the progression of effort required to become a producer went like this: Go to college, get an EE degree. Get a job as an assistant at a studio. Eventually become a second engineer. Learn the job and become an engineer. Do that for a few years, then you can try your hand at producing. Now all that's required to be a full-fledged "producer" is the gall it takes to claim to be one.

Calling people like Don Fleming, Al Jourgensen, Lee Ranaldo, or Jerry Harrison "producers" in the traditional sense is akin to calling Bernie a "shortstop" because he watched the whole playoffs this year.

The term has taken on perjorative qualities in some circles. Engineers tell jokes about producers the way people back in Montana tell jokes about North Dakotans. (How many producers does it take to change a light bulb?—Hmmm. I don't know. What do *you* think?

Why did the producer cross the road?—Because that's the way the Beatles did it, man.) That's why few self-respecting engineers will allow themselves to be called "producers."

The minimum skills required to do an adequate job recording an album are:

- Working knowledge of all the microphones at hand and their properties and uses. I mean something beyond knowing that you can drop an SM57 without breaking it.

- Experience with every piece of equipment that might be of use and every function it may provide. This means more than knowing what echo sounds like. Which equalizer has the least phase shift in neighbor bands? Which console has more headroom? Which mastering deck has the cleanest output electronics?

- Experience with the style of music at hand, to know when obvious blunders are occurring.

- Ability to tune and maintain all the required instruments and electronics, so as to insure that everything is in proper working order. This means more than plugging a guitar into a tuner. How should the drums be tuned to simulate a rising note on the decay? A falling note? A consonant note? Can a bassoon play a concert E-flat in key with a piano tuned to a reference A of 440 Hz? What percentage of varispeed is necessary to make a whole-tone pitch change? What degree of overbias gives you the most headroom at 10 Khz? What reference fluxivity gives you the lowest self-noise from biased, unrecorded tape? Which tape manufacturer closes every year in July, causing shortages of tape globally? What can be done for a shedding master tape? A sticky one?

- Knowledge of electronic circuits to an extent that will allow selection of appropriate signal paths. This means more than knowing the difference between a delay line and an equalizer. Which has more headroom, a discrete class A microphone preamp with a transformer output or a differential circuit built with monolithics? Where is the best place in an unbalanced line to attenuate the signal? If you short the cold leg of a differential input to ground, what happens to the signal level? Which gain control device has the least distortion, a VCA, a printed plastic pot, a photoresistor, or a wire-wound stepped attenuator? Will putting an unbalanced line on a half-normalled jack unbalance the normal signal path? Will a transformer splitter load the input to a device parallel to it? Which will have less RF noise, a shielded unbalanced line or a balanced line with a floated shield?

- An aesthetic that is well-rooted and compatible with the music, and
- The good taste to know when to exercise it.

3. Trendy electronics and other flashy shit that nobody really needs. Five years ago, everything everywhere was being done with discrete samples. No actual drumming allowed on most records. Samples only. The next trend was Pultec Equalizers. Everything had to be run through Pultec EQs.

Then vintage microphones were all the rage (but only Neumanns, the most annoyingly *whiny* microphone line ever made). The current trendy thing is *compression*. Compression by the ton, especially if it comes from a *tube* limiter. Wow. It doesn't matter how awful the recording is, as long as it goes through a tube limiter, somebody will claim it sounds "warm," or maybe even "punchy." They might even compare it to the Beatles. I want to find the guy that invented compression and tear his liver out. I hate it. It makes everything sound like a beer commercial.

4. DAT machines. They sound like shit and every crappy studio has one now because they're so cheap. Because the crappy engineers that inhabit crappy studios are too thick to learn how to align and maintain analog mastering decks, they're all using DAT machines exclusively. DAT tapes deteriorate over time, and when they do, the

information on them is lost forever. I have personally seen tapes go irretrievably bad in less than a month. Using them for final masters is almost fraudulently irresponsible.

Tape machines ought to be big and cumbersome and difficult to use, if only to keep the riff-raff out. DAT machines make it possible for morons to make a living and do damage to the music we all have to listen to.

5. Trying to sound like the Beatles. Every record I hear these days has incredibly loud, compressed vocals, and a quiet little murmur of a rock band in the background. The excuse given by producers for inflicting such an imbalance on a rock band is that it makes the record sound more like the Beatles. Yeah, right. Fuck's sake, Thurston Moore is not Paul McCartney, and nobody on earth, not with unlimited time and resources, could make the Smashing Pumpkins sound like the Beatles. Trying just makes them seem even dumber. Why can't people try to sound like the Smashchords or Metal Urbain or Third World War for a change?

There's This Band

There's this band. They're pretty ordinary, but they're also pretty good, so they've attracted some attention. They're signed to a moderate-sized "independent" label owned by a distribution company, and they have another two albums owed to the label.

They're a little ambitious. They'd like to get signed by a major label so they can have some security—you know, get some good equipment, tour in a proper tour bus—nothing fancy, just a little reward for all the hard work.

To that end, they got a manager. He knows some of the label guys, and he can shop their next project to all the right people. He takes his cut, sure, but it's only 15%, and if he can get them signed then it's money well spent. Anyway, it doesn't cost them anything if it doesn't work. Fifteen percent of nothing isn't much!

One day an A&R scout calls them, says he's "been following them for a while now," and when their manager mentioned them to him, it just "clicked." Would they like to meet with him about the possibility of working out a deal with his label? Wow. Big Break time.

They meet the guy, and y'know what?—he's not what they expected from a label guy. He's young and dresses pretty much like the band does. He knows all their favorite bands. He's like one of them. He tells them he wants to go to bat for them, to try to get them everything they want. He says anything is possible with the right attitude. They conclude the evening by taking home a copy of a deal memo they wrote out and signed on the spot.

The A&R guy was full of great ideas, even talked about using a name producer. Butch Vig is out of the question—he wants 100 g's and three points, but they can get Don Fleming for $30,000 plus three points. Even that's a little steep, so maybe they'll go with that guy who used to be in David Letterman's band. He only wants three points. Or they can have just anybody record it (like Warton Tiers, maybe—cost you five or ten grand) and have Andy Wallace remix it for four grand a track plus two points. It was a lot to think about.

Well, they like this guy and they trust him. Besides, they already signed the deal memo. He must have been serious about wanting them to sign. They break the news to their current label, and the label manager says he wants them to succeed, so they have his blessing. He will need to be compensated, of course, for the remaining albums left on their contract, but he'll work it out with the label himself. Sub Pop made millions from selling off Nirvana, and Twin Tone hasn't done bad either: fifty grand for the Babes and sixty grand for the Poster Children—without having to sell a single additional record. It'll be something modest. The new label doesn't mind, so long as it's recoupable out of royalties.

Well, they get the final contract, and it's not quite what they expected. They figure it's better to be safe than sorry and they turn it over to a lawyer—one who says he's experienced in entertainment law—and he hammers out a few bugs. They're still not sure about it, but the lawyer says he's seen a lot of contracts, and theirs is pretty good. They'll be getting a great royalty: 13% (less a 10% packaging deduction). Wasn't it Buffalo Tom that were only getting 12% less 10? Whatever.

The old label only wants fifty grand, and no points. Hell, Sub Pop got three points when they let Nirvana go. They're signed for four years, with options on each year, for a total of over a million dollars! That's a lot of money in any man's English. The first year's advance alone is $250,000. Just think about it, a quarter-million, just for being in a rock band!

Their manager thinks it's a great deal, especially the large advance. Besides, he knows a publishing company that will take the band on if they get signed, and even give them an advance of twenty grand, so they'll be making that money, too. The manager says publishing is pretty mysterious, and nobody really knows where all the money comes from, but the lawyer can look that contract over, too. Hell, it's free money.

Their booking agent is excited about the band signing to a major. He says they can maybe average $1,000 or $2,000 a night from now on. That's enough to justify a five-week tour, and with tour support, they can use a proper crew, buy some good equipment, and even get a tour bus! Buses are pretty expensive, but if you figure in the price of a hotel room for everybody in the band and crew, they're actually about the same cost. Some bands (like Therapy? and Sloan and Stereolab) use buses on their tours even when they're getting paid only a couple hundred bucks a night, and this tour should earn at least a grand or two every night. It'll be worth it. The band will be more comfortable and will play better.

The agent says a band on a major label can get a merchandising company to pay them an advance on t-shirt sales! Ridiculous! There's a gold mine here! The lawyer should look over the merchandising contract, just to be safe.

They get drunk at the signing party. Polaroids are taken and everybody looks thrilled. The label picked them up in a limo.

They decided to go with the producer who used to be in Letterman's band. He had these technicians come in and tune the drums for them and tweak their amps and guitars. He had a guy bring in a slew of expensive old "vintage" microphones. Boy, were they "warm." He even had a guy come in and check the phase of all the equipment in the control room! Boy, was he professional. He used a bunch of equipment on them and by the end of it, they all agreed that it sounded very "punchy," yet "warm."

All that hard work paid off. With the help of a video, the album went like hotcakes! They sold a quarter-million copies!

Here is the math that will explain just how fucked they are:

These figures are representative of amounts that appear in record contracts daily. There's no need to skew the figures to make the scenario look bad, since real-life examples more than abound. Income is underlined, expenses are not.

Advance: <u>$250,000</u>
Manager's cut: $37,500
Legal fees: $10,000

Recording budget: $150,000
  Producer's advance: $50,000
  Studio fee: $52,500
  Drum, amp, mic, and phase "doctors": $3,000
  Recording tape: $8,000
  Equipment rental: $5,000
  Cartage and transportation: $5,000
  Lodgings while in studio: $10,000
  Catering: $3,000
  Mastering: $10,000
  Tape copies, reference CDs, shipping tapes, misc expenses: $2,000

Video budget: $30,000
  Cameras: $8,000

Crew: $5,000
Processing and transfers: $3,000
Offline: $2,000
Online editing: $3,000
Catering: $1,000
Stage and construction: $3,000
Copies, couriers, transportation: $2,000
Director's fee: $3,000

Album artwork: $5,000
Promotional photo shoot and duplication: $2,000

Band fund: $15,000
 New fancy professional drum kit: $5,000
 New fancy professional guitars (2): $3,000
 New fancy professional guitar amp rigs (2): $4,000
 New fancy potato-shaped bass guitar: $1,000
 New fancy rack of lights bass amp: $1,000
 Rehearsal space rental: $500
 Big blowout party for their friends: $500

Tour expense (5 weeks): $50,875
 Bus: $25,000
 Crew (3): $7,500
 Food and per diems: $7,875
 Fuel: $3,000
 Consumable supplies: $3,500
 Wardrobe: $1,000
 Promotion: $3,000

Tour gross income: <u>$50,000</u>
 Agent's cut: $7,500
 Manager's cut: $7,500

Merchandising advance: $20,000
  Manager's cut: $3,000
  Lawyer's fee: $1,000

Publishing advance: $20,000
  Manager's cut: $3,000
  Lawyer's fee: $1,000

Record sales: 250,000 @ $12 = $3,000,000 gross retail revenue; royalty (13% of 90% of retail):$351,000
  less advance: $250,000
  Producer's points: (3% less $50,000 advance) $40,000
  Promotional budget: $25,000
Recoupable buyout from previous label: $50,000
Net royalty: (−$14,000)

Record company income:
Record wholesale price $6.50 × 250,000 = $1,625,000 gross income
Artist royalties: $351,000
Deficit from royalties: $14,000
Manufacturing, packaging, and distribution @ $2.20 per record: $550,000
Gross profit: $710,000

THE BALANCE SHEET

This is how much each player got paid at the end of the game.
Record company: $710,000
Producer: $90,000
Manager: $51,000
Studio: $52,500
Previous label: $50,000
Agent: $7,500
Lawyer: $12,000
Band member net income each: $4,031.25

The band is now a quarter of the way through its contract, has made the music industry more than three million dollars richer, but is in the hole $14,000 on royalties. The band members have each earned about a third as much as they would working at a 7-Eleven, but they got to ride in a tour bus for a month.

The next album will be about the same, except that the record company will insist they spend more time and money on it. Since the previous one never "recouped," the band will have no leverage, and will oblige.

The next tour will be about the same, except the merchandising advance will have already been paid, and the band, strangely enough, won't have earned any royalties from their t-shirts yet. Maybe the t-shirt guys have figured out how to count money like record company guys.

Some of your friends are probably already this fucked.

Baffler #5, 1993

MAURA MAHONEY

The Packaging of a Literary Persona

I'm Nobody!
Who are you?
Are you Nobody—too?
Then there's a pair of us?
Don't tell—they'd advertise—you know!
How dreary to be Somebody
How public, like a Frog
To tell one's name—
the livelong June
to an admiring Bog!
                                        —Emily Dickinson

SURELY YOU'VE HEARD of Donna Tartt? Judging from the hoopla surrounding the publication of her first novel, *The Secret History,* Tartt is definitely a somebody. Which is not to say that she would disagree with the sentiments in Dickinson's paean to obscurity. Tartt's ever-so-eccentric love of privacy—it's right up there with Michael Stipe's—naturally received plenty of press. In fact, Tartt could probably recite the poem for you. Her ability to recall reams of poetry ("I know 'The Waste Land' by heart. 'Prufrock.' Yeats is good.") was extolled with high seriousness in one national magazine's typical profile of the 28-year-old author—evidently to convey some sort of demonstrable Girl Scout badge of intellectual virtue.

But it's hard to imagine her quoting the decidedly unglamorous Dickinson. The Tartt media blitz made it abundantly clear that Emily simply doesn't rate as a literary model. In order to appeal to glossily literate, expensively educated consumers (usually neo-yuppies hearkening back to undergraduate intellectual purity), publicity packages like Tartt's (and McInerney's and Ellis's) must espouse a canon more narrow and more predictable than anything anywhere outside the campus of St. John's College.

To get Sam and Libby to put down the *New Yorker,* turn off PBS, and shell out the cash for a work of fiction, the book-hustlers have to present today's promotable "bright young things" as *serious artists.* It is a role that, spurious or not, cannot help but ring false—not only because it is premature, but because it is so clearly fabricated. This reification of the writer requires the author/product to pose on the literary landscape cloaked in ennui, incessantly (but carefully) invoking artistic influences, establishing an aura of consumer-friendly intellectual sophistication. The strategically chosen literary references the young writers spout reveal that the paramount goal is not artistry, but marketability, because the allusions consistently smack of café conversation—they're deep, but not too deep. They entice, rather than challenge.

The publicity frenzy that lifted Tartt and her colleagues to the top established a literary hierarchy ready-made for the ad pages. It created a world in which every neophyte author vies to be the Fitzgerald of the generation, a world in which indeed all writers from the twenties reign supreme, where Twain and Shakespeare (perhaps because they are so surpassingly famous) manage to get an occasional nod, and where Ayn Rand is actually considered to have merit. Personality triumphs over art, image prevails over intellect. And Donna Tartt, budding literati, cannot possibly invoke Dickinson to demonstrate possession of a lonely artistic soul. She has to stick to Salinger.

Writers have always cultivated a persona, of course. But Tartt, who received a $450,000 advance from Knopf, is not your ordinary first-time novelist. A Bennington College chum of gross-out-hack turned First-Amendment-martyr Bret Easton Ellis, she is represented by his agent, ICM's Amanda Urban. Her book soon grabbed the attention (and the cash) of Alan Pakula's Pakula Productions, which snapped up the screen rights. The novel was eclipsed by the event of its publication.

With all this money on the line, Tartt's handlers could not simply tout a "hotly awaited highbrow chiller" alone. Instead we got a full-blown portrait of the artist as a sort of post-punk, brainy Holly Golightly in the pages of *Mirabella, People, Entertainment Weekly, Vanity Fair, Esquire,* et al., and even in the more "serious" publications. She's what every swooning English major ever wanted to be—she's intellectual, and she's hip. She dresses in college-bohemian high style. Tartt may well turn out to be the best thing to happen to vintage clothing since Cyndi Lauper—in one spread she's prancing about in a black frock, long pearls, and of course, Doc Martens ("the author's winsome pose masks a wicked intelligence"), elsewhere she's sporting a severe tailored suit complete with trendy polka-dot necktie ("if her appearance offers any hint of the darkness within, it's in the way her pale face is framed by her nearly black hair, a contrast suggestive of something vaguely gothic").

Happily, no one quite brings up Louise Brooks while publicizing Tartt, but *Vanity Fair*'s James Kaplan comes close, describing her as

> a kind of boy-girl-woman in her lineaments, with lunar-pale skin, spooky light-green eyes, a good-size triangular nose, a high-pixieish voice. With her Norma Desmond sunglasses propped on her dark bobbed hair . . . and her ever-present cigarette, she is somehow a character out of her own fictive creation: a precocious sprite from a Cunard Line cruise ship, circa 1920-something.

All it then takes is talk of Tartt's answering machine, on which T. S. Eliot intones "The Waste Land," (!) and Kaplan is quite swept away. He breathlessly repeats much of the poetry she knows, mentions that she was a quirky, formal child, who used "I should like" instead of "I would like," (Tartt smugly comments about this riveting evidence of precociousness: "It was starting even then. Child is father to the man."), and rhapsodizes about the "small, hard-drinking, southern writer, a Catholic convert, witheringly smart, with an occluded past, sadness among the magnolias." In case readers don't get the message, the article is titled "Smart Tartt."

And the role was played out everywhere: her "eyes, animated by the pleasure of a good phrase, widen out of their squinty concentration into a clear and guileless green" as she confides her love of the T. S. Eliot answering-machine message to *Mirabella*'s Paul Gediman. She asserts that her life "is like Candide's," talks "cheerfully of life and death, dread and evil, in a voice both high and smooth, tuned to a fine Mississippi pitch," and carries on a determinedly post-modern conversation that "teems with references from Stephen King to Nietzsche."

Whew. Donna Tartt is likely to remind one of nothing so much as an English grad student who's been studying too long for her comprehensives. She was actually a classics student at Bennington, and her book is about a group of classics majors with distinctly Dionysian interests. So why not record her quoting Virgil at length (I'm sure she could) or photograph her standing beside a Doric column or a wine-dark sea? Because, faster than you can say Thucydides, someone in publicity recognized that Suetonius will lose to Stein in the image marketplace any day. There are a lot of former English majors out there, and Tartt was served to them as a reminder of the good old days when they, too, sat around and read the *Norton Anthology*. She is the embodiment of the post-collegian's intellectual fantasy.

This cultivated image does a great disservice to Donna Tartt, and to *The Secret History*. She is unquestionably one of the more gifted members of the new gliterati, and her book is an elegantly written, fast-paced read. Richard Papen, the narrator, gives the lyrical confession of a group of classics majors at a small Vermont college who idolize their professor and resolve to replicate a bacchanal. Four of his friends succeed in attaining Dionysian ecstasy, but their orgiastic embrace of the sublime results in the inadvertent slaying of a passerby. When it looks as though one member of the group may squeal, the others, with Richard, calmly plot to murder him. The novel is nothing if not sensational.

But a lyrical prose style and attention-grabbing plot cannot make up for serious literary deficiencies. The book is flawed by a pronounced lack of credibility. It is simply inexplicable why drippy, weak-willed Richard whose (what else?) suburban upbringing is supposed to be enough reason for his desensitized soul, not only would be drawn to this arrogant, smart-aleck lot, but also why he would go along with their chilling plans—and what, for that matter, any of them would see in him. The characters' putative glamour is a *donnée* in Tartt's eyes, but not in the reader's. We are informed of their charisma but do not experience it, in great part because the characters are remarkably clichéd; for example, it will come as no surprise that the Southern twins are (again, what else?) incestuous. The clique's hubris is utterly manufactured, and its fall therefore never transcends abstraction. Ultimately, what is meant to be a tale of innocence lost, glamour tarnished, and intellectualism gone berserk succeeds only as a page-turner, and as the nineties equivalent of Dungeons & Dragons or *The Dead Poets Society*.

And though *The Secret History* is certainly a testimony to the love of learning, what is intended to be viewed as the group's high-minded devotion to scholarship often merely comes across as irritating pretentiousness. The characters are lifeless imitations of what smart people are supposed to be like—and Tartt is far too impressed with them. Her frequently gratuitous classical and modern literary allusions could have been less grating if Tartt had injected even the slightest hint of self-knowing humor, but her tone is consistently reverent and annoyingly superior. You know you're in trouble when an author prefaces her list of acknowledgments with an apology that she's running "the risk of sounding like a Homeric catalog of ships." (Despite all the obscure and not-so-obscure classical allusions, don't bother looking for "semper ubi sub ubi," it isn't here; this is a *highbrow* chiller, remember?) And while there is nothing more enjoyable than an intellectual strutting her stuff (cf. A. S. Byatt's *Possession*), "Smart Tartt" gives ample demonstration that parroting and posing do not equal erudition. For all its references to Pliny, Homer, Milton, and others, its Fitzgeraldian glamor and mock-Eliot portentousness, and its great, big, flat-out Faustian themes, *The Secret History* is resoundingly a work of entertainment, not a work of art.

And yet in spite of all this, Donna Tartt was made a star. The celebrity-makers continue their inexorable march, and the commodification bandwagon rolls merrily along. Young, professional, liberal-arts alumni, nostalgic for the life of the mind while experiencing the harsh truths of the life of the paycheck, have been targeted to consume the Tarttian version of their most cherished myth—if it's elitist, it must be art.

Baffler #4, 1992

GARY GROTH

A Dream of Perfect Reception: The Movies of Quentin Tarantino

Americans love junk; it's not the junk that bothers me, it's
the love.   —George Santayana

QUENTIN TARANTINO is today's feel-good movie director, the
Frank Capra of the nineties. Moviegoers are as elated leaving show-
ings of *Pulp Fiction* as moviegoers must have been leaving *Mr.
Smith Goes to Washington* or *It's a Wonderful Life*. But whereas
Capra's movies were jolly, life-affirming affairs, Tarantino's are
jolly, death-affirming ones. And whereas 1938's audiences identified
with political reformer and populist Jimmy Stewart, today's audiences identify with petty criminals and murderers played by Har-
vey Keitel and John Travolta. This says considerably more about
the state of our culture than it does about Tarantino. So does the fact
that he is the most critically lauded, even fawned-over director to
emerge in the last few years—and a commercial powerhouse as
well. Tarantino, in short, has it all: the approbation of the tastemak-

ers of the popular press, the adulation of moviegoers, and the consequent clout that is so cherished in Hollywood.

In his short career, Tarantino has written four films, two of which he's directed himself (*Reservoir Dogs* and *Pulp Fiction*), the others having been directed by Oliver Stone (*Natural Born Killers*) and Tony Scott (*True Romance*). The critical establishment, such as it is, instantly crowned Tarantino an *auteur* upon the release of *Reservoir Dogs* and certified his exalted position with an effusive reception for *Pulp Fiction*. Movie magazines have trampled each other to rush obsequious profiles into print over the last two years, each chronicling his rags-to-riches story from movie enthusiast and video store clerk to Oscar-winning Hollywood whiz kid, his encyclopedic knowledge of movies, his excitement for all things filmic. He apparently talks faster than anyone this side of Camille Paglia and is a genuine connoisseur of trash. We are clearly living in the cinematic age of Quentin Tarantino.

But the age of Tarantino also appears to be Santayana's nightmare come true: Here is an American who doesn't merely love junk, but who proselytizes on its behalf every chance he gets. While he may be skilled as a writer and director, Tarantino's most important talent, the ability that has catapulted him to the top of the critical heap, is as an agent for commerce, a booster for the commercial values of industry product, a symbol of Hollywood Triumphant. The rare combination of mass popularity, critical acclaim, and industry adulation afforded his films represents the triumph of an economic/cultural order that aims to reduce both producers and consumers of film product into blithe and giddy Tarantino replicas. On the talk show circuit he prattles enthusiastically about a life spent watching and adoring junk, while his movies are feature-length advertisements for products that you can watch on TV or purchase at toy stores. Tarantino is the perfect shill—hip, comforting, and infectious—for both the passive ideology of spectatorship that the Information Age requires and for the product its leading industry manufactures.

It would be a different matter if Tarantino's movies were not empty rearrangements of Hollywood banalities. Despite his rule-breaking reputation, Tarantino's aesthetic is entirely predictable in its use of cliché and reverse-cliché: every film must include (a) a grisly torture scene in which a witty monologue is usually delivered by the torturer to the great discomfort of the torturee; (b) intense violence alternating with goofball humor, which more often than not derives from the characters' arcane knowledge of American junk culture; (c) an unending stream of "homages" or rip-offs of dialogue, scenes, or premises from a vast array of American and European movies; and (d) a Mexican stand-off in which everyone or nearly everyone dies.

Scratch the surface of one of Tarantino's dramas and the flimsy layer of moral electroplating that holds the story together disintegrates. The conflict that gives *Reservoir Dogs* what little human resonance it has—the struggle to reconcile an amoral life with moral impulses—seems almost intentionally shoddy when compared to a movie like *The Wild Bunch*, a Tarantino favorite, which is animated by the same moral conflict. The two films share similar bloodbath conclusions in which lone moral outlaws are slaughtered by overwhelming force. But it's the differences that are instructive. Unlike *The Wild Bunch*'s climactic eruption of violence, the moral backdrop to the actions in *Reservoir Dogs* doesn't convince. It is unlikely, for example, that the professional criminal played by Harvey Keitel would so obstinately jeopardize his safety or break with his old and trusted friend Lawrence Tierney, who's convinced (for good reason) that the Tim Roth character is a cop. To set this implausible situation Tarantino has Keitel exhibit a jerry-rigged paternalism toward Roth, claiming (wrongly) that, "It was my fault he got shot" and "The bullet in his belly is my fault." Keitel's sudden burst of profound moral responsibility seems more like a plot device mechanically inserted because Tarantino had seen the same theme used in another movie rather than because it makes any internal sense.

But the moral conflicts that run through *The Wild Bunch* are organic components of the film, attentively developed by director Sam Peckinpah, and consistently embodied, in various degrees, in the characters themselves. The film gets its meaning from the conflict between the decomposition of William Holden's gang and the moral imperative expressed in his exhortation, "When you side with a man, you stay with him, and if you can't do that, you're like some animal!" The much-celebrated violence in *The Wild Bunch* is explained as a matter of survival, but in *Reservoir Dogs* it is used purely to shock, to make for an effective scene, or to crank up the tension: Michael Madsen's torture of the cop, Roth's pointless killing of the civilian in the car, Chris Penn's irrational murder of the cop in the warehouse. And while the wild bunch's last act is one of willful redemption, Keitel's is a simple act of vengeance; it is both grandiloquent and trivial. So phony is Tarantino's moral attitudinizing that one begins to realize that the only reason he includes it in the first place is because it's the custom in Hollywood movies; it's how the product is made.

A glimpse of Tarantino's thinking about violence can be found in his response to questions regarding his repetitious use of the epithet "nigger" in *Reservoir Dogs* and, even more frequently, in *Pulp Fiction*. "I . . . feel 'nigger' is one of the most volatile words in the English language," he asserts, "and anytime anyone gives a word that much power, I think everybody should be shouting it from the rooftops to take the power away." By taking this same promiscuous approach to violence and callousness, he succeeds in draining any power or meaning they may otherwise have had as well. His films are a succession of torture scenes, murders, and tough-guy talk until the only possible response is one of disaffection. When Travolta's Vincent is machine-gunned by Willis's Butch in *Pulp Fiction*, one feels nothing because Tarantino didn't bother to sculpt Travolta's character into a human being we could care about. When Butch expresses indifference, even contempt for the opponent he just killed in the boxing ring, the audience easily accepts, maybe even enjoys his callousness; when he goes back to help Marcellus, the audience applauds his decency. One means no more or less than the other, the contradictory impulses nullifying the character's interest as a human being: He is no more than a plot convenience. When Samuel Jackson's Jules finds God, and gives Tim Roth his revelatory speech at the end of the film, we realize even God has been trivialized and reduced to a character in a sitcom.

Tarantino is well-known to be a most undiscriminating media buff. Consider, for example, his giddiness over the TV show *Baywatch*: "It's like, such a great show. I've been lamenting the fact that exploitation movies don't exist any more, but they do—they're just on television." He gushes about his favorite movie shoot-outs, listing *The Wild Bunch, Dillinger,* and John Woo in one breath—"And this has to be mentioned," he adds with dramatic urgency, "the restaurant shoot-out in *Year of the Dragon.* A true masterpiece of filmmaking." His familiarity with movies and TV has served him well; indeed, it's the application of this storehouse of knowledge— the references, "homages," characters, plot devices, etc.—that constitutes the reality of his films.

Tarantino learned a few things about name-dropping from his hero, Jean-Luc Godard. But while Godard has always kept his cultural references on the high end of the scale (Dostoevsky, Novalis, Sartre, Bakunin, Malraux, Apollinaire), Tarantino keeps his overt references decidedly low. His characters speak of Elvis, the Beatles, *The Brady Bunch, The Partridge Family, Bewitched, I Dream of Jeannie, Superfly, The Guns of Navarone, Green Acres, Kung Fu, Happy Days,* Lee Marvin, Sonny Chiba, and so on. When Tarantino's characters aren't invoking the names of movies or TV shows, they quote from them (such as Christian Slater in *True Romance* quoting John Derrick's nihilistic line from *The Harder They Fall*), or enact scenes that echo other movies. The prizefighter played by Bruce Willis in *Pulp Fiction* is a slick, witty, glamorized version of Robert Ryan's tragic prizefighter in *The Set Up;* Butch's and Marcellus's predicament at the hands of the rednecks is straight out of *Deliverance* (the difference, of course, being that in *Deliverance* the rape created the film's central moral dilemma whereas in *Pulp Fiction* it was merely "the single weirdest day of [Butch's] life"); *True Romance*'s voiceover and accompanying music is lifted from Terrence Malick's *Days of Heaven;* the structure of *Reservoir Dogs* owes a debt to *The Killing;* the much-praised looping narrative of *Pulp Fiction* is similar to Jim Jarmusch's *Mystery Train* (including title cards for the three separate stories); the mysterious attaché case in *Pulp Fiction* glows when opened, an homage to Aldrich's *Kiss Me, Deadly* (or to *Repo Man*). Even small gestures and routine camera placements are suspect. Madsen's funny gun gesture is the same motion used by a crook in *City on Fire* (from which Tarantino stole much of *Reservoir Dogs*), while the tracking shot of Buscemi running from the jewelry store is identical to tracking shots in *City on Fire* and *Los Delous*. And when he isn't knocking off characters or imagery, Tarantino's paying "homage" to dialogue from other films. Compare these excerpts from his oeuvre to Don Siegel's *Charley Varrick:*

(From the screenplay of *Natural Born Killers*)
Movie Mickey: Listen to me, Jimmy Dick! I want cash, lots of it, cars, fast cars! And I want it now! Not later, now! I wanna wail, baby, wail!

(From *Charley Varrick*)
Harmon: I got something I want to hang onto you, Jimmy-Dick! I've been waiting all my life to make a score like this, I ain't waiting no more. I mean, I'm gonna wail! And I'm talking about chicks, cars, clothes, a box at the races, and beefsteak three times a day!

(From *Pulp Fiction*)
Marcellus: I'm gonna call a couple pipe-hittin' niggers, who'll go to work on homes here with a pair of pliers and a blow torch.

(From *Charley Varrick*)
Boyle: They'll strip you naked and go to work on you with a pair of pliers and a blow torch.

After a while, all the scenes, references, dialogue take on an arbitrary cast: They're pieced together not from life but from twenty years of watching movies. Tarantino's characters—and Tarantino himself—inhabit a world where the entire landscape is composed of Hollywood product. Tarantino is a cinematic kleptomaniac—he literally can't help himself. Movies, TV shows, and ad jingles are all that there is on his earth.

Dialogue that goes nowhere; scenes borrowed in their entirety from other movies; endless invocations of TV past: The Tarantino aesthetic is a concentrated and streamlined rendering of the larger aesthetic of the culture industry. Like mass culture itself, which mutates opportunistically with the transient zeitgeist but stays always the same, Tarantino's films are always hip but scrupulously content-free. Literary critic James Wood writes that "Tarantino represents the final triumph of postmodernism, which is to empty the artwork of all content, thus voiding its capacity to do anything except helplessly represent our agonies (rather than to contain or comprehend). Only in this age could a writer as talented as Tarantino produce artworks so vacuous, so entirely stripped of any politics, metaphysics, or moral interest." And yet it's this very vacuousness, this disconnection from anything remotely resembling moral or emotional issues, that excites Tarantino's admirers. One of these insists that Tarantino's "greatness lies in the fact that his movies don't need the real world. Tarantino's head is already crammed . . . with a complete, distinct universe, which has its own reference points and its own moral compass"—a "distinct universe," a set of "reference points," and a "moral compass" that are all lifted from other movies.

This curious disconnection is true of his characters as well as the moral dilemmas that they so glibly confront. They inhabit a world bounded by movies and television. And when they are not defined by their own constant references to media, they are themselves characters familiar from other movies—gangsters, cops, prize fighters, talk show hosts, etc. (Though there aren't many et ceteras; that list pretty much covers the gamut of characters in Tarantino's four films to date.)

It would be one thing if Tarantino were using these filmic references and icons to comment on films or television, but one gets no sense that (unlike his idol Godard) he is engaged in social criticism or even has a discernible point of view. Nonetheless, he has endorsed the proposition ("one hundred percent") that "on one level [his] movies are fictions, but on another level they're movie criticism, like Godard's." His hagiographers tend to concur. But while his movies are certainly about movies, elevating them to the status of "criticism" would require distance, irony, and judgment, qualities of mind Tarantino has never displayed. When he writes a dance number for John Travolta in *Pulp Fiction*, he's not commenting on *Saturday Night Fever* but recreating it, and indulging in the ultimate dream of a movie buff.

Perhaps I'm misreading Tarantino entirely; perhaps I'm holding him to inappropriate standards. Perhaps his films are comedies, as many of his fans claim. Oddly enough, Tarantino himself denies this: "I always stop short of calling my work comedy," he has been quoted as saying, "because as funny as [*Pulp Fiction*] is, there are things you're not supposed to be laughing at. It takes the seriousness away from it if you describe it as comedy or black comedy . . . . " Two points are worth noting in this astonishing comment: (1) Tarantino does not think comedy or black humor is serious, and (2) he considers *Pulp Fiction* serious apart from its humor.

The neologism "comedy-drama" was coined by Columbia's publicity department to promote Capra's *It Happened One Night*. The film's success proved that naturalism and humor could coexist, creating and resolving a tension that seamlessly enhanced the possibilities of both modes. Lubitsch's masterpiece *To Be or Not To Be* had a similar effect. "One might call it a tragical farce or a farcical tragedy," the director said—"I do not care and neither do the audiences." Great comedy, including black humor, is always serious on some level: think of Chaplin and Keaton, Sturges and Cukor, or films like *My Man Godfrey* and *Private Lives*. In these films humor articulated the characters' social and political relationships, revealed their moral and emotional lives, and crystalized their conflicts. And their success grew from audiences' sheer joy in watching the play of wit at the service of universal human questions—love and death and the right way to live. Both required less a slavish mimesis than the creation of a world more or less analagous to our own, held together and made believable by an exquisite equilibrium between comedy and drama. Strictly speaking, they weren't realistic or naturalistic, but they were always emotionally, psychologically, or socially truthful.

Tarantino's comedy, though, is mostly a cheat. It is centered not around the doings of people we recognize from life or of archetypes extrapolated from life, but from the rarefied milieu of walking genre clichés—serial killers, Walter Mitty-adventurers, gangsters. Stylistically, the humor in *Pulp Fiction* is a hodgepodge of schtick, stand-up comedy routines, black humor, screwball comedy, and anything else he can get away with. Far from balancing humor and drama, his technique is to throw so much of this anarchic mess at the viewer that any critical apparatus is quickly dulled.

In one revealing episode, Uma Thurman's Mia overdoses on heroin, thinking it's cocaine (a case of mistaken identity, a classic screwball comedy device!), and Vincent and his drug source have to slam a needle full of adrenalin into her heart in order to revive her. It's a grotesque episode, but it doesn't suggest the complex wit or the rewards of screwball comedy so much as the kind of zany premise one expects from an episode of *I Love Lucy*: more sitcom than film art. Nor does the story bear any relationship to the rest of the film—soon afterwards Mia is just dropped. Then there's Tarantino's attempt at the blackest of black humor—when Vincent accidentally blows someone's head off in Jules's car, and the boys have to clean up the mess. But black humor requires more than mere goofiness to touch an audience; it demands an authorial point of view, a moral position staked out and defended by the filmmaker, or at the very least, a normative anchor from which we can get our bearings: Kubrick's *Dr. Strangelove* was clearly opposed to the madness of MAD just as *M*A*S*H* was opposed to priggish authoritarianism and hypocrisy. Cary Grant's and Raymond Massey's moral extremes provided the ballast that allowed us to see the irony in *Arsenic and Old Lace*. But there isn't any countervailing moral presence in *Pulp Fiction* to serve as contrast; since everyone in the film is a self-serving scumbag and everyone's motivations are selfish and sleazy, nothing is at stake and the humor is just momentary exercises in empty guffawing.

But whatever the mode, Tarantino seems determined to prevent his humor from cohering into a meaningful, thematic whole. It exists only in isolated or compartmentalized scenes, and his dialogue is usually spit out furiously by actors who are so constantly "on" that they appear not to be talking to each other, but directly and self-consciously to the camera in a kind of Bogosianesque routine. Ultimately it serves no function greater than as a bridging device between the violence, so the audience can chortle one minute and squirm the next, never bored. Having passively absorbed the "realities" of TV and movies, Tarantino regurgitates his favorite clichés and formulas, sometimes with a wink, sometimes with a straight face, sometimes with wit, but always with an unconditional love for the clichés and formulas that precludes the possibility of Godardian criticism or even incisive observation.

Tarantino is now everywhere, as ubiquitous as popcult itself, on talk shows, directing TV episodes, licensing his movies to a schlocky comic-book publisher, starting a production company to make television commercials (!), script-doctoring trashy Hollywood movies. In fact, American moviegoers' love affair with Tarantino may even have peaked. But there is no real danger of Tarantino's retirement from the public stage any time soon. He and his audience are as one insofar as they both demand of their entertainment shallowness, ease, familiarity, and as much sex and violence as an R rating can accommodate. Not only does Tarantino deliver these ingredients, but he makes the public feel good for wanting them in the first place. He is too valuable a symbol, too useful a metaphor, to be dumped anytime soon. In Tarantino and the enthusiasms of his audience the architects of the Mind Industry see their most fabulous aspirations made concrete: He represents the audience with its critical guard down forever, sucking it all up without reservation, commiting it to memory, building their lives around it. In Tarantino the titans of the Information Age see the world re-made in *their* terms, with *their* clichés, according to *their* formulas. He is pointing the way to a golden future in which there is no longer any difference between what people are told they want and what they think they want. In his frail, hyperactive body the industry sees the two great functions of "creative" and "marketing" coalesce seamlessly and ooze with sincerity; making, selling, and living junk; the dream of perfect reception fulfilled.

Baffler #8, 1996

THOMAS FRANK AND KEITH WHITE

Twenty-Nothing

I have read them all,
hoping against hope to hear the authentic call.
A tragical disappointment. There was I
Hoping to hear old Aeschylus, when the Herald
Called out, "Theo, bring your clowns forward."
That turned me sick and killed me very nearly.
—Hugh MacDiarmid

ALL ACROSS TV-land official America is caught up in a serious but amusing identity crisis. Not that you're having any difficulty with your own image, to be sure: Your problem is in deciding just how to nail down a large and influential group of consumers so we can be properly targeted for TV shows, movies, records, and above all, advertising. In a nation that idealizes youthfulness and demands that each generation bear a simple tag-line, the current crop of young people are proving difficult to corner. A nettlesome little problem, to be sure, one that has sent legions of Harvard grads through the revolving doors of ad agencies and Hollywood sound-stages, promising the key to the youth market, trying their hands at producing any number of briefly ubiquitous looks. This is the frenzy to define the "twenty-somethings," the summoning of the infotainment world's greatest minds (*Time* magazine, Oprah, Barbara Walters) to the burning question: How are we going to sell these people?

Pinning the label on the generation has always been one of the culture industry's favorite and most profitable games. Ever since the fabrication of the initial "youth movement" by people like Pepsi and adman Peter Max, you have sought names for the young, prefab identities by which people may be molded, manipulated, and sold for the rest of their lives. This process now seems so natural to you, the original TV-produced generation, that you have created a national pseudo-hysteria over our seeming lack of definition, publicly wringing your hands over the enigmatic youth of today, wondering if maybe you're finally on the wrong side of "the gap," and providing an enormous market for the tidal wave of magazines, movies, and sitcoms purporting to speak for the "twenty-somethings." Columnists churn out articles packed with meaningless speculation, anchormen shake their heads sadly, and sixties veterans intone gravely on the fleeting nature of youthful idealism, each contributing to the flood of silly ideas about "generations" and how they are constituted. Ordinarily this bizarre pseudo-debate would be amusing—what with its high, serious tone and its benevolent, advice-giving posturing—was it not so pathetically and openly just the simple whining of a people obsessed with youth about to approach middle age.

But try as you may, you can't seem to decide which label really fits us. Just a few years ago we were the violent, criminal generation, raised on a steady diet of TV crime and frightening the Eyewitness News crew with thrown rocks. Then we were the practical and conservative generation, happily corporate, voting by the herd for Reagan and voicing opinions whose lack of idealism was supposed to send Sixties People reeling in astonishment. How well we remember the colorful graphs that announced that version of the story from the front page of *USA Today*. But all too quickly we were the compassionate generation, the ones whose concern for the environment and poor folks was supposed to transform the 1990s. And now we're the "twenty-somethings," struggling against economic adversity, rejuvenating the record industry, providing the look and 'tude for movies like *Singles* and TV shows like *Friends*.

The most striking thing about this confused generational soul-seaching is that we haven't really participated in it much at all. Oh, sure, there was a fake novel called *Generation X* with a glossary of nonrelevant terms, but it was strictly a quick cashing-in on all the media hype, an effort more akin to *The Preppie Handbook* than *The Sorrows of Young Werther*. And yes, real live twenty-somethings have been interviewed for articles in the *New York Times, Time, Newsweek, Utne Reader, U.S. News and World Report,* and a Barbara Walters special that no doubt had parents around the country holding their hands to their mouths in mild approbation. But participation of this kind is to be expected, as many are easily lured by the shiny covers of your slick magazines and will happily accept the opportunity to appear as "authentic" members of the species. They are about as credible as the Monkees were when the network dressed them up and had them sing, "We're the young generation."

No, this is the doing of the baby boomers, with your bottomless need to compare all youth movements, real or imaginary, to your own. Generational categorizing comes naturally to you, since you yourselves have been the greatest beneficiaries of it, fairly monopolizing the talk shows and news magazines for the few years in which you kept the establishment gasping in collective outrage at your mock-threatening antics. Predictably enough, a good part of the "twenty-something" discourse is just plain insulting, consisting of solemn declarations by bona-fide Generation Authorities that the youth of today don't measure up to their world-shaking predecessors. We just have no vision, no ideas, no shiny features to redeem us. Then turn to the fashion pages for the rest of the discussion: a flurry of stories about grunge, descriptions of a cooptation technique so efficient that, you boast, styles make their way from "the street" to the boutiques quicker than ever before. Both interpretations are backed up with a weighty array of pop psychology, pop history, and, your infallible statistical divining rod, demographics. We certainly don't need this mass media affirmation of our lives. But why are you so concerned with this scrutiny?

As you learned from your own experience, youth sells, and even better to oldsters than to actual young folks. But first you must invent an easy generational stereotype in order to properly transform the allure of youth into concrete, salable products. And since people are what they consume, you go to great lengths to specify "our" music and "our" look—glossing over any real thoughts we might have—so that you can package an attractive "twenty-something" lifestyle complete with distinct, imitatable tastes and brand preferences. This is the real intent of the dozens of articles written about "our" generation that describe us whimsically in terms of the TV programs we are supposed to have watched in the seventies, the records we are supposed to have purchased, the gum we chewed, and the clothes we wore. In your hands this is our tawdry fate: a generation of people understood as the sum total of their hairstyles; an entire decade known by the popular records of the day.

Our history is rewritten even as it happens as part of your effort to package and market the "youth culture" commodity to hungry consumers. Even more disturbing is the thought of these products being sold in the form of nostalgia years from now. We can doubtless look forward to television shows like "Slammin'," chronicling the adventures of a group of alienated Washington, D.C., teenagers who use peculiar dance rituals to express their misunderstandings with their parents. "This Old Garage" will peek in on the coming of age of a homosexual vegetarian brother and his feminist sister as they clash and come together on the fringes of the Seattle rock world. More important than the shows will be the products sold along with them. As teens today sport the tie-dyed shirts of the sixties and the bell-bottoms of the seventies, so will our children model Doc Martens, special hair-griming formulas, and knee-exposing jeans in the year 2005.

For all the transparent absurdity of the "twenty-something" debate, we can't simply reject "generational identity" as a totally meaningless category: There have of course been small circles of people from particular age groups who have been shaped by specific events. But it *is* senseless to expect to find meaningful common ideas held by *everyone* born between 1960 and 1970. But we're talking more about demographics than culture, more about clues to mass-marketing than the thoughts of real live people, so this is exactly what your prattling TV, your news magazines, attempt to do. It's as though you thought the doings of the Young Hegelians were characteristic of the vast majority of their contemporaries, as though the "lost generation" had something to do with flagpole sitting, Amos 'n' Andy, and the religious revivals of the American 1920s.

When it comes to actually listening to our cacophony, you don't seem to like what you see and hear. So in the same way your monotone rock music industry has ignored the entire creative outpouring of the past fifteen years in favor of warmed-over versions of the pleasantries you listened to in the 1960s, you have ignored, suppressed, or just refused to consider the true concerns of youth. No wonder you're so badly confused.

And yet perhaps your confusion points directly to the most salient aspects of our thinking. If anything can be said to define us, it is that we are a generation that is wise to this game. The paramount theme of our extra-corporate cultural production (not significant data for marketing purposes, so of course you don't know about it) is resistance, negation of the officious everyday assault of this botched civilization. We don't worry about whether or not the bright futures and business opportunities and suburban spreads will someday be ours: We build barriers against the incessant stream of lies and stupidity that is your public culture. We aim to carve out autonomous space, to somehow free ourselves from the daily drivel that drones from all sides. It's a worldview that is necessarily incomprehensible to your standardized, mass-mediated ways of knowing.

While you spin your fantasies about a generation raised solely by TV, a youth so pliable and clueless that advertising and sitcoms are their common tongue, we have in fact been learning the utter falseness of these most revered institutions. You gloat that our understanding has long since been scrambled by the constant brainwash, you snicker that our identities are little more than a patchwork of lines remembered from episodes of the TV programs we watched as children. But in fact our youthful vision of the world was influenced more by Minor Threat than by the Partridge Family. We refuse to accept your central historical/televisual myth, the golden tale of the sixties and innocence lost, since we see it for the transparent suburban fantasy it is.

You find we are lacking in idealism, but in fact all we're really missing is your farcical public display of disillusionment. Having grown up under an astonishingly mean-spirited government, we regard people who pretend to see answers or even reason in your politics, your issues, your self-righteous hedonism, as simple at best, but more likely just dishonest. To us the idiocy, depravity, and soulcrushing cruelty of your human machine is so obvious, so plain and undisguised, that we set ourselves in opposition to it as a matter of course. It is not the sixties rosy bromides or revolutionary posturing that rings true for us, but the quiet determination of the twenties and thirties: Harold Stearns' call for intellectual secession, Dos Passos' recognition that "we are two nations." Nor were we granted the privilege of a long, fully-televised process of coming to these realizations. The "whole world" doesn't watch us because we aren't interested in your watching, aren't eager to ham it up for your cameras or begin a much-publicized dalliance with your bad taste and lunatic culture.

And you know none of this because our discourse takes place

not on audience-participation TV programs or in the hidebound pages of your glossy magazines, but in the small cénacles in college towns; the sub-movements of punk rock that you'll never hear about; the little magazines and independent record labels by the score that share nothing with the understanding of the world broadcast from everywhere by the official institutions of American speech. You would have to dig deep and listen carefully if you really wanted to know what we thought, but you'd rather hire the Red Hot Chili Peppers or River Phoenix to play the part for you, to tell you that it's OK; that all the twenty-somethings have come up with are a few stylistic innovations, a new sound and look that can be easily and fashionably imitated.

For each of us there came at some point a revelation, a sudden, astonishing realization of the way your world worked, of the purposes of your media, your politics, your academy. For many it came through rock music; from a hundred local scenes alive with enthusiasm and camaraderie and the promise of asylum. It was the knowledge that the music—and, by extension, the literature, the thoughts—that spoke most earnestly and honestly to our lives were virtually forbidden, barred from the record labels and airwaves choked with sixties-style liberationist pap. Here was both an expressive form that rang true and a means of resisting, an instrument of autonomy. Never again could we blithely file away the hours in your office complexes, listening dutifully to Madonna on the official radio. Never again could we read your newspapers uncritically, assuming their contents bore any relation to what went on in the world. Our generational compass was recalibrated instantly with a glimpse into the working of the machine: We were now *outside*, our tastes and thoughts automatically condemned by a smug alliance of hippies and businessmen.

It is this experience that you cannot seem to understand, nor will your co-optations, your manufactured replicas ever bring us back to the fold. Our resistance is not a hairstyle or a record or even a leather jacket with safety pins. You have created in us an implacable enemy of the worst kind: a foe that understands how your cultural machinery works, who you are not physically capable of retrieving.

You wonder about the nature of the "twenty-somethings": Here's your answer. We are twenty-nothing, forever lost to your suburban platitudes; lost to the simple blather of your TV; deaf to your non-politics; hopelessly estranged from your cult of "professionalism." We no longer flinch when the tough guys on the screen point their weapons our way. Nor do we nod when your intelligentsia instruct us in the fine points of indeterminacy. Our youth has been a classroom of resistance in which we have learned how to free ourselves from the grasp of your understanding, your manipulation.

Although your anointed authorities may not take it into account when they do their "studies" of the young, there is a vast cultural resistance underway. Your best and brightest want nothing to do with you. We were too cynical too young about your motives, your politics, your TV, your bad rock 'n' roll. This is a generation that will never again cooperate, will never make your coffee with equanimity or discuss happily the latest doings of your favorite sitcom characters.

We are a generation that finally says NO to your favorite institutions: not only will we not fight for oil, but we don't believe anything that you broadcast, we avoid your malls, we don't care about the free play of signifiers on your cable TV. Your feverish attempts at cooptation have begun far too late; too many will have defected long before your latest youth look hits the malls this spring. However you may demographically turn matters about in the future to convince yourselves that youth just isn't capable of your sophistication, your idealism, your credit limits, we'll be out there, slowly corroding the machine, filing down the teeth of the gears, readying your historical epitaphs.

The Baffler will not win this dispute by itself. You will believe what you choose to believe, and you will go on using your telephone surveys and your public-opinion polls to rationalize it. But then again, we don't care. We know who we are, no matter what labels you choose for us. Now leave us alone.

Baffler #4, 1992

Postscript

Looking back it's almost hard to believe the epidemic of stupidity that gripped American public discourse during the brief twenty-something furor. It just seemed to mount higher and higher, regardless of content, as though driven by some logic of its own. After months of delicate inquiry and painstaking attention to the subtleties of "our" generation's experiences, angsts, and deep longings, the nation's mind-makers announced the discovery of that most celebrated of American institutions—a virgin market niche! From the ashes of our fabled discontent arose opportunity of the most luminous sort. The mandarins of Washington received a new vocabulary in which to couch their empty platitudes, the men of Madison Avenue a panoply of new imagery, the masters of MTV a new array of "alternative" bands, and the kaisers of couture an entirely new palette of looks to exploit.

Our generation was even said to be suffering from an identity crisis because business had not yet nailed down a coherent consumer profile for us. But that was quickly remedied: With a great plethora of culture products having been specifically targeted just at us, we finally existed. And we soon enjoyed a legion of new "spokesmen," magazines, and political groups as well, mouthing the usual tepid stuff about "leadership" and the "vital center," droning predictably about the pure motives and clear-sighted nobility of youth, protesting about nothing with earnest ingenuousness, which of course they will auction off as quickly as possible for a place as a token "Gen Xer" on somebody's staff.

Perhaps most interestingly, *The Baffler's* skepticism toward Gen X stereotypes quickly became an important part of the Gen X stereotype, echoed in ads and editorials from Madison Avenue to Sunset Strip. But the sheer obscenity of a society—not just its admen, but its serious culture writers, its media columnists, its TV news shows—insisting on understanding cultural production as a question of demographics never became a part of the discussion.

THOMAS FRANK

Harsh Realm, Mr. Sulzberger!

NO ONE CAN SAY the *New York Times* is out of touch with the young. Like so many other organs of official culture, the *Times* in 1992 declared a newfound enthusiasm for all manifestations of the hip, launching a new "Styles of the Times" section in which the looks and sounds of youth culture and of risqué arty scenes around the country were admired and hungrily commodified. On November 15, 1992, "Styles of the Times" carried a feature on "Grunge," describing the music and bands that make up that genre, but more importantly focusing on the outward aspects of the new "subculture" and the ingenious ways in which these have been domesticated by high fashion designers for their upscale—but ever-so-cognizant—clientele.

Unfortunately, in its anxious scramble to rip off the Seattle kids' doings, the *Times* also printed a glossary of "grunge-speak" that is, as its originator Megan Jasper readily admits, completely fabricated. Convinced that "all subcultures speak in code," the *Times* went looking for some colorful argot from the Seattle rock scene and Ms. Jasper was only too happy to oblige them with some of the most inspired fake slang outside of Monty Python. Thus the Newspaper of Record dutifully repeated her comical assertions that youth in the Pacific Northwest regularly refer to their torn jeans as "wack slacks," platform shoes as "plats," people they don't like as "Lamestain" or "Tom-Tom Club" or "Cob Nobbler," and that they often spend time "Swingin' on the Flippity-Flop."

The prank began, Ms. Jasper recounts, when the British *Sky* magazine contacted her, as a former Sub Pop employee and hence a grunge expert, to help them construct a story about the Seattle youth movement they were certain existed. The British know better than any other people the commodity value of highly visible youth subcultures, especially imported ones, and naturally *Sky* was anxious to be the first to discover a new style that they could sell to unhappy English kids. Nonetheless, Ms. Jasper was surprised by the various journalists' "weird idea that Seattle was this incredibly isolated thing," with a noticeably distinct rock culture. The result of this credulity was that, as Ms. Jasper puts it, "I could tell [the interviewer] anything. I could tell him people walked on their hands to shows." After seeing the piece in *Sky* and recognizing the joke, members of the Seattle band Mudhoney were careful to use all the strange words in an interview with youth mind-molder *Melody Maker*, which is now planning a major feature on the (nonexistent) grunge movement. From Britain the story went to the *Times*, which so wanted to believe there was a new youth movement underway that it was apparently willing to forego the usual fact-checking.

Lexicon of Grunge: Breaking the Code

All subcultures speak in code; grunge is no exception. Megan Jasper, a 25-year-old sales representative at Caroline Records in Seattle, provided this lexicon of grunge-speak, coming soon to a high school or mall near you:

WACK SLACKS: Old ripped jeans

FUZZ: Heavy wool sweaters

PLATS: Platform shoes

KICKERS: Heavy boots

SWINGIN' ON THE FLIPPITY-FLOP: Hanging out

BOUND AND HAGGED: Staying home on Friday or Saturday night

SCORE: Great

HARSH REALM: Bummer

COB NOBBLER: Loser

DISH: Desirable guy

BLOATED, BIG BAG OF BLOATATION: Drunk

LAMESTAIN: Uncool person

TOM-TOM CLUB: Uncool outsiders

ROCK ON: A happy goodbye

Off the Record

It's not nice to fool *The New York Times*. So after a glossary of new grunge slang printed in the Nov. 15 edition of Styles of *The Times* was branded a hoax by *The New Republic*, the paper of record mobilized its forces to find out who had played the joke. In its Jan. 25 issue, *The New Republic* attributed its knowledge of the hoax to information printed in *The Baffler*, a small Chicago-based cultural magazine. The winter-spring 1993 issue contained an interview with Megan Jasper, a Seattle field representative for Caroline Records who was the source for *The Times'* grunge glossary. In the

Baffler article (entitled "Harsh Realm, Mr. Sulzberger!"), Ms. Jasper boasted that she had intentionally played a prank on the paper.

But when contacted last month by Styles editor Penelope Green and Rick Marin, the reporter who wrote the Nov. 15 story on grunge, Ms. Jasper denied ever having spoken with anyone from *The Baffler*. She further assured Ms. Green that the slang listed by *The Times* was indeed in use by members of the grunge subculture.

Thinking she had cornered the real hoaxer, Ms. Green called the editors of *The Baffler*. She gave them three hours, the editors said, to fax a statement explaining their side of the story to *The New York Times*. But instead of sending the apologetic message that *The Times* may have expected, the editors faxed the following:

"Of course *The Baffler* stands by its story, and we can document our conversation with Megan Jasper.

"Having seen *The New York Times*' misinterpretation of the Grunge 'phenomenon,' we are hardly surprised that you fail to understand the nature of this continuing prank.

"We at *The Baffler* really don't care about the legitimacy of this or that fad, but when The Newspaper of Record goes searching for the Next Big Thing and the Next Big Thing piddles on its leg, we think that's funny."

Ms. Jasper finally came clean in an interview with *The Observer*. She said she only lied to *The Times* a second time because Mr. Marin told her that if the slang terms proved to be bogus, Ms. Green's job would be in danger. "I would feel shitty if somebody lost their job over a stupid prank," Ms. Jasper said.

"Our piece was tongue-in-cheek, anyway, so I guess it works," Ms. Green said, when told of Ms. Jasper's confession. "But how irritating."

The article on grunge was ill-fated from beginning to end. In the opening lines, the article defined "grunge" as "a five-letter word meaning dirt." The word, however, has six letters. A correction in *The Times* concerning the printing of the bogus lexicon may well be moot at this point, however. Members of the Seattle-based band Mudhoney, who know Ms. Jasper, have been working some of the fake grunge slang—"cob nobbler" (uncool person), "swingin' on the flippity-flop" (hanging out) and "big bag of bloatation" (drunken person)—into recent interviews with *Melody Maker* and other magazines. T-shirts put out by C/Z Records in Seattle have the word "lamestain" (loser) printed on the front and *The Times*' bogus lexicon on the back.

Jim Windolf
New York Observer
March 1, 1993

PART IV

Wealth against

Commonwealth Revisited

THOMAS FRANK

Twentieth Century Lite

OH, THAT CYBER-REVOLUTION! It's turning out to be the long-awaited deliverer of American business from all the dreadful forces, riotous impulses, and malign social movements that have blocked its happy hegemony all these years. The "Third Wave," philosopher-king Newt Gingrich and his stable of third-rate thinkers proclaim, has finally liberated the wise entrepreneur not only from the grasp of Washington bureaucrats, with all their meddling demands about workplace safety and minimum wages, but from every other social institution that once threatened him. Labor unions, for example, the nightmarish Second-Wave organizations *par excellence*, are openly gloated to be a thing of the past, happily ruined by the near-total freedom of capital to move around the globe at will, wherever poverty severe enough to induce people to scab can be found.

Best of all, the advent of the Information Society seems to have accomplished the rosiest middle-class dream of all: It has freed us at last from the filthy grasp of the city and its teeming, huddling, criming, union-joining, welfare-cheating, liberal-electing masses. With the final perfection of the global computer net, place will become simply irrelevant: It will be as easy to transmit "information"—meaning all those human activities we used to call thought and culture—across three thousand miles as it is now to meet a client for lunch. As the cloying youngster intoned in last year's MCI commercials, "There will be no more there." No sooner was this profundity grasped by the Gingrichites (it probably helped to have it explained by a cute little tot with what sounds like an English accent) than they were declaring the millennium to be at hand: The metropolis had been abolished. Actual physical social interaction was a relic of the benighted past. No longer would we need to put up with the filth and dangers of the city to get our business done. This is the age of the "suburban entrepreneur hooked up to the Internet," David Brooks wrote in New York's *City Journal,* a quarterly propaganda sheet for the latest Republican fantasies. "In the Gingrichian world, cyberspace replaces urban space. Conversations are conducted over the modem instead of over dinner at a metropolitan restaurant or club." Whatever doubts had lingered about the wisdom of suburbanization (a product of New Deal social planning, but we'll overlook that for the moment) have now evaporated: *Distance doesn't matter.* The city is now officially obsolete. It has no further economic function. We "knowledge workers" can work anywhere we want. Let the proles commute.

But for all its exalted technotalk there's very little new about the recent anti-urban rumblings. The current frenzy is merely another outbreak of a chronic upper-middle-class allergy to the metropolis, the latest installment in that favorite affluent dream of attaining unchallengeable Olympian isolation from society while still retaining all the benefits of their privileged social position. For forty years Organization Man defined himself to his precipitate flight from the cesspools of social interaction, relocating himself to the fantasy land of suburbia where he could remake himself in any image he chose. That initial postwar geographic and demographic shift—which, not incidentally, wrecked the social fabric of twentieth-century America and read poor and working-class America out of the the country's official collective identity—has long been the inescapable stuff of national culture. Our televisual world already operates on an assumption of total detachment, of a pristine bourgeois universe into which nasty events like poverty and disaster intrude only as occasional oddities. And the latest cyber-development serves merely to make the fantasy seem that much more *natural,* to make the longstanding dream of upper-middle-class secession, of gated communities and zero contact between us and them appear an utterly practicable maneuver, to make the initial flight from the cities seem miraculously farsighted.

Meanwhile the now economically-outmoded metropolis—what business theorist George Gilder calls "these big parasite cities sucking the lifeblood out of America"—must learn to forsake the "dole" and accustom itself to a new role: The city is to be the ultimate form of entertainment for the suburban upper middle class, better than CD-ROM, even, and brought conveniently through the wonder of electronics into our ranch homes for our pleasure and consumption. Gilder et al. have no problems acknowledging the city's famous role as a meeting place for people of different ethnicities and walks of life; in fact, in accordance with the latest multicultural business theorizing, they actively celebrate the kind of cultural cross-fertilization that is believed to make American capitalism so vital. It's just that they don't think they should have to physically enter the place to partake.

In such a climate who will speak for the city? Why, *Utne Reader,* of course, which produced a special issue celebrating American cities in 1994. But if you came to the magazine expecting some sort of reaffirmation of twentieth-century American civilization, you'd be disappointed: The value of cities is that they are *Utne Reader* writ large, a non-stop alternative lifestyle carnival, where one can gawk at real-live Third-World peoples performing their colorful culture-stunts, consume all sorts of authentic treats, question dominant paradigms at a pricy disco, and then retreat—by public transportation!—to your hip urban abode, well-stocked no doubt with all of the gritty new products designed just for your hip urban demographic. The great achievements of the American metropolis? Such consumer delicacies as coffeehouses (which are, erroneously but somehow appropriately, identified with the 1930s snob term "café society"), street musicians, and, of course, rollerblading. The most perfect metropolis in the world that, after considerable thought, the magazine decrees we should emulate? You know without even opening the book—it's Prague.

Perhaps the most telling point of the issue is *Utne*'s summary of the joys of Boston, Massachusetts, which reads more like an ironic scoresheet of the fundamental emptiness of urban-hip than a celebration of the city. The author declares his affinity for, of all places, Harvard Square, where he consumes (of course) coffee and watches the "human potpourri." It's bad enough to describe humanity in terms of a popular yuppie house fragrance, but it's infinitely worse to actually believe, as the author declares he does, that the street musicians who accumulate in Harvard Square—perhaps the definitive urban fakers: the very most-privileged youths of the suburban heartland here to play-act at rock 'n' roll rebellion for four years before taking a position in daddy's firm—are actually *good*.

Thus do Americans debate the future of the metropolis, the basic issues of how we are to live together. There is no more fundamental question, and yet our most prominent dissenters can do little more than mimic the obscene verdict of the right-wing cyber-futurists: Cities are places of pleasure, theme parks for the lifestyle experimentation of affluent consumers with the rest of us around to provide colorful entertainment or to clean up after them if we can't sing and dance. The only real debate occurs over the ultimately minor question of whether we should enjoy lifestyle in person or whether, as Gilder puts it in a *Forbes* magazine article, the "tele-puter" will allow us to join in the fun—filtering out all the crime and filth—from our safe, suburban, "own living room."

-+->-<-+-

There is, of course, a vast critical literature on cities apart from the lifestyle-carnival tweedle-dum of Gilder and tweedle-dee of *Utne*. A host of enlightened commentary on our contemporary predica-ment sometimes finds its way into the public press: Mike Davis' writing on the curious civic culture of Los Angeles and the stag-geringly gigantic blunderings of California's policy-makers; Salaam Muwakkil's essays on race and urban America; David Har-vey's analysis of space, capital, and consciousness; Camilo José Vergara's graphic documentation of urban decay; and Robert Fitch's devastating account of the lucrative engineering of New York's decline in *The Assassination of New York*.

But by some weird inversion of intellectual value, this sort of re-sponsible discussion remains marginalized while the scatterbrained ravings of writers like Gilder, Alvin Toffler, Tom Peters, and Joel Garreau receive the attention and plaudits of the people who will actually be determining our collective future. Since it refuses to make the fundamental acknowledgment of business benevolence that is step number one in what Doug Henwood calls the pundit-licensing process, honest criticism can have no say in the matter. It's either pay your homage or get out of the game.

Our civic predicament, it seems, cannot be addressed simply by the straightforward identifying of problems and suggesting of so-lutions—any such approach will be resolutely ignored. It must also be a matter of identifying the disease that prevents difficult or crit-ical ideas from crossing the screens of our national consciousness. As ever, the problem is a cultural one, the devices by which our pe-culiar urban culture of decay, unconcern, lifestyle, and total segre-gation by class are made to seem *normal*. Our problems arise from a complex of never-to-be-questioned municipal faiths, bizarre assumptions about the public-mindedness of private industry, and a thought-squelching climate of competition between states and between cities. The waves may be lapping at the gunwales, but our officials seem to have convinced themselves that the answer is to crow loudly about how much drier it is over at their end.

We can't understand what's happening because we suffer from a deadly form of civic amnesia, a willingness of all interested parties to imagine themselves cut loose from the past, to forget about whatever it was that caused cities to be built in the first place in the frenzy of a headlong rush to attract conventions and corporate relocation. We can no longer comprehend the hard, basic urban reality of social class, we have no idea how these conglomerations of power and people that we inhabit ever came to be, and we cannot imagine our own pasts, except amid the jolly caperings of celebrities—cowboys and Indians, rubicund Al Capone, the homes of the Stars. To even suggest an alternative to business control of every aspect of life has become heresy unthinkable.

Even worse, the instant mobility of the "Information Age" has vastly intensified a certain cultural competition between cities. Boosterism has always been an underlying urban stupidity, of course, but in recent years it seems to have become the preeminent form of civic discourse, the omnipresent theme of every newspaper article, every business round-table, every sportsbar conversation. Cities are scurrying to transform themselves into consumer products, to substitute brand image for history, a carnivalesque "diversity" for ethnic identity, and to prosper not by, say, building things but by winning the loyalty of as large a market-share as they can.

→>-<←

Here in Chicago the South Side steel mills continue to be razed along with the lives and neighborhoods that surround them (never worth much more than a two-minute human interest segment on the TV news in the best of times). Buy a plasticized city map at any downtown store and look for the South Side on it: It isn't there. Drive around and try to find the neighborhood where the Memorial Day Massacre took place in 1937 (or better yet, find the "labor martyrs" web site); you can't. Here a tree grows through a roof, there a factory is dynamited for the cameras of a visiting Hollywood movie crew. Down here civilization is over; The City is an obscene joke.

Oblivious to it all, the new order is prospering out on Navy Pier, just east of the glittering North Michigan Avenue shopping district. The city has finally completed there a monumental embodiment of its new civic vision: a gigantic ferris wheel from which the town's towers can be viewed to advantage. The city cannot guarantee that fog will obscure the smoke and fires of the South Side on every day of the week, but the wheel suffers no shortage of customers nonetheless.

Baffler #7, 1995

EDWARD CASTLETON

Post-Urban, Post-Industrial but Never Post-Elite

"How are ye blind, ye treaders-down of cities!"
—*The Trojan Women* but in the spirit of John Horne Burns

ONCE, A LONG TIME AGO, there was an analog world, goes the contemporary bromide of the new cyber-elite. Now, they enthuse, the world has transformed itself into a "place without space," where time zones are more important than trade zones, and where an address on-line is a thousand times more significant than any petty street coordinate. Busying themselves with faxes, voice-mail, e-mail, and the Internet, this new class couldn't care less about where they physically happen to be. Geography and community must come to them. "Being digital" is the crucial thing, insists Nicholas Negroponte, MIT media lab guru and high priest of the new corporate age: Every remnant of the analog world must bend to meet his needs or be abandoned. There is, for example, no difference between Sunday and Monday in Negroponte's workweek. Work follows him everywhere and he follows it, jacking in with his laptop wherever he happens to be. As for those topographic mundanities that would imply that something exists outside the solipsistic self, forget it. The digital world has freed this entrepreneurial narcissus from the surly bonds of place, class, and context—and also, if we are to believe the bombast, from the grip of those nasty relics of the past known as cities.

Nowhere has this been made more clear than in the February 1996 special edition of *Forbes*. The magazine's cover story is a face-off over "the city vs. the country" featuring the apostle of entre-prenurial overcoming, Tom Peters, and George Gilder, author of the futuristic *Microcosm: The Quantum Revolution in Economics and Technology*. Gilder is all pessimism, predicting "the death of cities" due to the dread inevitability of Gordon Moore's (you know, the founder of Intel) Law, which asserts that because the number of transistors on a chip double every 18 months and because capital now depreciates in real value faster than ever before, there is an organic centrifuge—a "constant pressure distributing intelligence to the fringes of all networks"—out there somewhere that is breaking down all concentrations of power. The law does not seem to apply to the relationship between management and labor, but Gilder freely speculates about its consequences for the physical conglomeration of the metropolis. "Big cities are left-over baggage from the industrial era," he insists, "dirty, dangerous, and pestilential" places that only survive on a $360 billion life-support system courtesy of government subsidies. But with the coming of the information revolution this ultimate concentration of power can be painlessly amputated while all its advantages are retained and delivered safely and cleanly through the glories of ever-expanding bandwith. The leveling of the distinctiveness of different cultural activities will bring a "culture of first choices" where you can watch operas at the Met or order books on the computer from Borders without having to move your lazy ass.

Peters, though, is all WASPish optimism, the positive counterpoint in a rigged rendezvous. At first, his argument seems surprising: The city is "the perfect market" and thus the site of perfect competition. The accumulation of capital has never undermined the growth of the urban metropolis, he points out. In fact, the occurrence of the one has historically been concomitant with the development of the other. Strangely, though, the proof to which Peters points is not a city in any traditional sense; it's Santa Clara County in California, the site of the illustrious Silicon Valley. Here we can experience "the ascendancy and relevence of the new city-state," a veritable Renaissance Italy of "clusters of exuberant variety" where entrepreneurship and progress arise from the interaction between innovative high-tech Indians and Vietnamese, a tribute to the vitality of American pluralism as well as to the competitive milieu that blurs all the boundaries in the heat of "the passion to one-up the other guy." Needless to say, Peters adds, San Francisco and San Jose are not separate cities anyway; they form an enormous "zesty network" ("the 50,000 person city is history"), the product of a sucessful merger, a sort of cosmopolitan joint venture.

According to Peters, human interaction will triumph over Gilder's vision of a domesticated techno-utopia. Yet the sort of human interaction he has in mind is not entirely clear. In a characteristic fit of amphetamine-fed bombast coupled with his usual millenarian opacity, this consultant's consultant blurts out,

> As far as I am concerned, the greatest thing in the world would be the dispersion of the suburb. You should either be in places where there are two people per square mile or places where there are two million per square mile. I have a great deal of difficulty imagining a vibrant society with no opera companies and no ballet companies, no Cafe Veronas in Palo Alto, and I doubt whether we can have a cyberspatial Cafe Verona with the sweat dripping all over the machines.

Never mind imagining Peters as an enthusiast of such generic emblems of high culture as either opera or ballet: What's really revealing is his choice of Palo Alto as the desirable "vibrant society"—Palo Alto, the seat of Stanford Univerisity and its Hoover Institute, a sterile, affluent shopping mall community that even forced its eastern, more Hispanic half (the half that cleans the toilets and does the gardening) to secede and form East Palo Alto.

For those who didn't get the message of the Gilder/Peters pseudo-debate, another hint of the post-urban future came in the next feature story, "Tele-City on a Hill" written by Peter Huber of the Manhattan Institute. Warning any New York readers who aren't yet panic-stricken that *Omaha,* "the 800 Number Capital of the World," is threatening to transform Gotham into just another "fly-over community" with its cheap labor, taxes, and real estate, Huber insists that the only hope for urban sprawl is to reorganize itself and interactively export its "intellectual capital" via "long-distance antennas and transcontinental glass, switches, routes and multiplexes, the eyes and ears of the electronic age." But by "intellectual capital" Huber and his fellow urban theorists don't mean the editorial staff of the *New York Review of Books.* A *Business Week* story on urban cyber-rejuvenation is more specific: What's desirable about Manhattan is "Silicon Alley," where venture capitalists can get turned on by "the most diverse pool of intellectual capital anywhere" in the form of new "edutainment" and CD-ROM game "industries."

At the behest of Newt Gingrich's think tank, the Progress and Freedom Foundation (PFF), Gilder coauthored with fellow futurists Alvin Toffler, Esther Dyson, and George Keyworth "Cyberspace and the American Dream: A Magna Carta for the Knowledge Age," an alarming little pamphlet that encapsulates all the pseudo-emancipatory and anti-urban fantasies of the new corporate right. See, the "Third Wave" economy, whose central resource is "actionable knowledge" (e.g., "data, information, images, symbols, culture, ideology, and values"), has replaced the "static competition" of the Machine Age with "dynamic competition," "demassification," and more quality (albeit expensive) customized goods. The "Third Wave" has also millennialized the way we understand geography. Now we are to witness "the creation of 'electronic neighborhoods' bound together not by geography but by shared interests" as "Third Wave policies permit people to work at home, and to live wherever they choose"—unless, of course, backward-looking Second Wave policies interfere and encourage urbanization.

Michael Vlahos, one of the PFF's leading thinkers, predicts that by the year 2020 we will inhabit a glorious realm he calls "Byte-City," ruled over by "Brain Lords" like Microsoft's Bill Gates, followed consecutively in the suburban hierarchy by "Upper Service" workers (lawyers), "Industrial" workers, and then the "Lost" people "who can't cope" and must do menial jobs. Old understandings of the metropolis give way to a city that is nothing more than "a node in the network of our lives." Vlahos's vision of the cyber-future in which everyone serves one another from their living rooms is perhaps the most fleeting mirage in the GOP's dream of a meritocratic utopia. "All job worth must be proven in Byte City," Vlahos boasts, insisting that the "Brain Lords," those "kinder, gentler robber barons" of tomorrow, will not constitute a "heritable class," heaven forbid, but "will make it as individuals." Old-style cities brought *anomie* and caused a "loss of identity" amidst the tyranny of mass production and mass consumption. But in the next century, every home will possess a "virtu-screen" that "doesn't take us to the city, it brings the city to us. The city is in our living room, or wherever we want it to be."

Of course the obsequious Democrats are no less hallucinatory. In a pathetic fantasy of future urban bliss published in *Business Week*, the same platform chosen by the Republicans, Joel Kotkin of the Democratic Leadership Council and David Friedman of the *L.A. Times* proclaim Hollywood to be the ideal. This hallowed place, where small, non-union companies compare themselves to "medieval craftsmen" and produce masterpieces of high-tech

American stupidity. The heroes of their story are the props makers at tiny firms with names like Cinnabar and the independent contractors who make customized xenon lights for the cinematic trashmen that rule the town. These bold but minuscule innovators, brilliantly solving problems for the big producers, hail from a different race altogether than the more vulgar and resentful Second-Wave type that occasionally blow up federal buildings or computer scientists. As Jonathan Katz, the founder of Cinnabar, warmly reminisces about his first job in an uncreative unionized Hollywood, "I remember one producer saying to me, 'What is a nice Jewish boy like you doing making props? I'm used to rednecks in overalls.' " And so, because of "intelligent" freelancers like Katz, a ship scene from *Free Willy II* can thankfully be shot at an outdoor pool next to the L.A. Coliseum: The "here-today-gone-tomorrow production strategy" is manifest destiny in this age of productive chaos.

Apart from the fact that Kotkin's capitalist-multicultural babble is being uttered by a Democrat, his narrative of a CD-ROM future is nearly identical to the one favored by Vlahos and the other starry-eyed pseudo-intellectuals at the PFF. But regardless of whether the new order is cultural or organic, urban or suburban, or even whether the half-baked metatheory comes from the right or the center, the rhetoric of necessity, it seems, must be invoked. Byte City or no Byte City, the important fact is that the rule of the post-analog business theorists who make up the new power elite be legitimated and profit margins increased.

As for our existing cities, without their accumulated "intellectual capital" they are only dens of "welfare cheats" and other such riff-raff, places where New Age freak Arianna Stassinopoulos Huffington and Texas journalism professor Marvin Olasky can go cruising the ghetto on anthropological culture runs while looking for charitable organizations to practice "effective compassion" with the funds of their newly-founded PFF affiliate, "Center for Human

Compassion." Newt himself phrased the new vision of the city best. On the one hand, the city is dangerous and horrible: "As a father of two daughters, I can't ignore the terror and worry of parents in our inner-cities must feel for their children . . . Within a half-mile of this Capitol, your Capitol, drugs, violence and despair threaten the lives of our citizens." On the other hand, the solution is empty block grants for those marginalized by the Third Wave while we commute across the new "borderless" world from our safe suburbs in Maryland and Virginia. And what could be a better place for a test-run of the cyber-civis than Washington, D.C.: a penal colony for the descendents of slaves run by inept overseers amid Mussolinian architecture and precious boutiques for the precious bourgeois commuters to preciously idiotic Georgetown. Unable to govern itself, deregulated *avant la lettre,* and faced with a $722-million budget shortfall and junk bond status, the Capital is today run by an independent finance board that delights in lowering property taxes and voiding the union contracts of those lazy, surly, "pensioned to the hilt" city workers that live on the wrong side of the Anacostia.

But for other Third-Wave thinkers, the inner city is just the place for the capitalism of the future to flourish. Certainly, it is the only part of the metropolis the business press and the mainstream press are willing to talk about, albeit with the paternalistic benevolence of a mint julep. Before the advent of the Republican rollback, the inner city could be conveniently branded as an autonomous ecosystem all of own. Blatant geographical disparities in wealth could be dismissed as part of a larger, natural social order. But with the "end of history" the memory of urban political struggles can be tossed along with the welfare state, and the problem of urban poverty can be handed over to the mercantile experts in profitability. The vultures are poised and ready to go.

Baffler #7, 1995

TOM VANDERBILT

Revolt of the Nice: Edge City, Capital of the Twenty-First Century

> In the convulsions of the commodity economy we begin to recognize the monuments of the bourgeoisie as ruins even before they have crumbled.   —Walter Benjamin

> You want rich. You got it.   —Joel Garreau

WITH ITS LONELY office towers standing sentinel on one side of I-94, Hoffman Estates, Illinois, is the last outpost of activity before the billboard-dotted stretch of farmland that eventually becomes Wisconsin. It's a familiar sight for anyone driving north of Chicago. But what is Hoffman Estates, and what is it doing way out here? For a number of urban scholars and sociologists, there was something about Hoffman Estates and similar developments that make them more than suburbs, yet not quite cities, and they flocked to the drawing board to sketch its form. A slew of interpretations followed: Robert Fishman called them "technoburbs," for their high-tech companies and facilities; Kenneth Jackson called them "centerless cities"; "middle landscape" was suggested by Peter Rowe; while Edward Soja favored "exopolis." Others weighed in with more clinical terms like "multinucleated metropolitan region."

But it was Joel Garreau, with his 1991 book *Edge City: Life on the New Frontier*, who seized the zeitgeist and captured the imagination of the journalists and opinion makers who were watching places like Hoffman Estates. Edge City, a brand identity for a phenomenon urban scholars had long been trying to name, was born, and Garreau instantly became brand manager. Since writing *Edge City*, Garreau, a *Washington Post* reporter, has built himself a virtual cottage industry of post-suburban boosterism. In magazines from *American Demographics* to *Inc.* to *The New Republic* to *The Edge City News*, Garreau blankets the intellectual turf like a propaganda pamphlet drop, issuing new installments in his paean-in-progress to Edge City—those curious corporate campus towns with strange hybrid names like the Katy Freeway-West Houston Energy Corridor or the Reston-Herndon-Dulles Access Road Area, which sometime in the 1980s went from being outposts of managerial synergy and decent parking to, in Garreau's mind, full-fledged urban entities.

For Garreau, Edge Cities are not merely another soulless expression of corporate relocation and disposable exurban sprawl. Nor are they suburbs in new clothes. Garreau identifies his product as any place that has at least five million square feet of leasable office space, at least 600,000 square feet of leasable retail space ("the equivalent of a fair sized mall"), "more jobs than bedrooms," is "perceived by the population as one place," and was "nothing like 'city' as recently as thirty years ago." Given this liberal definition, Edge Cities turn out to be the creators of most of the wealth and employment in the U.S. today, and in their jumbled agglomeration of mixed-density retail and often indistinguishable office towers Garreau sees the future of America itself.

Garreau's odyssey from objective chronicler to Edge City partisan is an unlikely one, as he recounts in the introduction to his book. When high-rise office buildings began to appear near his home in the Virginia suburbs, putting "Houston" cheek-by-jowl with the pastoral glens of Fairfax County, he set out to find out "who was doing this to us." Somewhere along the path of investigating this "clear and present danger to Western Civilization," he met the "enemy," he says, and the enemy "was us." Heading in to the heart of blandness, steaming slowly upriver past New Jersey malls and California planned developments, Garreau began to see order among the chaos, hope among the natives, a glimmering future in the wilderness. In short, Garreau began to like Edge Cities. Somewhere between a food court in Newport Beach and a chunk of Class-A office space in Atlanta, our trusty Marlowe became Kurtz.

Now, as a "principal" in *The Edge City News* (an expensive newsletter designed to deliver "need-to-know" information to Edge City decision-makers) and a "stakeholder" in Edge City (TECN's term for what used to be called "citizens"), Garreau delivers his by-now-familiar pitch: Edge Cities are the bustling new frontier of America, the next wave in the process by which "we" first moved to the suburbs to escape the city, then moved the city's marketplaces to the suburbs for convenience's sake, and now, in a triumph of democratic will, have "moved our means of creating wealth, the essence of urbanism—our jobs—out to where most of us have lived and shopped for two generations." There are, as he points out, 190 Edge Cities larger than Orlando, Florida, but only forty downtowns the size of Orlando. Edge Cities make up the top thirteen spots for median 1990 household income, and eighteen of the top forty largest job centers in the U.S. are in places like the Santa Ana Freeway/Anaheim or the Dallas Galleria/LBJ Freeway Area. Edge Cities now have the bulk of the nation's population, create the majority of jobs, have less crime, are safer and more comfortable, and are the standard residence of choice for most Fortune 500 headquarters. These developments, by all reasonable estimates, seem destined to continue.

Like other historical modes of urban life, Edge Cities are perfect expressions of the prevailing economic order. Today business theorists theorize about a world without boundaries, a world of nonparticularity, a world of "telepresence" and the "virtual office," a world of dispersed corporations. As Garreau admits, "the reason there are no 'Welcome to' signs in Edge City is that it is a judgment call where it begins and ends." In his book, Garreau writes excitedly that the Edge City model is sweeping Europe as well, despite "immensely different" political, economic, and cultural systems; what he fails to consider, however, is that the corporations creating these complexes are units of the same multinational parents—IBM France, Colgate Palmolive, British Petroleum—that create Edge Cities in the U.S. Is it any wonder that as corporations become less site-specific, relying on an abstract global labor force and "universal brands," the enclaves they construct should be any less homogeneous?

Edge Cities are where corporations go to "reengineer," free from the labor unions, tight regulation, and tax burdens of traditional downtowns. According to Garreau, it is also where people go to reinvent themselves, free from the rigid structures of the city, which maintain fixed and frozen relations between the very poor and very rich. Garreau writes enthusiastically that "Edge Cities are for entrepreneurs, while downtowns are for old-fashioned Organization Men." Out here in the supposedly classless and fluid Edge Cities, Garreau says, "we invent new institutions to create community, new ways to connect with each other." But, as he concedes, it's a tenuous and contradictory notion of community upon which Edge City is built. The same entrepreneurial flux and rapid growth that gives economic life to Edge City is the same force that undermines the notion of a stable community. Community, in the sense of those seeking to preserve a set way of life they have established for themselves, thus becomes "the enemy of change—and the growth of Edge City." Edge City is fundamentally hostile to community in a more concrete sense as well—it is designed to keep others out aggressively. Christopher Lasch calls it "a revolt of the elites" and Robert Reich a "secession of the successful": What Edge City boils down to is an economic and cultural distancing not only from people of a different race and class, but a purposeful withdrawal from involvement in and responsibility for the greater politic of the city. In Edge City, the architecture perfectly embodies the principles upon which these communities are being built. Driving across the George Washington Bridge from New York into the Edge City of Fort Lee, New Jersey, one faces straightaway the intimidating specter of defensible corporate space: the dull-metallic reflective armor of one tower sits atop its own stacked parking garage, a fortress unto itself; while nearby another building—resembling a vertical ice cube tray—looms like a violent and utterly alien blemish on the landscape.

The associations that de Tocqueville so marveled at ("Americans are forever forming associations") have now become homeowner associations, another expression of what political scientist Evan McKenzie calls "privatopia"—the privately run and financed developments that make up most of Edge City housing. For Garreau, homeowner associations are innovative solutions to the problems of life on the frontier. A less charitable view would see them as an attempt to localize government so it only serves a small number of homogeneous residents; and, as they contract out for services, an attempt to render the city obsolete altogether. A letter in *TECN* from the chairman of an Atlanta Edge City coalition exemplifies this: "Seventy-five chief executive officers of major firms joined together (paying annual dues of $5,000 each) to substitute for and supplement governmental actions affecting quality of life . . . funding equipment needs for mall policing, lobbying for improved roadway access, providing support for the public high school, marketing the community through an annual guide book . . . . "

And what becomes of public expression in the privatopias of Edge City? Garreau apologizes for the censoring of free speech in Edge City shopping malls ("public spaces that are really private property," he says, seemingly without irony) by saying "it's a question of how much we value safety and comfort." Shopping malls, for Garreau, are actually a sign of cultural vitality, modern day public squares where the classes can mingle, if not shop at the same store (or on the same floor). In his usual booster tone he waxes enthusiastic about a mall in Bridgewater, New Jersey:

> The mall's a doozy. The first floor (The Commons Collection) caters to the affluent with Brooks Brothers, Laura Ashley, Godiva, and major-league indoor trees. The third floor, by contrast (Campus), is neon "under twenty-five" heaven. It has an enormous Sam Goody's record store, a store that sells nothing but sunglasses, a store that sells nothing but artifacts from cartoons . . . (You want village green? You got it. Squint a little. This is what it looks like in the late twentieth century).

So an authentic and vigorous civic life is now built around the promise that a store exists that sells "nothing but sunglasses." In his grand civic delusion, Garreau can call a mall a village green if he likes—but remember, if it looks like a mall, has a Body Shop and a Banana Republic, and has security guards who would escort anyone out who so much as brandished a political flyer, it's probably just a mall. Unlike the village green, the mall is designed to orient the consumer in one direction: to consume. It is built for no other reason.

But there is one thing that has kept Edge City from meeting its true realization as an urban place: culture. Culture is the Holy Grail of the inscrutable Edge City category Garreau calls "Nice." The elements of the "nice"—lakefront vistas, schools with "astonishingly high SAT scores," golf courses, country clubs—are why Garreau says Edge Cities arise where they do, for if cheap development were the only issue, blue-collar white ethnic suburbs closer to the city would suffice. Garreau knows that many people find Edge Cities aesthetically and culturally appalling. But he is optimistic. "Edge City is the creation of people with money," he writes. "If they want 'culture,' they'll get it." In *American Demographics*, Garreau continues excitedly that they are in fact beginning to "get it": Yes, seven of the top ten places with the highest ratio of bars-to-employed people are Edge Cities (all ten are in Texas). One is loathe to imagine the places, though: a franchise "theme" bar where the highlight of the week is Goldschlager night and maybe jello shots and karaoke; where junior symbolic analysts can imbibe the European flavored-vodka-of-the-month and pass along today's O.J. joke as funneled through the emerging markets desk. In the Edge City of Irvine, the owners of the first bar to open there described it to the *Los Angeles Times* as an "upscale, traditional Jamaican plantation . . . where patrons can graze on appetizers including fresh oysters injected with Stolichnaya." (One hesitates to speculate where the indigenous labor of a "traditional plantation" fits into this scheme.)

And that's not all. Edge City professionals now have a variety of "fragrant, intriguing, and tasty cuisines" at their disposal. This thanks to Vietnamese and El Salvadoran immigrants—the ones many suburban voters would like to send back but whose economy increasingly can't seem to do without. But beyond bars, ethnic restaurants, and malls, Edge City culture gets a little hazy. *TECN* describes a New Age ritual in which people gather around the Quorum office complex near the Dallas Galleria to watch the vernal equinox ("And people say Edge City has no soul," they chuckle), leaving one to wonder if the ancient Druids might not have some leadership secrets to pass along.

To cloud the "culture" issue just a little more, Garreau likes to trot out the singularly unconvincing claim that by giving people a place to flex their entrepreneurial spirit, Edge Cities actually revitalize downtowns, since moneyed Edge professionals can now (presumably they couldn't before) spend their disposable income as tourists to the city's museums, theaters, and retail centers. In fact, Edge Cities have had profound cultural effects on traditional downtowns, but in far more malign ways. The architectural and planning lessons, the mass retailing strategies, and nascent "shadow governments" of Edge City are, in a brutal twist of irony, being reapplied to central cities. From New York's South Street Seaport to MCA's CityWalk in Los Angeles to Baltimore's Harbor Front, the metropolis of old is rapidly becoming a retail museum (or a living museum gift shop), a denatured festival marketplace inorganically grafted onto an old industrial district.

In New York, the private security and maintenance forces of Edge City are used to patrol the business improvement districts in enclaves across town. Residents can even inhabit their own Edge City preserve: the decidedly Dallas-like Battery Park City. The pseudo-culture of Edge City now infects New York as well, as themed restaurants offering generic food and pricy merchandise sprout up to offer safe havens for Edge City tourists. The whole spectacle recalls what Henry James called "the hotel world," that great cultural contrivance at the pinnacle of American civilization in which an entire environment is created, based not on nature and history but on satisfying and elevating desires.

Now that Edge City has entered the "real city," its triumph on the world stage of history would seem to be complete. But there are cracks in the facade. As Charles Lockwood reported in the *Wall Street Journal,* some Edge Cities, or "suburban downtowns," are having the economic problems long associated with decaying urban centers. Lockwood argues that American corporations are finding that with telecommuting and "hoteling" that they no longer need the massive 1980s-style office complexes of Edge City. Other corporations are pulling up stakes in favor of ever more distant realms, some even relocating back to downtown (with Boston's vacancy rate dropping to 12% from 19% in 1991). Indeed, the notion of the flight of jobs and industry to Edge City, while often taken as a fait accompli, can be misleading. Just recently, the Prodigy Service Corporation, a leading on-line provider exemplary of the high-tech Edge City landscape, announced it was relocating from White Plains, New York, to New York City, apparently to be closer to the multimedia companies growing in the downtown area. Of course, there was nothing inevitable about business's great move away from downtown into the great sprawl beyond. Inner cities are not by their own logic bound to fail: They are pushed into their problems by business's concerted withdrawal into private sanctuaries of nice.

Nevertheless, when movements like regional tax sharing try to redirect some of the fruits of "nice" back to the less privileged segments of the metropolitan region, Edge City cries "backlash." As the *TECN* notes: "Many people, including Edge City stakeholders, view such redistribution of revenues as in effect penalizing neighborhoods that work in order to bolster districts—and, in some cases, policies—that don't." Edge City thus justifies itself in moralistic terms as a "community that works," as if this were some inherent condition apart from the billions of dollars in corporate investment that makes Edge City viable.

We can glimpse an Edge City future different from Garreau's optimistic vision in the problems that are now plaguing many old suburbs. Mike Davis, writing in the *Los Angeles Times*, lists a number of inner-ring suburbs that are now faced with the same problems of crime, homelessness, and unemployment as the inner city. As Davis argues, these suburbs, which once took jobs and revenues from downtowns and were heralded with the same enthusiasm that Edge Cities are now, have in turn seen their jobs and tax revenues move to more favorable elsewheres. The decline of the older suburbs triggers a new kind of populist resentment toward the new suburbs, whose sparkling postmodern towers stand in contrast to the tract housing of yesterday, which suffers from what Davis calls "premature physical obsolescence."

There is something particularly sad about a dying suburb, or a struggling Edge City. While Garreau and others contend that Edge Cities are "works in progress," raw and ragged like the frontier cities of the past, and that in time, they will blossom into virtual Venices, this now seems unlikely. In Edge City there is no vision beyond the immediate production and distribution needs of corporate America. Nor is there any history, apart from highway rest stops named after heroes from the past. It is not merely their newness that makes Edge Cities so ahistorical: They are erected as an image of managerial capitalism, places of innovation and obsolescence. Like the outmoded computer chip of last year, they and their Information Age residents will be deemed vestigial as soon as they lose their competitive edge.

Planners argue that, to prosper and flourish, Edge Cities require "fill-in" development, the kind of mixed-use, high-density public places that would create some island of community amid all the parking lots. But lacking a viable governmental structure, bereft of civic feeling, restrained by scant tax bases, and devoid of any overarching vision, it is hard to imagine such development happening. While it is true that nineteenth-century American cities had governments as fragile as Edge City, they also had the public works projects of millionaire industrialists, who, robber barons though they were, felt some impulse to create civic structures. The high-tech captains of industry in Edge City share no such sense of responsibility. Rather than a Rockefeller building art museums for collective enjoyment, we have Bill Gates building for profit an Internet system that allows people to download digitized art images into their own homes.

And if some unimaginable economic or social "destabilization" someday renders Edge City hostile to the needs of business, business will simply relocate, and citizens will scarcely feel compelled to save what is left behind. It's a scorched earth development policy whose motto might well be: Destroy the village to save the company. Left behind are the shortsighted efforts of planners and the disposable exoskeletons of aesthetically appalling office parks.

However inspired he may seem, Garreau is as banal and moribund as the suburban downtowns themselves. In breathlessly evoking the quantitative superiority of Edge Cities, Garreau becomes a sort of uber-booster, ignoring the democratic decay and the triumph of marketplace values that Edge Cities represent, enthralled with a corrupt form of populism that paints Edge Cities, because they house and employ so many people, as the undistilled American spirit. But unlike suburbia, which spawned a litany of jeremiads, Edge City has settled across the landscape with little more than an acknowledgment that it has done so. It is as if critics, leery of being labeled elitist, were afraid to challenge what is construed as the popular will; i.e., people are living there, so they must like living there. But as Herbert Muschamp has written, Edge Cities are founded not on populism but on the negation of the popular will, built where they can stand beyond planning, beyond government, beyond taxation. In the great DMZ of deregulation they sprout, in baleful testament to the failure of municipal politics and the triumph of the corporate ethos.

Baffler #7, 1995

KIM PHILLIPS

Lotteryville, USA

WHAT WOULD YOU do if you won a million dollars? Forget the revolution: This is your ticket to the Kingdom of Freedom. No matter how many hours you log in at a fast-food restaurant or behind a secretary's desk, it's unlikely you'll ever save enough to buy a house or have credit-card companies calling up with prime offers, let alone get your hair and thighs to look like those of the Aaron Spelling actresses who tantalize you every Monday and Wednesday night. Dream a little dream . . . for Parisian vacations, little gifts for the wife, a chance to start the business you've always dreamed of, a chance to give it all away. The classless society is happening right now, at a party at a mansion in Beverly Hills. And a lottery ticket might buy you an invitation.

In Grand Crossing, a neighborhood on the South Side of

Chicago, the average monthly spending on the lottery is $60 per household. Grand Crossing lies just west of the South Shore neighborhood, home of the much-lauded community-development-oriented South Shore Bank. Jeffery Boulevard, the busy commercial thoroughfare where the Bank's headquarters are located, is lined with thriving small businesses—hair salons, pizzerias, Black-owned clothing stores. But traveling from South Shore to Grand Crossing you pass a boarded-up apartment building, an abandoned grocery store, a deserted TV repair shop. A little bit further and you come to Stony Island Avenue. The businesses here are distinctly different than on Jeffrey—there's a Checkers, a Church's Fried Chicken, a Burger King; a neighborhood has started to become a ghetto. Next to a shuttered bar there's an ad for a pawn shop—"Need Cash Fast? Top Dollar for Broken Gold." Go under the highway that passes over the neighborhood; you'll find a sudden proliferation of storefront churches one of which, the House of Deliverance, has obviously been abandoned. At Cottage Grove there's a Currency Exchange and a store that advertises itself as selling liquor—and, as an afterthought, food. Beyond, there's nothing but ramshackle buildings, no businesses as far as the eye can see. Only the passing of an occasional bus reminds you that you're connected to the rest of the city.

Compare Grand Crossing to Bronzeville, the famous *Black Metropolis* described in 1945 by St. Clair Drake and Horace Cayton, with its "continuous and colorful movement" among locally-owned businesses. A neighborhood, a city, is a concentration of people, goods, money, drawn in from the hinterlands; if much of this abundance is collected only to be dispersed again, a sizable portion remains and circulates within the closed system of the city. Drake and Cayton describe the neighborhood's policy wheels, illegal private precursors to the lottery, which were run by primarily Black syndicates—the white mob took them over during the fifties—and were ways of amassing capital within the community, of making sure a few people would have enough money to support local businesses and even invest. As a way of redistributing money within the neighborhood, policy wheels didn't work too badly. It's not a coincidence that policy has been replaced by the lottery just as the local department stores and restaurants have been replaced by Burger King.

A monthly average of $4.48 is spent on the lottery per household in Flossmoor, Ilinois, a wealthy suburb where the average income is $117,000 a year. In Posen, Illinois, a poor suburb where average household income is $33,000, the monthly average is $91.82. Although people of all incomes play the lottery, and the indigent, of course, can't afford to spend much, it remains overwhelmingly true that lottery players, like the policy wheel players of the past, are overwhelmingly poor. But in every way the lottery serves a wholly different function than its predecessor. On the one hand, it scrapes up revenue for starved state coffers. On the other, it inoculates the urban poor with a stiff ideological dose of eternal possibility and personal mobility. The one thing it does *not* do is collect money for local investment. In an era when Enterprise Zones and tax cuts for businesses are all that is offered to heal the wounds of the cities, the lottery is America's perverse way of dealing with poverty and ignoring the plight of its urban poor.

Lotteries are part of a long and vigorous tradition in American life, going back to the colonial period when lotteries were used to amass funds for the construction of many of the hallmarks of colonial architecture—the Harvard and Yale campuses, Fanueil Hall—and even for getting supplies to Revolutionary troops. During the nineteenth century, private lotteries took in millions of dollars; the last of these, a fabulously corrupt money-making machine in Louisiana, was shut down in 1896. Yet even after the last of the official lotteries was shut down, illegal wheels continued to turn great profits, and instant sweepstakes à la Publisher's Clearinghouse took the place of the lottery among the law-abiding—especially when times got rough.

The lottery came back as a tool of public finance in the late sixties and early seventies. Today, thirty-nine states have lotteries. After a few years of slow growth between 1975 and 1980, the Illinois lottery exploded: ticket sales climbed from 98 million in 1980 to 1.5 billion in 1990. Your lottery dollar breaks down like this: about 50 percent goes back in payoffs, 40 percent goes to the Common School Fund, 5 percent goes to commissions for lottery vendors, and 5% goes to operating the lottery. The transfer to the school fund in 1994 was $552,111,416. Of course, it's something of an accounting fiction to say that the lottery made half a billion dollars for the school fund—if the money hadn't come from the lottery it would have had to come from somewhere else in the tax structure. A more accurate way to put it might be to say that the lottery saved local property owners half a billion dollars.

State revenues shouldn't be thought of as absolute figures; the crucial question about state taxes isn't whether they're "high" or "low," but who pays them. Since every state gets its revenue from somewhere, the important question is which part of society is expected to foot the bill, and looking at the tax bill of an individual or the amount of revenue collected from a single source transforms taxes from a political matter into one of bookkeeping. Tax structures, as Orange County, California, is reminding the world, are ways of distributing financial power. For example, sales taxes are regressive not only because they take a more sizable cut of a poor person's income than that of someone in the upper middle class, but because they reduce the cumulative purchasing power of working people and hence the bargaining power workers have over the economy as a whole. Tax structures also indicate the roles different parts of society play in the functioning of the state, not only a bureaucratic government in Springfield but a set of obligations connecting different parts of society. The lottery is perhaps unique in that it is one of the few revenue sources that applies solely to poor and working people and doesn't affect business or property owners at all. In this it seems closer to pre-Revolutionary France, a system in which peasants picked up the brunt of the Crown's bill, than to the United States before the progressive income tax. To the policy wonk it may seem absurd to bring up feudalism in a discussion of taxes, but the comparison is more appropriate than it might seem. "Regressivity" is usually used to describe a state revenue source that exacts a larger proportion of a poor person's income than that of a rich person. However, many common state revenue sources—like excise taxes on cigarettes and the lottery—go farther than this; they take a larger *absolute* amount from the poor than the well-off, while other kinds of tax relief programs give businesses industrial parks and factory buildings at outrageous discounts.

Despite its vast ghettos, in Chicago the poor are easy to forget. Wealth is everywhere, as immanent and unreachable as the spires of the Loop seem from the South Side—a fairy city, forever hovering out of reach. Money hangs over the city like an unfulfilled promise, beckoning in the department stores, the glass skyscrapers, the taxi-cabs, a whiff of expensive perfume. "Get from Grand Boulevard to Easy Street," read a lottery advertisement put up in Chicago's poor-est neighborhood a few years ago. "This could be your ticket out." Lottery stories sometimes eat up fifteen minutes of a half-hour news program; the ubiquitous pot of Illinois State Lottery gold at the end of a rainbow sits in the window of liquor stores all over the South Side. The message blares from the newspapers that print winning numbers, "hot" numbers, "overdue" numbers, from the hysterical screams of winners on TV. Anyone can be a millionaire. You gotta play to win. Everybody gets another chance.

A chance for what? Lottery marketing firms such as Scientific Games—which make millions from state contracts—devise scenes of wealth so surreal that they seem like Donald Trump's nightmares. An ad on the New York City subway a couple of years ago showed a throne room in an island mansion, the turquoise waves of some tropical sea visible through a window behind a velvet throne; a middle-aged man in tattered bathrobe with glasses and slippers sat reading the paper while a small poodle stood at attention before him, a peculiar mixture of suburbia and imperial Russia. Yet Chicago's Kimbark Liquors, a little Hyde Park establishment that serves the South Side, sells 2,700 tickets the day before a $20 million drawing, and the purchasers don't seem to be thinking about poodles to wait on them. "It's just a dream, something to think about before you fall asleep, something to take your mind off its everyday hassles," says Larry, a salesman at Kimbark. What people think of when they play the lottery doesn't seem to be the fancy cars, the racks of CDs, the fabulous new house, the private jet; not the freedom that comes with unlimited consumption, but instead the quieter comfort of financial security, a security that is no longer obtainable through work. A middle-aged Black man at Kimbark who plays twenty dollars worth of tickets every day says that if he wins he'll go to Georgia, where it's warm. An older woman tells me she'd just like to pay off her bills. Mike Lang of the Illinois Lottery says, "Winners often buy a new car, not a Ferrari but a Buick or Cadillac." It's not being a millionaire that people long for, it's simply not being poor any more.

Statistically speaking, nobody ever wins the lottery. The chance of picking 6 random numbers out of 54 is one in 12,913,582. Philosophers of capitalism from Adam Smith to Milton Friedman have long been perturbed by the phenomenon of people playing a game they ought to know they can't win. But sneering at the lottery as "a tax on the ignorant," claiming that people who play the lottery are poor fools, deluded and uneducated, manipulated into buying false promises of wealth, fame, and glory, is an attempt to bypass the possibility that maybe poor people actually have a good understanding of what their life chances are; maybe lottery players are *right*. At issue here is not the lottery *per se* but the chance of personal mobility, the question of where you can get ahead in life by saving up money; the lottery should make sense to anyone for whom the answer is nowhere. Lottery tickets aren't like investments in the stock market; they are tickets to a dramatically different kind of life, the kind of life you'll never be able to save up to just by working nine to five.

In fact, the lottery is a perfectly rational investment for a person facing a lifetime of drudgery and uncertainty. The dictums of the economists—that saving can ultimately buy you a better life, that accumulation toward reinvestment ought to be the practice of any rational utility-maximizer—fail to take into account that money means one thing for the rich and quite another for the poor. Poor people's money doesn't work right. It doesn't save, it doesn't accumulate, it doesn't invest. For most people, money is simply a means to an end, a way to get food, clothing, shelter, and a little TV on the side. It gets traded in, given away, stolen, lost. Elusive and slippery, you can't put it somewhere it will stay—like a house or a pension plan—until you can make the down payment. The working man's purchasing power is just the boss's variable capital, so the saying goes. Money, the form both take, is a neutral medium. To compare the cash under the mattress of the poor to the investments of the wealthy is to postulate a continuum where there is in fact a radical break.

As the progression from Bronzeville to Grand Crossing indicates, what makes a ghetto a ghetto is not so much a lack of money but the lack of institutions in which money can collect. With no local businesses through which to circulate, the green stuff disappears from poor neighborhoods into the cash registers of the few remaining chain supermarkets. It goes to the makers of Olde English 800, to the tobacco millionaires, the fast-food chain owners, the landlords in the suburbs, the currency exchanges. The lottery is hardly unique in siphoning money out of a poor community—

compared with most businesses that "serve" the poor it looks almost innocuous. If the model for the lottery isn't Robin Hood, it's not quite Ronald Reagan either—it robs the poor to give to the school system. That it goes to the state is perhaps a sign of how desperate state governments are for revenue, but for the players it's no different than other systems that suck their money away. To refer to the lottery as a swindle or a cheat on the poor ignores the basic truth about being poor, which is that you get cheated all the time.

Yet there is a lucky winner. The lottery is perhaps the most painless and narrow form of redistribution, taking money from the poor to enrich one of their own. While the lottery may, in a sense, be rational for the individual, it is clearly irrational for the class. Rather than simply manipulating ignorance, the lottery teaches a sly lesson: For people in desperate situations, fantasy is the answer. Reinforcing the message of personal mobility, lottery playing teaches that you're on your own, that organization and politics are loser's games. Unlike the liquor salesmen or absentee landlords, the lottery sells a vision of the future—a future imagined in terms of an unchangeable class system. The poor donate money to make a poor person rich, at which point that person and their newfound wealth pack up and move out. And the rich pay nothing for this self-containing system of political quiescence—in fact, they get a tax cut.

When people are laid off, budgets are tight, crime is rampant, and social dislocation is the norm, a microeconomic model explaining why this is the best of all possible worlds can't be far behind. The early 1980s found a new theoretical model afoot in the antiseptic world of sociologists and political scientists that suggested that a city is not an economic unit in its own right, much less a place where people work and live, but rather a "service provider"—a place offering skyscrapers, office buildings, three-martini lunches, shoeshine boys. The earliest theorizers applied rational choice theory to urban life: People shop for cities the way one might look at a J. Crew catalogue, ultimately selecting the town with the ideal mix of services and taxes for them. Later academics contented themselves with explaining the only important thing—why cities should be prostrate and powerless vassals before the lord of corporate money. Since attracting big business to the city, where it will create jobs and pay (some) taxes, is by definition good for all the members of the city, it follows that all responsible city policies aim to attract private capital, with tax breaks, infrastructure, and perks like free electricity. Cities should compete for the privilege of housing the headquarters of Sears, the factories of U.S Steel. And any micro-economist can tell you what the result of all this competition is—a better deal for the consumer.

Debates in academia rage—do "incentives" actually attract business to an area? How much do taxes matter? *What does business want?*—questions that business publications happily answer. The *Site Selector Handbook,* for example, is quite straightforward on this intricate and difficult subject. In a recent article called "Incentive Lures: Firmly Embedded in the Location Equation," the president of a Colorado economic development council says, "I'd have to say incentives are brought up in discussions of prospects virtually 100% of the time today." Voltaire is brought in to defend the practice: "A little evil is often necessary for obtaining a great good." And the states and localities whip themselves into masochistic lathers to demonstrate that they provide a perfect setting for *your* company. "To say our state is 'pro-business' is a little like saying the Sistine Chapel is 'kinda pretty,' " reads an ad for North Carolina, touting the state's right-to-work law, its balanced budget, and its favorable bond rating. An ad for the Gateway Area, towns in Northern Illinois, Southern Iowa, and Northern Missouri, goes even farther, advertising the "Nordic stock" of the locals—"A Work Force that Earns Its Pay"—who, despite their Old World work ethic of "not just accepting hard work, but taking pride in it," come for lower wages than any workers in the surrounding cities. No sassy Black folk in Southern Iowa, no sir!

A state budget is a tricky thing to unpack, containing such oddities in its murky depths as a steep sales tax on illegal drugs so that drug dealers can be busted for tax evasion, and sales tax exemptions for all kinds of goodies ranging from manufacturing equipment to semen used for the artificial insemination of livestock. But a number of things are unmistakably clear about the lottery and the Illinois tax structure—the state has one of the highest sales taxes in the nation (6.25 percent) and one of the lowest income taxes (a flat tax of 3 percent; of the seven states with flat taxes, only Pennsylvania's is lower). The lottery, which makes up 5 percent of total state revenue, grosses about 15 times the tax on real estate transfers ($28 million a year), about 5 times the tax on corporate franchises ($93 million a year), and is gaining apace on the corporate income tax ($851 million a year). In fact, total state revenue from all forms of gambling—riverboats, the racetrack, bingo, and the lottery—now exceeds the corporate income tax, at $864 million a year. ("A tantalizing source of revenue," reads a brochure from the Comptroller's office.) When you look at the lottery and gambling alongside the variety of other revenue sources that fall most harshly on the poor—steep taxes on cigarettes, on liquor, and sales taxes—it seems evident that Illinois wants to increase taxes on working-class people, while easing up on corporations and their rich employees. But what else can they do? Chicago can't move, capital can. Rather than enact new income taxes Illinois has decided to soak the poor.

While urban governments kow-tow to capital, local property owners have staged semi-revolts at any hint of increased property taxes, leaving cities and states with a vacuum where there should be revenue. Public goods and services are needed to attract businesses and investors, yet cities keep trying to undercut each other, each offering a better deal, lower taxes, more freebies, more docile workers. The "populist"-conservative ethic of personal responsibility and lower welfare payments dovetails nicely with the businessman's dream of a "flexible" labor market and a proliferation of low-wage workers—workers whose pockets can be picked, at least in the short run, to make up for the dwindling piles of gold in state coffers. The only thing cities have plenty of these days is poor people. And the lottery is a way of exploiting that human resource, the one taxable group in a state that won't move out and whose numbers are growing.

→>–<–

A British academic named Barbara Goodwin has written extensively about an imaginary "just society," which is organized around a mechanism called the Total Social Lottery. The lottery, held every five years, will determine which job you have, where you live, who has children, who governs. Every citizen will receive a basic social minimum—food, health care, a place to live—and all other income will be randomly redistributed every five years in Lifestyle Packages, which include random amounts of cash. The first question my friends in the primitive 1990s have about this society is not about its instability or lack of flexibility, but whether they would have to be treated by an untrained dentist every five years. While it's similar to the kind of fantasy kids dream up in the backseat during a long car ride, Goodwin's utopia sheds a little light on our own "meritocratic" society and the dozens of belief-systems, from Andrew Carnegie's benevolent social Darwinism to the ramblings of Murray and Herrnstein, it has spawned in self-defense. The basic assumptions Goodwin makes about the lack of connection between the social importance of work and the size of one's income may not be so far from the mark. After all, the function of many jobs may have more to do with social discipline and profit-making than with the social importance of the work itself; people who work at McDonalds' don't make hamburgers as much as they make money for the people who own the fast-food chain.

There's a strong tendency among lottery players to use numbers that have personal or numerological meaning, which are invariably random numbers in genesis—birthdays, for example, are perhaps the most random numbers of all. Numbers can have occult meanings as well—for example, 769 equals death, which for some reason makes it a lucky number. Images in dreams have numerical meaning; "abdomen" is 28-33-54, according to some dream-book publications, and "accident" is 4-31-50 if you witness one, 1-37-50 if you're in one. Other players seek order in absolute randomness; thousands of Illinois players let the Quick-Pick random-number generator pick their numbers for them. The world is moved by strange forces, irrational passions, dreams, and the randomness of birth, and wealth is largely a matter of chance, luck, and the uncontrollable variable of life-choices dictated by who your parents are. While this emphasis on the blind hand of fate, which causes some people to be born rich and others poor, may obscure the logic of a social system that keeps them that way, it poses a direct challenge to any perceived link between wealth and morality, between intellect and income, between productive power and money.

Because the real lucky breaks don't have anything to do with chance. America is a country built on a gamble; from the flash in the pan of the California Gold Rush to the liar's poker of the stock exchange, the American myth crowns those who risk all for precious metals, mouthwatering spices, towering condominiums. Chicago is a city of dreams, of elaborate fantasies, settled in a mad rush of real estate speculation, propering in a financial heyday spent trading the prices of fictional bales of wheat. Yet speculation and lucky breaks, whether those of the explorer or the junk bond trader, hide a curious balance of power; Chicago's futures market was possible because of the railroads built with Eastern capital, the financial wizards of the eighties can fall back into the wide open arms of the federal government. Who will the winners be when Mayor Daley talks of bringing riverboat gambling to Chicago—the out-of-work steelworker who makes a killing at the casino, or the downtown property owner who faces a tax hike if the boats don't open soon?

The peasants pay taxes while the noblemen joust; the unproductive economy feeds off an abundance of frustrated hopes. Instead of coming to grips with the harsh realities of poverty and urban decay, our empty cities exist in a hazy dream of riches. The lottery doesn't solve the problems of the city or cure the plight of the poor, and the lottery's fog of fantastical riches can't survive forever in the harsh reality of ghetto life—which, if nothing else, may mean that someone else will have to subsidize the school system. The answer lies in the very bond the lottery tries hardest to break—the bond of solidarity, whether of class or of neighborhood or, finally, among cities. Imagine a kind of union of cities, a political unit that refused to compete for companies, instead working as a group to lay down terms for business—adequate wages for workers, laws mandating that a company remain in a given location for a specified number of years, consideration for the urban environment—rather than allowing business to lay down terms for them. The ideology of the lottery is the ideology of competition, in which each man is for himself and only one wins. Yet the only way cities can hope to win in the future is through solidarity. To get from Grand Crossing to Easy Street, cities will have to do better than the lottery—it's a loaded gamble, a fixed game, a bet which only capital can win.

Baffler #7, 1995

TOM VANDERBILT

The Gaudy and Damned

California is a place in which a boom mentality and a sense
of Chekhovian loss meet in uneasy suspension; in which the
mind is troubled by some buried but ineradicable suspicion
that things had better work here, because here, beneath that
immense bleached sky, is where we run out of continent.

—Joan Didion

SOMEHOW THE PURSUIT of the American Dream is always most
poignant in California. When it crashes here, it seems to do so with
epochal fury, and no place has experienced a more fiery crash than
Orange County, California, the storied locus of virile, "B-1" Bob
Dornan conservatism and entrepreneurial might. Here, in this
theme park of a county (the theme, as one tourist brochure put it,
is "you can have anything you want"), the meeting of boom and
loss played itself out in the daily papers: The *Orange County Reg-
ister,* the most reliable barometer of local opinion, ran stories only
pages apart that contrasted life under the penumbra of bankruptcy
against the place in the sun that we had always known Orange
County to be. Tales of personal depression and "bankruptcy blues"

cast a shadow on the passing parade of upbeat economic indicators that everyone else seemed to be enjoying.

Nowhere was that "uneasy suspension" more strikingly manifested than the Crystal Cathedral, the immaculately-maintained headquarters of televangelist Rev. Robert Schuller, set in the modest, Eisenhower-era suburb of Garden Grove, where the John Birch Society once sold its pamphlets in the Knott's Berry Farm amusement park, and where Newt Gingrich's book sells briskly in the Richard M. Nixon Memorial Library and Birthplace. The Cathedral, in the shadow of Disneyland, is a metaphorical motherlode in the otherwise inscrutable terrain of post-suburbia. Walking through the parking lot, past the silver railings and concrete of the private family gardens ("offering the finest in memorial property"), my first thought was of the Cathedral's fidelity to the environment outside. Designed by Philip Johnson, it is an immense building of white steel trusses and glass-paneled walls. Its mirror exoskeleton glares crisply, like any one of the corporate headquarters ringing the highway interchanges near Irvine. Flanking the Cathedral is a giant "Tower of Power" made up of steel tubes thrust upward into the sky, terminating in a set of sharp, jagged points, their metal surfaces glimmering menacingly in the sun like a phalanx of missiles at a desert military installation. Inside, a smooth piece of crystal set in a larger mass of unpolished rock rotates under glass like a jeweler's display in Fashion Island, one of the county's more exclusive malls. An inscription marking the fortieth anniversary of the Crystal Cathedral (1955–1995 A.D.), which is situated nearby, reads like a distillation of the history of suburbia itself: "This was also the era of the birth of television, the building of nuclear weapons of warfare, an age of hope and fear."

The Cathedral is a sprawling "megachurch," with all the trappings of mass entertainment: indoor stadium-style seats for 2,862 (but not—at least not yet—skyboxes), Sony JumboTrons adjoining both sides of the pulpit, and an array of broadcasting equipment used to beam Schuller's "Hour of Power"—the country's most popular religious program—to its estimated three million weekly viewers. Just past the church entrance lies the "Drive-In Worship Center." On that day it was empty parking lot, but each Sunday it swarms with Schuller's vehicular flock, who watch from their cars as the Cathedral's 90-foot high doors slide open; a peculiar homage to the preacher's first house of worship, a drive-in movie theater. In the gift and book shop one may find Crystal Cathedral cocktail napkins and keychains, a "Motivational" book section, and myriad postcards and t-shirts bearing Schuller's copyrighted homilies, the most popular of which seems to be: "Tough Times Never Last, But Tough People Do!" Unlike his more inflammatory neighbor in Anaheim, the Rev. Lou Sheldon of the Traditional Values Coalition, Schuller is interested less in morality and sin than a libertarian inspirational uplift, designed to soothe those who have reaped the rewards of success and console those who haven't yet, hinting broadly that economic salvation is just round the corner. It's a message worth millions of dollars a year from viewers, and one that he delivers across the country in places like Flint, Michigan, where he is shown in Michael Moore's 1988 film *Roger and Me* pronouncing his regenerative slogans to a room full of unemployed autoworkers.

In a local library, I found what was perhaps, in light of the county's fiscal catastrophe, the most ironic piece of the Schuller merchandising empire, a slim volume called *The Power of Being Debt-Free*, written by Schuller and an undistinguished economist. After thanking Milton Friedman, Arthur Laffer, and a number of others in the introduction, Schuller notes that the book began over a dinner with Robert and Elizabeth Dole. The national debt, it seems, had been vexing him, so he set about drafting a recovery plan based on his self-help doctrines; the book, accordingly, is a litany of exhortations and bold pronouncements, a forest of exclamation marks interspersed with statements like: "America is a superpower with superpeople who have superpotential for superproductivity."

But outside the library, Orange County seemed gripped not by "super" anything but rather the less empowering dynamic of "hope and fear." Under the bankruptcy, the county seemed to inhabit a dual world; one a gray dystopia of uncertainty and falling property values; another, the accustomed bright and buoyant showcase of affluent citizens who were forming start-up software firms in small industrial parks and shopping at Coach and Hermés. It was home to one of the country's most profitable Mercedes-Benz dealers, yet ominous talk loomed of massive cuts in bus service to help bail out the county—and just how would those nannies and gardeners from Santa Ana make the daily commute to Big Canyon Villas or Belcourt? In Orange County, such paradoxes run deep and jagged like irrigation ditches: Only there did it seem to make sense that the soft-spoken and earnest editor of the new "alternative weekly," itself housed next to those software firms in a commercially-zoned office park, would meet me for lunch wearing a three-piece suit, and then drive me in his BMW to a cafe at "the Lab." Known as the county's "anti-mall," the former canning factory is a perfect fabricated bohemia—with rusted post-industrial debris as strategically chosen as the "environmental" music at the county's real malls—made possible through the generous cooperation of a local surf/-skate-wear tycoon.

Popular ideas of Orange County still revolve around gated communities, golf villas, yacht clubs, and European signature boutiques. The picture is of a sylvan suburban paradise—just a shade less blanched than Sun City—where places like Coto de Caza, an equestrian rising-property-value preserve of the rich, stretch for miles along the breathtaking backdrop of the Santa Ana mountains. Media coverage of the bankruptcy focused on this sort of opulence fixedly, with a stream of TV dispatches from high-end Newport Beach shopping centers, where the point that Orange County was a "wealthy deadbeat" could be driven home more effectively. But a twenty-minute drive replaces the glimmering things of F. Scott Fitzgerald's imagination with the cluttered barrios of Santa Ana, the shabby procession of strip malls selling fish tacos and "$1 Chinese food," and the repeated binary clusters of attached homes (from $85,900) in Tustin Ranch for what Richard Ford once called "starter people." Minus its two or three wealthiest enclaves, it has been pointed out, Orange County barely makes the state's median income level.

And yet it's certainly easy to find pockets of privilege and prosperity in Orange County, places where the better-off can cocoon in relative safety as everyone else frets about the ground-level impact of the "Citron crater." One night in Newport Beach, I rode to dinner on the thirty-foot yacht of a Corona del Mar investment banker. As we motored slowly through the still waters of Newport Harbor, past the former estates of John Wayne and Gene Autry, past the second or third homes of international industrialists, the banker would turn away from the wheel every so often, pointing with awe to one of the multimillion-dollar vessels resting in their exclusive berths. "That boat cost more than God!" he would gush, conjuring up immediately the entwined supplication to religion and money that Schuller's ministry also seemed to suggest. Returning to the dock, the banker's assistant asked if I had enjoyed the ride, and then, gesturing to the panorama of bobbing boats and harborfront property, said with a smile, "See, not all of Orange County is bankrupt."

Baffler #8, 1996

Closing Salvo

THOMAS FRANK

Dark Age

The Cultural Miracle

HAVE YOU HEARD? The "affluent society" is over! Virtually every respectable organ of public opinion has now officially acknowledged its demise: The warm old world of general prosperity is gone forever; poverty and economic insecurity have made a triumphant comeback; the wealth of the nation has concentrated itself rapidly into fewer and fewer hands. Meanwhile every innovation in public policy further impoverishes those who work for a living: "Welfare reform" turns out to mean creating a docile workforce, desperate for any kind of employment; so does any change in labor law; so does "free trade"; so does the explosion of the prison population; so does the growth of the temp industry. But for our cyber-masters, displaying their lifestyles in the *New York Times Maga-zine*'s 1995 special issue on "The Rich," things just keep getting better and better. Tiring of our lo-res problems, they have decided that it's best simply to secede from Second-Wave notions of public responsibility altogether, to seal the perimeter of the gated community, climb into their skyboxes, and jet off into the fully-secured sunset.

For all its great cable channels, the excellent new global cyber capitalism is turning out to be a lot like the simple, grinding, exploitative capitalism of a hundred years ago. The astonishment that so many commentators express at this fact, however, is in one sense profoundly dishonest. Only the most naive can be surprised when a decade of policies designed to crush organized labor, enrich the rich, and render our entire national life subservient to the whims of the market achieve exactly those ends. But in a broader sense the alarm so commonplace on today's editorial pages is genuine. As we learned in the "Deprivation Theory" unit back in Sociology 101, inequality of this kind always begets social upheaval. It's virtually a mathematical certainty: Immiseration brings radicalization. We're walking blithely down the road to disaster; we're asking for a replay of the 1930s, for strikes and interfering brain-trusters; we're pushing what's known euphemistically in this country as "the middle class" to the known limits of its complacency, and this time it won't just be a bunch of suburban kids flipping us off and smoking pot when we told them not to.

And yet the seismographs of public opinion show barely the faintest signs that Americans are preparing to redress what's been done to them. Instead, we on the receiving end of the new inequality are turning out majorities that reaffirm the very politics that have so afflicted us, we are tuning in enthusiastically to hear millionaires and their hired spokesmen pose as rebels, revolutionaries, defenders of the forgotten man. We're rising as one, a song on our lips, to strengthen the hands of those who smite us; we're up on the rooftops of our flooded homes praying fervently for rain; we're offering smiling shoeshines to the people who have come to take possession of our foreclosed farm.

Were the man in the skybox inclined to view events in long-term perspective, perhaps he would be more impressed by the world-historical cultural wonder of which he is the beneficiary. Perhaps he would get on his cell-phone *right now* and pledge ten or twenty thousand to the local televangelist. For this is the doing of the Almighty Invisible Hand as surely as were the "economic miracles" of postwar Germany and Japan, a deliverance from the fate of the strife-and-strike-fatigued Mexicans, French, and British that is so ineffable it can only be attributed to divine intervention. By some act of economic providence the American population seems to have become incapable of acting on its own behalf; "rational choice," at least for us sub-CEOs, has disappeared without a trace from the sociological radar screen. Every day the market commits some new outrage, offers some new demonstration of its worthlessness as a way of ordering human civilization; and every day the organs of official opinion respond with louder and louder declarations of faith in the providence of the market, tributes to the glory of the global economy, zealous denunciations of any organization that would check the market's omnipotence.

Call it, then, the Cultural Miracle, an unprecedented unlinking of economic cause and social effect: a parting of impoverishment and action, of social reality from political consequences. It's the cultural equivalent of the economists' "black box": In one side go the objective circumstances—the most vicious attack on the public well-being by private wealth in decades; and out the other comes the mysterious response—the most abject reverence for private wealth to characterize our public culture in decades. The nation's owners are free to do their worst now, since there's no longer any substantial force out there that can counterbalance, challenge, or even question their choices. The only political "incentives" we have created encourage them to make things worse for us still. Layoffs and lowered wages not only increase profits, they appear to translate directly into hosts of new converts to the Limbaugh Legion, fresh ranks of grumblers vowing revenge against the "politically correct."

We've all heard about the problem of conformity in flush times. The Cultural Miracle, though, is complacency in years of economic privation; it is the spectacle of both parties in free-fall to the right; it is Cold War military policies that, though now lacking any external justification, continue to propel themselves along for no reason but inertia; it is armies of temps and junior executives and blue-collar workers who imagine that the correct response to their own newfound economic precariousness is to smash what's left of the welfare state.

The Cultural Miracle is the Great Disconnection of the American intellect, the virtual extinction of popular thinking in terms of social class at the exact moment when social class has made a most dramatic return. It is a prodigious uncoupling of the language and imagery of everyday life from that whole plodding Second Wave world in which "interests" were organically connected to action and in which economics provided identifiable "motives" for social behavior.

Even economics, it seems, is no longer concerned with the production of things but with the manufacture of imagery, with the health of a Culture Trust whose every arcane fluctuation or celebrity-swap receives the instant scrutiny of both business and lifestyle editors nationwide. Culture causes and simulacrum is in the saddle to a degree that perhaps only Jean Baudrillard can imagine, that the laughably archaic studies linking TV to real-world violence can only begin to suggest. Notions of objective social reality have themselves become objects of easy retro derision, as distant and clichéd as the strange impulses that once prompted our ancestors to attempt to control the world around them.

What desultory feelings of discontent that manage to penetrate the veil quickly assume a savagely retrograde aspect. As in previous hard times, the language of rebellion, of class resentment, and of egalitarianism have taken center stage; once again the elemental battle of the People against the Elite is joined. But don't look for a Clifford Odets comeback or a Eugene Debs postage stamp anytime soon. The characteristic political expression of these miraculous times is a stunningly misguided variant of the old populist formula, this time turned neatly inside out. When we talk about the People we're talking about businessmen; when we heap scorn on snobbish elites, it's those meddling unions and their pals in the government who are our target.

Vox Mercatus, Vox Dei

Right-wing populism has a long history, marked prominently by the racism with which earlier leaders sought to turn the working class against its own interests. But whether its current avatar is Steve Forbes, Newt Gingrich, or Rush Limbaugh, the Cultural Miracle is driven by a different and far more powerful ideological fuel, an anti-intellectualism that is almost metaphysically resolute in its hostility to ideas. However its various nostrums and slogans—the flat tax, the Contract with America, the gold standard, the protective tariff—flicker across the national media consciousness, the guiding impulse of the new cultural dominant remains the same: to think about exerting human control over the marketplace (unless you're a CEO) is somehow elitist. Sometimes, of course, the language that its Republican devotees use is familiar Jacksonian stuff: rantings against effete Harvard, ravings against treasonable experts and their values-eroding expertise, and boasts of their own offensiveness to established policy institutes and schools of government administration. And, as usual, they make their announcements of cultural mistrust not in small-town PTAs and letters to sundry editors, but from positions of real power: magazines and newspapers subsidized by some of the largest fortunes in the country, radio and TV programs that reach vast audiences, the floor of the House of Representatives.

But the latest bearers of the proud tradition of Joe McCarthy,

Billy Sunday, and Davy Crockett unleash their powerful new version of the assorted old prejudices not simply against thinkers or the college-educated—many of the inquisitors hold assorted Ph.D.s and MBAs themselves—but against particular kinds of thought. Nor is it merely tradition or that Old Time Religion that they want to defend from the ravages of modernity: On the contrary, for the new Right these are Second Wave ideas as obsolete as ink and paper. The adepts of the Cultural Miracle are fundamentalists of a different sort, prophets not of the angry God of Jonathan Edwards but of the omnipotent market. Read a handful of the sharp-edged editorials of the *Wall Street Journal,* through which the faithful are called to action; scan the pages of the latest business advice books: The market is eternal, the market is unchanging, the market is all-solving, the market is all-seeing, the market is everywhere. The market is both the natural condition of mankind and the unique blessing of the American Eden. The market is also synonymous with democracy: Since it gives the People what the People want, the market is, by definition, the incarnation of the People's will. Those who speak for the market speak with the *vox populi.* Most importantly, though, the market is a fantastically jealous god, deeply offended by the puny efforts of mere mortals to improve on its creations with government, tariffs, unions, or culture.

Having replaced God with the market, the new anti-intellectuals take on targets more colossal than their forebears could have ever imagined. For Gingrich and Co., the elitist enemy is not mental ability per se but Enlightenment itself, portrayed now as the exclusive affectation of bureaucrats and professors, as an intolerable affront to Nature and the omnipotent market. The heresy that must be rooted out is the basic notion that people can control their world, can, through exertion of human intelligence, improve their situation; the bedrock value with which it must be replaced is a Zen-like doctrine of no mind, of bodily and spiritual attunement to the deep rhythms of the market. Buying and selling are holy acts, the source and end of human meaning; all else is empty sophistry and deceptive tricks by which scheming professors propose to get themselves ahead.

This, then, is the new consensus worked by the Cultural Miracle: The market is natural, normal, and irresistible. Efforts to control its vagaries, however, are artificial, dictatorial, arrogant—and undemocratic. One can watch the new faith that buttresses the Cultural Miracle emerging in documents like Terry Teachout's reworking of H. L. Mencken, in which the great scoffer is no longer the hated tormentor of the booboisie, but the ally of the market-wise peasants in their eternal battle against the verbal prestidigitations of the know-it-all bureaucrat. Or in Rush Limbaugh's recent statement of theoretical principle, borrowed almost verbatim from the stripped-down Social Darwinism of William Graham Sumner: Nobody has any obligation to anyone else, under any circumstances (unless they've signed a contract). With a contemptuous snort he dismisses a hundred years of social theory as so much airy fantasy, needless complexities taking us away from the straight and true faith of Gilded Age capitalism. Or consider the bizarre speech given a few years ago by P. J. O'Rourke to the Cato Institute, the thinking Hun's think-tank, in which he declared himself for "no political cause whatsoever" and hailed the group's dedication to "nothing," all of which he derives from a hostility to intellect and a relativism that should make those hated deconstructionists envious:

> I don't know what's good for you. You don't know what's good for me.
> We don't know what's good for mankind. And it sometimes seems as
> though we're the only people who don't.

But while the public is coached with a steady chant of *stop thinking*, the market proceeds on its benevolent way, unhindered by the corrosive disbeliefs of the New Right: It *does* know what's good for us. The errant ways of bureaucrats and the hubris of policy makers are to be excoriated in resentful small-town editorials without number, but the market moves serenely along, now and forever, beyond our earthly powers of reckoning. Its booms and busts are as natural as earth and sky, and our duty is not to engage in insolent schemes by which we might control the market, but to reconcile ourselves to its majestic ways; to make our own culture as "flexible" as Third Wave capitalism demands; to offer up unquestioningly the prosperity of generations when "competitiveness" calls. To appease the market we will surrender every vestige of self-government, abandon the ways and beliefs and tastes and faiths of centuries, turn our cities into warehouses of the "amenities" by which the mobile, transnational yuppie can be served. And history is the baggage needed least of all, the dethroned god whose every trace the zealots of the market seek to efface, rationalize, or enclose conveniently in a glass display case.

It's a strange species of populism that declares the people's will to be the destruction of the people's way of life. But the crowning mind-fuck of this panorama of intellectual obscenity has to be the perversity of the label fancied by the architects of this chaos—they like to call themselves "conservatives."

The People, Maybe!

If the characteristic political maneuver of the Cultural Miracle is a Buchananesque transformation of inchoate public resentment of business depredations into support for pro-business policies, its characteristic intellectual maneuver is even more counterintuitive: endless lessons about "reality" and adjusting ourselves to it. The cover story of the January 8, 1996, issue of *Newsweek,* a choice bit of pseudo-history penned by journalist Robert Samuelson, offers a useful glimpse of the mental processes of the Cultural Miracle in action. Things *have* gotten worse for ordinary people in the last few years, the pundit admits. But the problem is not business ("what we today call 'the market,' " Samuelson notes in a pious aside)—it's us. All these years we've been thinking about things wrong, expecting too much, waltzing irresponsibly through an "Age of Entitlement" during which we believed that prosperity was somehow our right. Most importantly, we never understood "the market" correctly: For years we thought of it as a big "machinery" that we could adjust and control.

Now we know better, Samuelson smugs. The market is not something we can alter, but an elementary force of nature that stands outside history altogether, "a vast river" that floods and recedes regardless of our petty desires. But it's a well-meaning deity, if its ways seem whimsical: When it fires people, puts others on twelve-hour shifts, and smashes wage scales, we must remember that it is acting in the best possible interests of all, that "the process can be harsh and crude, and although some suffer, more benefit." Our response to these petty misfortunes should not be to challenge the market's omnipotence, but to reconcile ourselves to its overarching wisdom. And there is a long litany of lessons that we must relearn as we humble ourselves, do our penance, and prepare to resume the path "toward reality" that was forsaken after World War II: everything from shopworn notions about "human nature" (you know, that basic acquisitive urge that never, ever, ever changes) to the entrepreneur-worship of Tom Peters to the fundamental tenets of the new apostle's creed. Government cannot help and must stop trying; if we're poor, it's our own fault.

More importantly, there are a few historical facts that we must forget. We must not think about where we came up with this mistaken social system in the first place. Apparently it just happened one day when that abstract and irresponsible entity, Big Government, started promising people things. Above all we must not remember that social change happened because people organized themselves in unions, co-operatives, and political parties and *made* them happen; that the non-rich once had power because they *took* power. Such behavior is doctrinally impossible, and any evidence that ever occurred must be ignored: Only the market has the ability to act with historical effect. And we must strive to erase any recollection of events that were not filmed in color, to convince ourselves that Big Government is a product not of the 1930s but of the misguided generosity of the postwar boom; now that prosperity has departed, so must that Government.

Clifford Odets' 1935 drama of economic information and its forgetting, *Till the Day I Die,* is a populist fantasy of exactly the phenomenon Samuelson denies. The play opens on a group of German communists surreptitiously cranking out leaflets with which to plaster Nazi Berlin. One hero boasts to a comrade that "This particular leaflet's going to make some of our Nazi friends perspire once it gets into the workers' hands. Workers might like to know . . . wages are down one-third and vital foods are up seventy-five per cent." The Nazis, meanwhile, maintain their grip on power by keeping such inherently explosive facts from the people and by torturing to the point of mental collapse those who dissent openly. Information is connected unproblematically to unrest in Odets' world; if the people know what is happening to them, the people act.

The Cultural Miracle is Odets' 1930s turned upside down, information severed from action and populism itself tamed and in the service of its old archenemy. The people can have all the data they want, but it turns out they'd much rather have the sappy Hollywood screenplays Odets was eventually hired to write. The culture of the nineties looks a lot like that of the thirties, with all the old genres intact but—just as the daily terrors, political battles, and strange passions of that time now seem as mysterious to us as events on another planet—with the poles of meaning neatly inverted, the symbols and the metaphors magically reversed.

It's not that we don't feel the old anomie: Just as the audience at the first performance of Odet's *Waiting for Lefty* joined the actors chanting "Strike!", we can be easily worked up against the mysterious forces that make life so unfulfilling. But for us rebellion has come disconnected from the tangible change it once promised. Now it only appears publicly as an existential thing, a sort of limp craving for self-expression so closely associated with consumer products and brand loyalty that we are virtually incapable of imagining it without a corporate sponsor of some kind.

Just as in the 1930s, we push the envelope of "realism" ever farther, but reality seems to work differently now. Bigger Thomas reappears as Clarence Thomas, surviving a persecution mounted by crazed leftists this time. Studs Lonigan is back as a character on *Cops*, a selfish union worker being gratifyingly taken down by the market he tried to defy. Forget the millionaires who run the place; what we want is TV vengeance against the poor Lonigan next door, we want his union broken, we want his unemployment benefits stopped, we want his health care taken away, we want stiff laws demanding that he behave just so, we want him locked up; and we want to watch the resulting tragedy on television, see him hauled off half-naked and bleary from drinking too much Colt 45, pleading pathetically with some stern law enforcement officials.

Broadcast demagoguery, never in eclipse for long, has made a triumphant comeback. Limbaugh battles Buchanan for Father Coughlin's old market niche and the antidemocratic nightmare from Frank Capra's *Meet John Doe* is acted out in real life, with thousands of common folk crowding into convention centers and mouthing empty slogans at the behest of some power-mad millionaire. But the Cultural Miracle does Capra one better—not only are the millionaires no longer required to conceal their involvement or hire "John Does" to do their populist fronting, but we find it hard to imagine mass movements (or magazines, for that matter) that have arisen *without* a responsible millionaire at their helm. Being men of the market, millionaires *are* the people, and we cheer them ecstatically as they ascend their skybox to watch the performance of the Gary Cooper character, played by Bruce Springsteen, of course.

The saga of Everyman continues during the commercials, filmed always in Olympian slow-motion as he relaxes on the jet plane, gazes out the window of his office, carries the way of the market to all those benighted lands that have yet to experience American culture. It's hard times, so the thing to do is to get those CEOs up on those pedestals as fast as possible, take that federal government apart as quickly as we can, surrender any notion of controlling the market, and learn our place in the great global scheme. You'll get that raise when you stop thinking about that union.

The Will to Forget

Only the most unabashed partisans of business supremacy are willing to boast openly about the larger change that has made the Miracle possible, to speak the name of the great foe whose vanquishing now permits the market to stride the globe unchecked. Francis Fukuyama, the right's favorite pre-Limbaugh intellectual, put it most plainly in a famous 1989 essay: Business has *ended history*. Not just in the Hegelian sense, the simple victory dance over the corpse of the Soviet Union that was the essay's primary purpose, but in a philosophical way as well. While America's arms expenditures triumphed over the Red Menace, its comfortable consumer banalities triumphed everywhere over local and inherited culture, language, and ideas, and literally ended people's ability to think historically. The visibility of Western consumer goods throughout the world signals the success of what Fukuyama hails as the combined Western effort "to create a truly universal consumer culture that has become both a symbol and an underpinning of the universal homogenous state." And while Fukuyama readily admits that "The End of History" does not mean that all economic and social conflict has been resolved, that universal capitalism means universal happiness, he gloats that without the faculty of cultural memory our unhappiness, however grinding, just doesn't matter. People can no longer think about their social position in a manner that might lead to conflict, that might threaten Western business interests.

Fukuyama's pronouncements may have marked a new hostility to history but pastlessness is as American as Microsoft. Visiting the new country in the mid-nineteenth century, de Tocqueville was deeply moved by its willful rejection of the class rankings and tastes of the European past, by the settlers' tendency to forget the Old World and to abandon the ways of the countless generations before them. Casting off the dead weight of the ages has always been a favorite conceit of American writers less frightened by democracy than was the aristocratic de Tocqueville: Deracination has in many ways been the centerpiece of the nation's self-understanding. The golden fable of opportunity—of an empty land where anyone could, like Jay Gatsby, remake himself unhindered by the artificial constraints of civilization—is, after all, the basic theme in the great American stories of immigration and western expansion. Even our atrocities obeyed this primal cultural impulse, this imperative to forget: Slavery demanded a cultural uprooting of those who did not come to the New World willingly. But by and large our literature praises the power of the melting pot, celebrates the democracy of the frontier, sings the glories of getting out of the Old and into the Cold.

For ideologues of American business, the suspicion of history is a longstanding article of faith. In the frequent denunciations of the past voiced by the great Captains of Industry one finds not mere assimilationist longings, but profound disdain for any entangling traditions that could interfere with efficiency and restrict the absolute freedom of every individual to pillage every other individual. Henry Ford's famous outburst, "History is bunk," was a statement of fundamental business ideology, not merely a response to an immediate annoyance. According to the great capitalists' "practical" worldview, as Richard Hofstadter has noted, "The past was seen as despicably impractical and uninventive, simply and solely as something to be surmounted." In its quest for efficiency, the pre-Information business "community" set itself against the peculiar and backward-looking ways of tradition and human particularity in almost every way it could. Its famous time-motion studies aimed to suppress factory workers' humanity, transforming them into robots like the hapless line worker in Charlie Chaplin's *Modern Times.* Its glass-and-steel office towers were efficiency-maximizing machines for the paper-shuffling labor of its Organization Men, stripped of any concessions to human tastes and comfort; its suburbs and tenements, sterile boxes for the propagation of obedient underlings.

Alongside the hyper-rational, hyper-efficient Organization envisioned by America's premier managers there also developed an emotional and religious conception of business practice, a cult of positive thinking that was even more hostile to cultural memory than was the dominant cult of efficiency. In the writing of the positive thinkers, anti-historicism reached a new plateau of sophistication. The annoyances of history and cultural particularity were not just to be over-paved, but *leveled,* reduced to a convenient flatness where every epoch was exactly like the present as far back as the eye could see. The economic struggle of daily life was and had *always been* a matter of individual men and God, a question of just how positively each up-and-coming entrepreneur could think, just how blindly he could pursue success. The cold statistics of the bureaucrats were ultimately insignificant, nor did social class or local economic conditions really matter: All you needed to succeed was a salesman's disposition and an open-faced readiness to work. All human history—and especially the doings of its big figures, favorites like Jesus, Lincoln, Charlemagne, and Joan of Arc—could be understood as parables for the struggling executive of the twentieth century. Theories of efficiency may have intentionally ignored history, but positive thinking went them one better. For its believers the past was fundamentally identical to the now. Capitalism is the immutable way of God and nature, the unchanging condition of mankind. To wonder how things ever got to the sorry state they were was to engage in idle and even counterproductive conjecture: Society *never* developed or changed (although, as Samuelson would point out, it would occasionally embark on some sort of folly like the New Deal), it simply produced a series of interesting executives and leaders from whose exploits we might learn a thing or two.

With the coming of the Age of Information this anti-historicism has blossomed into a full-blown secular antinomianism. Cause and effect itself is a meaningless illusion, the new business thinkers argue, for the Information Age is an *Age of Unreason,* of instant, world-wide change and constant flux. The world is mad, they insist, it's spinning chaotically out of control, and to remain profitable, businessmen must become mad themselves, become creatures immersed totally in the present (or, better still, the future) and intentionally ignorant of whatever developments have put us where we are. "How people and companies did things yesterday doesn't matter to the business reengineer," write the authors of 1994's ubiquitous management text, *Reengineering the Corporation.* The hero of the Information Age, according to its authors, is the businessman who is able to violate most violently, to separate himself most completely from both his own and his company's past—to *forget.* The virtue of forgetting is the book's essential message. Its dust jacket carries this enticing legend: "Forget what you know about how business should work—most of it is wrong!" With total seriousness its authors recommend that businessmen adopt an epistemology of constant forgetting, of positive militancy against cultural memory. "At the heart of business reengineering," they write, "lies the notion of *discontinuous thinking*—identifying and abandoning the outdated rules and fundamental assumptions that underlie current business operations." In the wave after wave of manuals that have appeared since then the language of permanent-overthrow is simply ratcheted up a few notches. Now we fill our commuting time penetrating the mysteries of concepts like "Thinking outside the box," "radical change," and "transformation." So thick have the ranks of the corporate Jacobins grown that "The will for change has itself become banal," advertising executive Jean-Marie Dru writes—just before proposing his own scheme for more effective and total corporate deracination: "disruption." ("If a brand rests on its heritage, fails to question itself, and builds only on its past, before long it will come to appear complacent or static.")

Unlike his Organization predecessors, who merely wanted to destroy annoying obstacles to efficiency like city blocks and the sleeping habits of laborers, the information businessman dreams of what Russell Jacoby once called "social amnesia," a collective inability to recall who did what *yesterday*, never mind last year or last century. Freed from the gravitational pull of worldly history, he floats deliriously on a rushing stream of detatched signifiers, the flotsam and jetsam of centuries of civilization having become just so many shiny trinkets floating meaninglessly by (it's not a coincidence that Dru quotes appreciatively from Baudrillard and Tom Peters from Ludwig Wittgenstein). The constant flux that supports us all, consumerism's endless piling of new upon new, can be bound by no tradition, reason, language, or order other than the simple mandates of ceaseless, directionless change.

Among media decision-makers themselves the curtailment of our historical attention span is assumed quite matter-of-factly, with what one imagines is a fair amount of pride, to be an accomplished fact. Thus the convention on "objective" news programs of discussing events of last week or a few months ago as though they were dim memories of the distant, unenlightened past: References to Iraq must be prefaced by the reminder that the U.S. was at war with that nation a few years ago; news from Somalia must begin by informing us that, quite recently, this country was occupied by American soldiers. Otherwise, it is understood, we just wouldn't remember: Naturally we're too caught up in whatever the current patriotic frenzy is to recall those of the recent past. If we're lucky the logistical problems associated with this need to constantly remind viewers of what was once common knowledge may one day expand to the point where TV news becomes impossible altogether, with almost all of the 45-minute program devoted to telling us what country we live in, that other cities and nations exist, who our

elected officials are, and so on. The only thing that will never require explaining, of course, is the glowing box itself, the central position it occupies in our dwellings, and the reasons why we come
back to stare at it, day after day.

The Apocalypse that Refreshes

Freedom from the past, however, does not necessarily bode well for
other freedoms. In fact, no effective challenge to the rule of business can be mounted without solid grounding in precisely the sort
of cultural memory that Information Capitalism, with its super-
sonic yuppie pan-nationalism and its worship of the instantaneous,
has set itself out to destroy. Without memory we can scarcely understand our present—what strange forces in the dim past caused
this agglomeration of seven million unhappy persons to be de-
posited here in the middle of a vast continent, clinging to the shores
of this mysteriously polluted lake?—much less begin to confront
the systematic depredations of the system that has made our lives
so miserable. In contrast to American business's insistent denial of
pastness, Richard Hofstadter continues,

> In Europe there has always existed a strong counter-tradition, both ro-
> mantic and moralistic, against the ugliness of industrialism—a tradition
> carried on by figures as diverse as Goethe and Blake, Morris and Carlyle,
> Hugo and Chateaubriand, Ruskin and Scott. Such men counterposed to
> the machine a passion for language and locality, for antiquities and mon-
> uments, for natural beauty; they sustained a tradition of resistance to
> capitalist industrialism, of skepticism about the human consequences of
> industrial progress, of moral, esthetic, and humane revolt.

Without an understanding of particularity, of the economic con-
structedness of our lives, this kind of critical consciousness becomes impossible. All we can know is our own individual
discomfort, our vague hankering for something else—an else that
can be easily defined away as a different product choice, a new

lifestyle, a can of Sprite anti-soda, or a little rule-breaking at Burger King.

This century's technological advances are often described as victories over the primal facts of nature: hunger, cold, disease, distance, and time. But the wiring of every individual into the warm embrace of the multinational entertainment oligopoly is a conquest of a different sort, the crowning triumph of the marketplace over humanity's unruly consciousness. The fact that the struggle has been a particularly long one does not alter the fact that business authorities seem to be on the verge of a spectacular and final victory. It is fitting that, as this century of horrors draws to a close, our masters rush to perfect the cultural equivalent of the atom bomb, to destroy once and for all our ability to appreciate horror. With no leader but the "invisible hand," with no elite but the mild and platitudinous Babbittry of the American hinterland, Western capitalism will soon accomplish what the century's more murderous tyrants, with all their poisonous calculation, could only dream of doing: effacing the cultural memory of entire nations. For there is no tradition, religion, or language to which business owes any allegiance greater than momentary convenience; nor does any tradition, religion, or language remain that can muster a serious challenge to its cultural authority. It is capitalism, not angry workers, unhappy youth, or impoverished colonial peoples that is "the bull in the china shop of human history," David Rieff wrote in 1993. "The market economy, now global in scale, is by its nature corrosive of all established hierarchies and certainties . . . ."

When the twentieth century opened, business was only one power among many, economically and culturally speaking, a dangerously expansive but more or less contained participant in a larger social framework. While it might mistreat workers, break unions, bribe editors, and buy congressmen, its larger claims and authority were limited by an array of countervailing powers. It does not require a rosy sentimental view of any past period to recognize that today there are no such countervailing forces. Not only is labor toothless and feeble, seemingly capable only of slowing its own demise, but there is no cultural power on earth—save maybe the quixotic imagination of each isolated "reader" of the corporate text*—that can stand independent from or intrude upon the smooth operation of capital. With its advanced poststructuralist power-train, its six-barrel rock 'n' roll assimilator, and its turbo-charged fiber-optic speed, multinational capital is able to run cultural circles around our ponderous old notions of democracy, leaving us no imaginable means through which the culture of business might be resisted, no vantage point from which "the public" might be addressed, not even any way to approach the subject without lapsing into cliché. It's night in America, and we can feel ourselves slipping into a sleep from which we can't imagine ever waking.

Meanwhile the last twenty years have brought a palpable undoing of the American fabric, a physical and social decay so unspeakably vast, so enormously obscene that we can no longer gauge the destruction with words. We all know this: there it is every night on TV, there it is as you drive through the South Side of Chicago on your way to work (thank God for the virtual office!). And yet it matters nothing, because we don't live in that America anymore: Our home is *literally* the TV, the interactive wonder, the simulation that is so much more exciting, fulfilling, and convenient than any possible permutation of physical reality. We can do nothing but watch the world crumble because—our collective imagination being as much a construct of business necessity as the government's various trade agreements—we cannot imagine it being any other way.

Out here in the great flyover, ground zero of the Information

---

*Fukuyama's dismissal of Cultural Studies' argument about reception of Western culture-products is significant: "For our puposes, it matters very little what strange thoughts occur to people in Albania or Burkina Faso . . . . " Not being "embodied in important social or political forces and movements," they just aren't "part of world history."

Revolution, you can *feel* the world dissolving, everything from the hard verities of the industrial past to the urban geography beginning to melt away in the pale blue CRT fog. Our archetypes and ideas and visions and memories, the accumulation of centuries, are yielding as easily to corporate reengineering as has our landscape, built and torn down and renamed and reshuffled, everything forgotten instantly and relegated overnight to the quaint land of sepia-tint. This year we'll live in beautiful Passiondale, just down the road from Cambry Estates. Next year the noise and mud aren't so charming; wreck it down and move to a new box in a better fortified enclave: meaningless upon meaningless, stretching out across the infinitely malleable Illinois prairie.

Even while we are happily dazed by the mall's panoply of choice, exhorted to indulge our taste for breaking rules, and deluged with all manner of useful "information," our collective mental universe is being radically circumscribed, enclosed within the tightest parameters of all time. In the third millennium there is to be no myth but the business myth, no individuality but the thirty or so professionally-accepted psychographic market niches, no diversity but the happy heteroglossia of the sitcom, no rebellion but the preprogrammed search for new kicks. Denunciation is becoming impossible: We will be able to achieve no distance from business culture since we will no longer have a life, a history, a consciousness apart from it. It is making itself unspeakable, too big, too obvious, too vast, too horrifying, too much of a cliché to even begin addressing. A matter-of-fact disaster, as natural as the supermarket, as resistable as air. It is putting itself beyond our power of imagining because it has *become* our imagination, it has *become* our power to envision, and describe, and theorize, and resist.

Baffler #6 and 8, 1995–96

Contributors

STEVE ALBINI is a recording engineer and writer from Chicago.

BILL BOISVERT, former editor of the *Grey City Journal*, has written for the *Village Voice*, *In These Times*, and the *Chicago Reader*.

JENNIFER BROSTROM lives in Washington, D.C.

EDWARD CASTLETON is a graduate student in France.

STEPHEN DUNCOMBE is the author of *Notes from Underground: Zines and the Politics of Alternative Culture* (Verso, 1997). He teaches American Studies at SUNY-Old Westbury.

THOMAS FRANK is co-founder and editor-in-chief of *The Baffler* and the author of *The Conquest of Cool* (University of Chicago Press, 1997).

GARY GROTH is the publisher of Fantagraphics Books and the editor of *The Comics Journal*.

GREG LANE is the publisher of *The Baffler*.

MAURA MAHONEY is a writer and editor in Washington, D.C.

DAVE MULCAHEY is a senior editor of *The Baffler* and associate editor of *In These Times*.

KIM PHILLIPS is an *enfant terrible* in Chicago, Illinois. She has written for the *Washington Post*, *Grey City Journal*, and *In These Times*.

TOM VANDERBILT is an associate editor of *The Baffler*. His work has appeared in *The Nation*, *Lingua Franca*, and *London Review of Books*.

MATT WEILAND is the managing editor of *The Baffler* and an editor at The New Press.

KEITH WHITE, a co-founding editor of *The Baffler*, recently fled a career at a popular internet company to work for a newspaper. He is perhaps the only member of his generation to have turned down a job with Microsoft.

Index

Index

The Baffler is a literary and cultural review published in Chicago, Illinois. In addition to essays like these it includes short fiction, art, photographs, poetry, and a selection of disconcerting text-objects found in out-of-the-way cultural crannies. But for all the genius of the free market, The Baffler can be unusually difficult to find in stores. If you're interested in seeing more we recommend that you write us directly. Our address is P. O. Box 378293 Chicago, Illinois 60637.

NÜRNBERG ("far in rear")
DRESDEN ("1 mile behind")
GNEISENAU
SCHARNHORST

German ships close 1 poi.

Open fire

Resume southerly course

One point off.
7:26, Cease fi
7:45, 3mƱ

FINLAND

Anchorage for Merchant Ships Under Examination

FLOW

AREA

INNER PATROLLED AREA

SWONA

OTRANTO
GLASGOW
MONMOUTH
GOOD HOPE
73 TONS

1907

A, 105-3" 273 TONS

L. A. 135-3"

GOOD HOPE hit.

OTRANTO
capes S.W.

MONMOUTH
ceases fire, 7:20;
sunk by NURNBERG, 8:56.

GOOD HOPE
ceases fire, 7:23;
sunk, 8:20.

GLASGOW
capes S.W.

1910

1911

1913

548 TONS

Firing a Salvo

sts of the simultaneous firing of all the guns of a ship's battery. All

LEGEND

lish cruiser Yarmouth
Sunk
Sunk
Captured. Loaded with other ships and ther
Sunk
Sunk
Sunk
Sunk
Sunk
Sunk 315 mile

Sunk

Sunk
Captured. Recaptured press of Japan and Padang

2nd LIGHT CRUISER SQUADRON
2nd BATTLE SQUADRON
1st LIGHT CRUISER SQUADRON
2nd CRUISER SQUADRON
3rd BATTLE CRUISER SQUADRON
2nd BATTLE CRUISER SQUADRON
1st BATTLE CRUISER SQUADRON
BATTLE CRUISER FLEET
3rd LIGHT CRUISER SQUADRON